THE WORLD'S CLASSICS

JOHN DONNE

Selected Poetry

Edited with an Introduction and Notes by
JOHN CAREY

Oxford   New York
OXFORD UNIVERSITY PRESS

Oxford University Press, Walton Street, Oxford OX2 6DP

Oxford New York
Athens Auckland Bangkok Bogota Bombay
Buenos Aires Calcutta Cape Town Dares Salaam
Delhi Florence Hong Kong Istanbul Karachi
Kuala Lumpur Madras Madrid Melbourne
Mexico City Nairobi Paris Singapore
Taipei Tokyo Toronto
and associated companies in
Berlin Ibadan

Oxford is a trade mark of Oxford University Press

British Library Cataloguing in Publication Data
Data available

Library of Congress Cataloging in Publication Data
Data available

ISBN 0–19–282499–6

3 5 7 9 10 8 6 4 2

Printed in Great Britain by
Mackays Ltd
Chatham, Kent

Contents

EPITHALAMIONS

EARLY VERSE LETTERS

EPIGRAMS

Introduction

CRITICS have traditionally drawn attention to the forcefulness of Donne's poetry, the outrageous comparisons, the vehemence, the explosive openings. These traits are certainly present, but they are relatively superficial. His poetic greatness issues far more securely from the subtlety of his tones and rhythms, the inflections and modulations, the haunting but elusive significances, the glancing light that one word sheds on another. It is in these respects that he far excels his imitators later in the seventeenth century—and, indeed, most other English poets.

A distinctive feature of his poems is that they are usually addressed to someone or something else. Poems where the poet simply talks to himself, in the 'I wandered lonely as a cloud' mode, are common with other poets, but rare in Donne. He projects himself by talking to a woman, or to the sun, or to death, or to God, or (in 'Mad paper, stay') to the paper he writes on. This means that his poems seem to exist not just as writings but as speech-acts, with all the complications that speech brings—the emphases, the duplicities, the ironies, the persistent shadow of the unsaid.

In Donne, addressing something or someone else is a means both of expressing and of concealing a self. We, the readers, are left to guess what lies behind the voice, as we always are with voices. Take, for example, 'The Blossom' (p. 120), a poem in which the speaker addresses first a flower, and then his own heart:

> Little think'st thou, poor flower,
>   Whom I have watched six or seven days,
> And seen thy birth, and seen what every hour
> Gave to thy growth, thee to this height to raise,
> And now dost laugh and triumph on this bough,
>   Little think'st thou
> That it will freeze anon, and that I shall
> Tomorrow find thee fall'n, or not at all.
>
> Little think'st thou, poor heart,
>   That labour'st yet to nestle thee,
> And think'st by hovering here to get a part
> In a forbidden or forbidding tree,

> And hop'st her stiffness by long siege to bow:
>> Little think'st thou,
> That thou tomorrow, ere that sun doth wake,
> Must with this sun, and me a journey take.

What kind of speaker is this? A grave, considerate man, it seems, who watches flowers grow, and tells them sadly of coming frost. He cares for small, helpless things, and enlivens them by his imaginings. A blossom on a tree seems to him to 'laugh and triumph'. The tone suggests someone solicitous, mature, resigned.

Yet as the poem goes on we find that none of this is quite right. It turns out that it is a poem of thwarted lust and self-pity. The speaker cannot get the woman he desires to yield to his advances, and he complains about it. But because he addresses other things—the flower, the heart—he seems detached and magnanimous, rather than complaining. Telling the heart that it wants to 'nestle' in the woman (the 'forbidden' and 'forbidding tree') seems different from saying that he wants to 'nestle' in her himself. Yet that is what he must mean, for it is his own heart he is talking to. By addressing the heart as if it were a poor, unsuspecting little creature, distinct from himself, he retains his masculine superiority, whilst simultaneously exposing the need and vulnerability that lie behind that façade.

But then again, the pathos ('poor flower', 'poor heart') may not be as self-revealing as this reading supposes. It may be an aid to seduction. The speaker may be using it simply to work on the woman's feelings—if, that is, we imagine the finished poem as being meant for her to read. In its later stanzas the poem grows—or seems to grow—jaunty and flippant. The speaker tells his innocent little heart some home truths about women and their desires:

> A naked thinking heart, that makes no show,
> Is to a woman, but a kind of ghost.

The word 'naked', used of the disembodied heart, bawdily suggests the kind of nakedness that women (according to the speaker) really want. This jibe, and the bravado of the poem's ending (where the speaker vows that he will find another woman 'As glad to have my body, as my mind') could certainly be read as defiant or threatening by the 'forbidding' woman (still flatteringly and hopefully described as a 'sun' even though the poet is ostensibly relinquishing hopes of her). If the poem is for her to read, then its whole purpose may be to warn her that this is her last chance. If she will not yield, he will go—and tomorrow.

But, after all, we do not know that it is for her to read. Poems that simulate speech-acts inevitably prompt our speculation about the person spoken to, as well as the person speaking. But they thwart our speculation as well: that is a factor in their complication. Perhaps it is as well to add here that in talking, as I have done, about a woman who might have seen the poem, I am not suggesting there ever was a real-life woman in this situation, any more than there needs to have been a real-life flower behind the first stanza. What we are concerned with is not the relation between Donne's life and his poems (about which very little is known) but the context of imaginary possibilities that the poems create by their words and tones.

Questions like those raised by 'The Blossom' crowd around almost all the poems in this book—which is why Donne's poems, though mostly short, are unending. What is in the mind behind the voice is always intriguing, always unanswerable. The tones engage and frustrate us. Like 'The Blossom' in its pathos, and in its possible oblique appeal to a desired woman, is 'A Jet Ring Sent', where the tone, as often in Donne, flickers and changes between one line and the next:

> Thou art not so black as my heart,
> Nor half so brittle, as her heart, thou art.

The first line is a cortege of tragic, hollow monosyllables—fit for any hero-victim of Jacobean drama to intone. But with the sardonic crackle of 'brittle' the second line awakens to resentment and satire. At the poem's end, as the speaker croons over the little black ring the woman has sent, we have the same displacement of pity from himself to an external object that we found in 'The Blossom':

> Yet stay with me since thou art come,
> Circle this finger's top, which didst her thumb.
> Be justly proud, and gladly safe, that thou dost dwell with me,
> She that, oh, broke her faith, would soon break thee.

The rocking motion of 'justly proud, and gladly safe' suggests a cradling protectiveness, as if the ring were a surrogate child, and only the sob ('oh') that breaks the last line betrays (or, perhaps, is shrewdly calculated to suggest to the reprimanded woman) that the speaker has not been able wholly to transmute his suffering into care for his little keepsake.

Another, and typical, kind of subtlety in this stanza is the fleeting memory of the woman's body, and of its slenderness, compared to the man's. It is the fleetingness, not the memory, that is typical. Despite the lists of female parts in 'Love's Progress' or 'The Comparison', the norm in Donne (strangely, given that he is popularly thought of as a sexually explicit poet) is for the woman's body to be omitted or minimally registered—a fingernail in 'The Flea', a hand in 'The Ecstasy', a thumb in 'A Jet Ring Sent'. The rest of the body is present by inference only, if at all. In *Satire 2*, for example:

> words, words, which would tear
> The tender labyrinth of a soft maid's ear . . .

Here the word 'soft' makes as if to spread the tenderness of the inner ear over the rest of the maid's body, as if she were all as raw and sensitive as an exposed eardrum. But it is only a passing suggestion. Even the celebrated lines about Elizabeth Drury's body in *The Second Anniversary* uncover no more than her cheeks:

> we understood
> Her by her sight, her pure and eloquent blood
> Spoke in her cheeks, and so distinctly wrought,
> That one might almost say, her body thought . . .

The thinking body, suffused with eloquent blood—one of Donne's most powerful images of femaleness—remains discreetly shrouded beneath pure, dead Elizabeth Drury's clothes. Only her cheeks show. As we might expect, Donne's most famous line about a woman's body reveals no part of it at all, but is composed entirely of prepositions:

> Licence my roving hands, and let them go
> Behind, before, above, between, below.

> (*Elegy 2*)

The roundnesses and clefts over and into which the stroking hands rove are invented by us as we read, not by Donne.

Rhythm and its subtle changes are another and major means of conveying the unsaid in his poetry. Sometimes he makes rhythm work against meaning, altering the written words:

> Go, and catch a falling star,
>   Get with child a mandrake root,
> Tell me, where all past years are,
>   Or who cleft the Devil's foot . . .

The tripping measure, like a children's game, sweeps the bitterness from a poem which—if we paid attention to its words as distinct from its rhythms—would carp at women for falsehood. The often-quoted 'attack' on modern science and the new astronomy in *The First Anniversary* could be read as an attack only by the tone-deaf:

> . . . of meridians and parallels,
> Man hath weaved out a net, and this net thrown
> Upon the heavens, and now they are his own.

The rhythm triumphantly acclaims scientific achievement, whatever crusty obscurantism the words may, in context, subscribe to.

'A net, and this net', winding up to a pitch of excitement, exemplifies another of Donne's commonest and most versatile tonal devices—repetition. He uses awkward or ugly repetitions as an earnest of commitment, a silent message that the poem's speaker is too engrossed in what he or she is saying to have any truck with prettiness. The tactic can produce lines so tuneless that only Donne would have risked them:

> Me to me; thee, my half, my all, my more,

for example, in 'Sappho to Philaenis'—a line which sounds like a foreign student trying to master English personal pronouns. Less grotesquely, repetition can yield steely concision:

> His only, and only his purse
> May some dull heart to love dispose . . .
>   ('The Curse')

or clanging rancour:

>   my man,
>   Can be as happy as I can; if he can
>   Endure the short scorn of a bridegroom's play . . .

                                        ('Love's Alchemy')

or clinching neatness:

>   My picture vanished, vanish fears . . .

                    ('Witchcraft by a Picture')

or simple-minded certitude:

>   Good we must love, and must hate ill,
>   For ill is ill, and good good still . . .

                                        ('Community')

or soothing condolence:

>   Sleep sleep old sun . . .

                    ('Resurrection, imperfect')

These, of course, are only some of the tonalities Donne's
repeated repetitions access. His rhymes, too, resonate with tonal
implications. No poet ever used rhyme-schemes more designedly.
In 'The Anniversary' rhyme is like another voice, striving to bear
out what the speaker speaks:

>   All kings, and all their favourites,
>   All glory of honours, beauties, wits,
>   The sun itself, which makes times, as they pass,
>   Is elder by a year, now, than it was
>   When thou and I first one another saw:
>   All other things, to their destruction draw,
>   Only our love hath no decay;
>   This, no tomorrow hath, nor yesterday,
>   Running it never runs from us away,
>   But truly keeps his first, last, everlasting day.

The first six lines set up an expectation of couplets; but the last
four resolutely adhere to the same rhyme, as accompaniment to the
changelessness that the poem's speaker proclaims. These persistent
rhymes can be read as a valiant show of constancy, backing up the

speaker's boast. Yet they are also an illustration of its emptiness. For they cannot go on for ever. After their four defiant blasts they peter out, just as the last line, though strung out, as no previous line in the stanza is, to twelve syllables, falls silent even while announcing everlastingness. In this way the rhymes participate in the darkening drama of the poem, which admits, in the end, that some fears are 'true' (l. 27), though it decides to ignore them.

Donne's rhymes have their say in his poems not only in such large-scale orchestrations as this, but also in their routine line-to-line negotiations. Indeed, the first two lines of 'The Anniversary' illustrate this. The full-mouthed 'favourites', rhymed with the feeble monosyllable 'wits'—a bare, shorn remnant of its rotund rhyme-word—provides a sound-picture of the process of decay that the lines describe. There is a lovely example of rhyme-word contribution in 'Twickenham Garden':

> Alas, hearts do not in eyes shine,
> Nor can you more judge woman's thoughts by tears,
> Than by her shadow, what she wears.

In the third line here, the lingering resonance of 'shadow' reaches forward to 'what she wears', so that fleetingly the woman's clothes seem diaphanous and insubstantial, no more than shadowing flesh. What the rhyme, 'tears . . . wears' contributes is that (though the sounds may have been closer in Donne's day than ours) it is not a perfect rhyme. You cannot tell a woman's thoughts by her tears or her clothes, and the ear's suspicion of some mis-match in the rhyme, despite the eye seeing it as a rhyme, compounds the aura of doubt.

Pace, like rhyme and rhythm, is a decisive constituent of tone. We notice Donne's attentiveness to it in *Satire 4* where, creating the character of a sinister, beggarly gossip, he invents not only turns of phrase and tones of voice for the man (the familiar use of 'your'; a squeak of indignation 'like to a high-stretched lute string') but also a portentous slowness of delivery when it comes to imparting his bits and pieces of high-life scandal:

> He takes my hand, and as a still, which stays
> A semi-breve, 'twixt each drop, he niggardly,
> As loth to enrich me, so tells many a lie . . .

In his lyrics, as here, Donne slows pace by pausing between phrases, or by line-breaks that cut across sense, or by long mono-syllables ('stays', 'loth') or by polysyllables ('semi-breve', 'nig-gardly') that exact distinct articulation. The last two of these expedients create the freezingly slow line in 'A Litany':

> The cold white snowy nunnery . . .

In this line, it is worth noting, the first two adjectives could not be justified by meaning. 'Snowy' implies 'cold' and 'white', so renders them superfluous. But they are needed to retard the pace.

The other two types of pace-slower exemplified in the *Satire 4* excerpt, line-breaks and inter-phrasal pauses, create the awed gradation from phrase to phrase at the start of 'The Funeral':

> Whoever comes to shroud me, do not harm
> Nor question much
> That subtle wreath of hair, which crowns my arm;
> The mystery, the sign you must not touch,
> For 'tis my outward soul . . .

The pause between 'sign' and 'you' in the fourth line—a pause extended indefinitely by wonder, and trepidation, and reverence—is not signalled by any punctuation. It is encouraged partly by the lingering echo of the second line ('Nor question much') which inclines us to make 'you must not touch' into a matching, sepa-rate, rhyming, four-syllable line. But more emphatically, the pause is enforced by tone of voice—by, that is, the need for the implica-tions of 'mystery' and 'sign' to sink in before the prohibition consequent upon them—'you must not touch'—can be allowed to fracture our meditations.

By contrast with these line-stoppers, a device Donne uses to increase pace is the catalogue—the string of words without con-junctions—which can be observed performing its imitation of hurry in strikingly different contexts. Imagining, in *Elegy 11: On his Mistress*, the nightmares that may afflict her when he is away on his travels, he warns:

> . . . nor in bed fright thy nurse
> With midnight's startings, crying out, 'Oh, oh
> Nurse, O my love is slain; I saw him go
> O'er the white Alps, alone; I saw him, I,
> Assailed, fight, taken, stabbed, bleed, fall, and die.'

Half-awake, snow-dazed wonderment ('O'er the white Alps, alone') gives way to mounting panic as the remembered dream crowds itself into words in the last line. Far removed in meaning, but dependent on the same catalogue device for acceleration, is the impatient anticipation of the Last Judgement at the beginning of Holy Sonnet 4:

> At the round earth's imagined corners, blow
> Your trumpets, angels, and arise, arise
> From death, you numberless infinities
> Of souls, and to your scattered bodies go,
> All whom the flood did, and fire shall o'erthrow
> All whom war, dearth, age, agues, tyrannies,
> Despair, law, chance, hath slain . . .

The sonnet's tonal structure depends wholly on the shift, at the start of the sestet, from this impetuous staccato to a foot-dragging procession of monosyllables:

> But let them sleep, Lord, and me mourn a space . . .

The components of tone we have been noting are what Donne makes his voice out of. The value of what his poems say, regarded as an extractable or paraphrasable content, may at times be negligible, drawing, as he does, on a hackneyed stock of sighs, tears and broken hearts. But even when content is at its slightest, the poems themselves are not negligible because of the vitality and subtlety of their tone. How they are said, not what is said, is what matters. The originality of their phrasing distinguishes them and quickens them with implications.

As we have seen with 'The Blossom' and 'A Jet Ring Sent', the implications can modify, or run counter to, what the poems at first seem to profess. We are unsure quite how to interpret them. Though commonest in the *Songs and Sonnets*, this happens throughout Donne's poetry—in an elegy like 'The Autumnal', or in the apparently obsequious verse-letters to the Countess of Bedford, or in the dizzily hyperbolic *Anniversaries*. Sometimes the same poem can be read in diametrically opposed ways. 'Woman's Constancy' is an example.

> Now thou hast loved me one whole day,
> Tomorrow when thou leav'st, what wilt thou say?

> Wilt thou then antedate some new made vow?
>> Or say that now
> We are not just those persons, which we were?
> Or, that oaths made in reverential fear
> Of love, and his wrath, any may forswear?
> Or, as true deaths, true marriages untie,
> So lovers' contracts, images of those,
> Bind but till sleep, death's image, them unloose?
>> Or, your own end to justify,
> For having purposed change, and falsehood, you
> Can have no way but falsehood to be true?
> Vain lunatic, against these 'scapes I could
>> Dispute, and conquer, if I would,
>> Which I abstain to do,
> For by tomorrow, I may think so too.

Taken at face value, this is spoken by a man to a faithless woman. He anticipates the excuses she will make for her faithlessness, and admits, at the end, that he is quite likely to prove faithless himself. Alternatively, the speaker may be a man who is obsessed by women's inconstancy, and who directs his paranoid vituperation at an innocent and loving woman, who has no intention of leaving him. The arguments he dreams up for her bear no relation to her ideas but are born of his own twisted logic. There is no way of deciding between these two readings: both are equally possible. Yet they are also mutually irreconcilable, since in one the woman is innocent, in the other guilty.

We might say that the poem is in two minds about itself, and this condition is widespread in Donne's poetry—though seldom quite as blatantly as in 'Woman's Constancy'. That his poetry can be seen as the representation of two- (or three- or four-) mindedness accords with the changeability which, on his own account, was one of his most prominent character-traits. Even when he was at prayer, he found that his mind wandered, and his piety blew hot and cold:

> Oh, to vex me, contraries meet in one:
> Inconstancy unnaturally hath begot
> A constant habit; that when I would not
> I change in vows, and in devotion . . .

This consciousness of instability seems to have led him to question the concept of human personality as a definite or knowable thing.

So far as we can tell, he was the first English poet to have given thought to such matters. Who or what he was—whether he amounted to any kind of single entity—were questions that his examination of his own consciousness suggested, it seems, no conclusive answers to. That he wrote the highly moral *Satires* and the highly immoral love elegies during the same period of his life, the 1590s, and that his *Songs and Sonnets* express widely divergent attitudes to love, may be taken as an index of the disparities that expression of the inconsistencies within him seemed to demand. Writing to the Countess of Bedford at New Year's Tide, it is his ignorance of what he is that he brings to her notice:

> This twilight of two years, not past nor next,
>   Some emblem is of me, or I of this,
> Who meteor-like, of stuff and form perplexed,
>   Whose what, and where, in disputation is,
>   If I should call my anything, should miss.

The unwillingness to give a name to himself belongs to the same circuit of ideas as the poem 'Negative Love', where the impossibility of isolating what it is that he loves defeats the explicitness normally associated with love-avowals. Another poem circling round the same absence of centre is 'Air and Angels', where the opening lines claim that the speaker has loved the loved woman even before he saw her:

> Twice or thrice had I loved thee,
> Before I knew thy face or name;
> So in a voice, so in a shapeless flame,
> Angels affect us oft, and worshipped be . . .

This seems to say that the loved woman does not inhabit the loved woman's body. She is, to her lover, something different from what she is—and something intangible, a voice (but not her voice), a flame (but not a real flame). The disintegration of personality, which we have been observing in other poems, here spreads to and eats away the personality, and person, of the loved.

It was not only in his poetry that Donne was intrigued by questions of this kind. He discussed them with friends. We may gather this from a letter he wrote to Sir Henry Goodyer, where he distinguishes between diseases of the body and of the mind. The former, he observes, are relatively definite, being subject to medical diagnosis: 'But, of diseases of the mind there is no criterion, no canon, no rule, for our own taste and apprehension and interpretation should be the judge, and that is the disease itself.' The impasse acknowledged here (that you cannot know your mind because you have only your mind to do the knowing with) belongs to the same problematic area of self-definition and self-analysis that we have found the poems enquiring into. Reading Donne's poetry in this context allows us to see its subtleties and ambivalences of tone, and its simulation of spoken discourse, as a continuation of his remarkably modern awareness of the doublings, instability, and insubstantiality of the self.

Chronology

1572   Born between 24 January and 19 June in parents' house in Bread Street, London; third of six children of John Donne, a prosperous ironmonger, and Elizabeth (*née* Heywood).

1576   Father dies (between 16 January and 8 February); mother remarries (by July) John Syminges, a doctor, and ex-President of the Royal College of Physicians.

1577?   Elder sister Elizabeth dies.

1581   Two youngest siblings, Mary and Katherine, die (buried 25 November).

1583   Uncle Jasper Heywood, head of Jesuit mission in England since 1581, captured and imprisoned (December).

1584   Jasper Heywood sentenced to death (9 February) and sent to the Tower pending execution. Donne and younger brother Henry (age 10) matriculate at Hart Hall, Oxford, 23 October.

1585   Jasper Heywood released and banished to France (January).

1588   Stepfather Syminges dies (7 July).

1588–9 Perhaps studies at Cambridge.

1589–91 Perhaps travels abroad, visiting Italy and Spain.

1590?   Mother marries third husband, Richard Rainsford (certainly before 7 February 1591).

1591   Admitted as law student to Thavies Inn (? May). Earliest surviving portrait painted (a miniature, possibly by Nicholas Hilliard).

1592   Transfers from Thavies to Lincoln's Inn (6 May).

1593   Appointed Master of the Revels at Lincoln's Inn (6 February, the Christmas revels having been cancelled because of plague in London). Now aged 21, signs receipt at Guildhall for his share of his father's estate (19 June). Brother Henry dies in Newgate of plague, having been arrested (early May) for harbouring a Catholic priest, William Harrington.

1594   Harrington hanged, drawn, and quartered at Tyburn (18 February). Donne chosen Steward of Christmas at Lincoln's Inn (26 November) but declines to act.

1596   Volunteers for military service under the Earl of Essex; serves with English force that storms and sacks Cadiz (21 June) and burns Faro (July); returns with fleet to Plymouth (August).

1597   Sails (10 July) with fleet to attack Ferrol, but ships are dispersed by storm, returns to Plymouth; sails (15 August) on the 'Islands Expedition' to the Azores (September), where the English force captures Fayal but fails to intercept the Spanish treasure fleet; returns to England (October). Appointed secretary to Sir Thomas Egerton, Lord Keeper (? November, or 1598), and moves to quarters at York House, the Strand, Egerton's London residence. Ann More, Lady Egerton's niece, is also a member of the household.

1599   Bears the sword at the funeral (26 September) of Egerton's son, Sir Thomas, who had been his companion-in-arms on the 'Islands Expedition'.

1600   Lady Egerton dies (20 January); Ann More returns to her father's house at Losely, near Guildford; Egerton remarries (October) Alice, Countess of Derby.

1601   Donne sits in Parliament (October–December) as MP for Brackley, Northants, a borough in Egerton's control. Ann More returns to London with her father, Sir George More (in or before October). Donne secretly marries her (December).

1602   Breaks news of marriage to Sir George More (2 February); is briefly imprisoned in the Fleet and dismissed from Egerton's service. The Donnes, in financial difficulties, go to live with Ann's cousin Francis Wolley at Pyrford, near Losely.

1603   Daughter Constance born. James I and his Court, on progress, stay with Wolley at Pyrford (10 August).

1604   Son John born (May, or earlier).

1605   Travels on Continent, leaving England probably in February, as companion to Sir Walter Chute. Visits Paris and perhaps Venice. Son George born (May), probably during Donne's absence abroad.

1606   Returns to England (April or earlier). Moves with family to a two-storied cottage ('a little thin house') at Mitcham.

1607   Son Francis baptized, 8 January. Donne takes lodgings (till 1611) in Tincomb's house in the Strand; applies unsuccessfully (June) for a post in the Queen's household.

1608   Daughter Lucy baptized, 8 August; godmother, the Countess of Bedford. Donne seeks State employment (November) as secretary in Ireland; unsuccessful. While confined to bed with neuritis (winter, 1608/9) writes 'A Litany'.

1609   Applies (February) for colonial posting as secretary with the Virginia Company; unsuccessful. Daughter Bridget baptized, 12 December.

1610   (January) Publishes *Pseudo-Martyr*, dedicated to James I and supporting government policy in the Oath of Allegiance controversy; journeys to Royston to present a copy to James. Receives honorary MA from Oxford (April).

1611   Daughter Mary baptized, 31 January. Publishes *The First Anniversary* (in or before November), with 'A Funeral Elegy' appended, in memory of Elizabeth Drury. Travels to Continent (November) with Sir Robert and Lady Drury, leaving wife and family with relatives on Isle of Wight; stays in Amiens.

1612   *The First Anniversary* republished, along with first edition of *The Second Anniversary*, while Donne is abroad. Wife delivered of stillborn child (buried 24 January). Stepfather Richard Rainsford imprisoned in Newgate (February, or earlier) for refusing to take Oath of Allegiance. Donne and Drurys move to Paris (? March), Frankfurt (April), Heidelberg, Spa (July), Maastricht, Louvain, Brussels (August), and return to England (September). Moves with family to Drury Lane house provided by Sir Robert.

1613   Wedding (14 February) of Princess Elizabeth to Frederick, Elector Palatine, for which Donne writes 'Epithalamion'. Son Nicholas baptized, 3 August (died in infancy). Donne 'almost blind' (September) with disease of eyes.

1614   (February–March) Donne and family stricken with illness; daughter Mary dies (18 May), and son Francis (buried 10 November). Donne sits in Parliament (April–June) as MP for Taunton (seat in gift of the Master of the Rolls).

1615   (23 January) Ordained deacon and priest. Appointed (? February) a royal chaplain. Made Doctor of Divinity at Cambridge by royal mandate (March). Daughter Margaret baptized (20 April).

1616   Receives rectory of Keyston, Hunts., from king (16 January), and rectory of Sevenoaks, Kent (7 July). Daughter Elizabeth born (14 June). Chosen Divinity Reader at Lincoln's Inn (24 October).

1617   Wife gives birth to stillborn daughter (10 August) and dies (15 August).

1619   Leaves England (12 May) as chaplain with Viscount Doncaster's embassy to Germany. Travels to Heidelberg, where Donne preaches before Elector Palatine and Electress (16 June); continues with embassy to Stuttgart, Munich, Salzburg (5 July), Frankfurt, Nuremberg, Vienna (October), returning through Holland where Donne preaches at The Hague (19 December).

1620   (1 January) Returns with embassy to London.

1621   Elected and installed Dean of St Paul's (22 November).

1622   Chosen honorary member of the Council of the Virginia Company (3 July); preaches to the Company (13 November).

1623   Arranges daughter Constance's marriage (3 December) to celebrated Elizabethan actor, theatre-manager, and founder of Dulwich College, Edward Alleyn (aged 57). Seriously ill with relapsing fever (November).

1624   *Devotions upon Emergent Occasions* published. Appointed vicar of St Dunstan-in-the-West.

1625   Death of James I (27 March). Donne preaches at Court (3 April). Stays (July–December) in Chelsea, while plague rages in London, at house of Lady Danvers, George Herbert's mother. Meets Herbert.

1626   Coronation of Charles I (2 February). Donne preaches at Court (24 February).

1627   Daughter Lucy dies (buried 9 January). Sir Henry Goodyer dies (18 March) and Countess of Bedford (31 May). Lady Danvers dies (buried 8 June).

1630   Daughter Constance marries Samuel Harvey of Aldborough Hatch, Essex (Alleyn having died in 1626). Donne falls ill while visiting her and makes will (13 December).

1631   Donne's mother dies (buried 28 January). Preaches last sermon at court, 25 February (published posthumously as *Death's Duel*). Dies 31 March.

Note on the Text

IN preparing the modernized text of Donne's poetry and prose in this selection I have made use of the old-spelling editions listed below, but I have sometimes restored readings from the seventeenth-century editions, particularly the 1633 edition of Donne's poems, where Donne's editors have discarded them. I have generally retained the seventeenth-century punctuation, but have modified it where it might mislead a modern reader.

The Elegies and The Songs and Sonnets, ed. Helen Gardner (Oxford University Press, 1963).

The Satires, Epigrams and Verse Letters, ed. W. Milgate (Oxford University Press, 1967).

The Divine Poems, ed. Helen Gardner (Oxford University Press, second edition, 1978).

The Epithalamions, Anniversaries and Epicedes, ed. W. Milgate (Oxford University Press, 1978).

SATIRES

Satire 1

Away thou fondling motley humourist,
Leave me, and in this standing wooden chest,
Consorted with these few books, let me lie
In prison, and here be coffined, when I die;
Here are God's conduits, grave divines; and here
Nature's secretary, the Philosopher;
And jolly statesmen, which teach how to tie
The sinews of a city's mystic body;
Here gathering chroniclers, and by them stand
Giddy fantastic poets of each land.   10
Shall I leave all this constant company,
And follow headlong, wild uncertain thee?
First swear by thy best love in earnest
(If thou which lov'st all, canst love any best)
Thou wilt not leave me in the middle street,
Though some more spruce companion thou dost meet,
Not though a captain do come in thy way
Bright parcel gilt, with forty dead men's pay,
Nor though a brisk perfumed pert courtier
Deign with a nod, thy courtesy to answer.   20
Nor come a velvet Justice with a long
Great train of blue coats, twelve, or fourteen strong,
Wilt thou grin or fawn on him, or prepare
A speech to court his beauteous son and heir.
For better or worse take me, or leave me:
To take, and leave me is adultery.
Oh monstrous, superstitious Puritan,
Of refined manners, yet ceremonial man,
That when thou meet'st one, with inquiring eyes
Dost search, and like a needy broker prize   30
The silk, and gold he wears, and to that rate
So high or low, dost raise thy formal hat:

That wilt consort none, until thou have known
What lands he hath in hope, or of his own,
As though all thy companions should make thee
Jointures, and marry thy dear company.
Why shouldst thou (that dost not only approve,
But in rank itchy lust, desire, and love
The nakedness and barrenness to enjoy,
Of thy plump muddy whore, or prostitute boy)   40
Hate virtue, though she be naked, and bare?
At birth, and death, our bodies naked are;
And till our souls be unapparelled
Of bodies, they from bliss are banished.
Man's first blessed state was naked, when by sin
He lost that, yet he was clothed but in beast's skin,
And in this coarse attire, which I now wear,
With God, and with the Muses I confer.
But since thou like a contrite penitent,
Charitably warned of thy sins, dost repent   50
These vanities, and giddinesses, lo
I shut my chamber door, and come, let's go.
But sooner may a cheap whore, that hath been
Worn by as many several men in sin,
As are black feathers, or musk-colour hose,
Name her child's right true father, 'mongst all those:
Sooner may one guess, who shall bear away
The Infanta of London, heir to an India;
And sooner may a gulling weather spy
By drawing forth heaven's scheme tell certainly   60
What fashioned hats, or ruffs, or suits next year
Our subtle-witted antic youths will wear;
Than thou, when thou depart'st from me, canst show
Whither, why, when, or with whom thou wouldst go.
But how shall I be pardoned my offence
That thus have sinned against my conscience?
Now we are in the street; he first of all
Improvidently proud, creeps to the wall,
And so imprisoned, and hemmed in by me
Sells for a little state his liberty;   70
Yet though he cannot skip forth now to greet
Every fine silken painted fool we meet,

He them to him with amorous smiles allures,
And grins, smacks, shrugs, and such an itch endures,
As 'prentices, or schoolboys which do know
Of some gay sport abroad, yet dare not go.
And as fiddlers stop lowest, at highest sound,
So to the most brave, stoops he nigh'st the ground.
But to a grave man, he doth move no more
Than the wise politic horse would heretofore,   80
Or thou O elephant or ape wilt do,
When any names the King of Spain to you.
Now leaps he upright, jogs me, and cries, 'Do you see
Yonder well-favoured youth?' 'Which?' 'Oh, 'tis he
That dances so divinely'. 'Oh,' said I,
'Stand still, must you dance here for company?'
He drooped, we went, till one (which did excel
Th' Indians, in drinking his tobacco well)
Met us; they talked; I whispered, 'Let us go,
'T may be you smell him not, truly I do.'   90
He hears not me, but, on the other side
A many-coloured peacock having spied,
Leaves him and me; I for my lost sheep stay;
He follows, overtakes, goes on the way,
Saying, 'Him whom I last left, all repute
For his device, in handsoming a suit,
To judge of lace, pink, panes, print, cut, and pleat,
Of all the Court, to have the best conceit.'
'Our dull comedians want him, let him go;
But Oh, God strengthen thee, why stoop'st thou so?'   100
'Why? he hath travelled.' 'Long?' 'No, but to me',
(Which understand none), 'he doth seem to be
Perfect French, and Italian'; I replied,
'So is the pox'. He answered not, but spied
More men of sort, of parts, and qualities;
At last his love he in a window spies,
And like light dew exhaled, he flings from me
Violently ravished to his lechery.
Many were there, he could command no more;
He quarrelled, fought, bled; and turned out of door   110
   Directly came to me hanging the head,
   And constantly a while must keep his bed.

Satire 2

Sir; though (I thank God for it) I do hate
Perfectly all this town, yet there's one state
In all ill things so excellently best,
That hate, towards them, breeds pity towards the rest.
Though poetry indeed be such a sin
As I think that brings dearths, and Spaniards in,
Though like the pestilence and old fashioned love,
Riddingly it catch men; and doth remove
Never, till it be starved out; yet their state
Is poor, disarmed, like papists, not worth hate.   10
One (like a wretch, which at Bar judged as dead,
Yet prompts him which stands next, and cannot read,
And saves his life) gives idiot actors means
(Starving himself) to live by his laboured scenes;
As in some organ, puppets dance above
And bellows pant below, which them do move.
One would move love by rhymes; but witchcraft's charms
Bring not now their old fears, nor their old harms:
Rams, and slings now are silly battery,
Pistolets are the best artillery.   20
And they who write to lords, rewards to get,
Are they not like singers at doors for meat?
And they who write, because all write, have still
That excuse for writing, and for writing ill.
But he is worst, who (beggarly) doth chaw
Others' wits' fruits, and in his ravenous maw
Rankly digested, doth those things out-spew,
As his own things; and they are his own, 'tis true,
For if one eat my meat, though it be known
The meat was mine, th' excrement is his own.   30
But these do me no harm, nor they which use
To outdo dildoes, and out-usure Jews;
To out-drink the sea, to outswear the Litany;
Who with sins' all kinds as familiar be
As confessors; and for whose sinful sake,
Schoolmen new tenements in hell must make:
Whose strange sins, canonists could hardly tell
In which commandment's large receipt they dwell.

But these punish themselves; the insolence
Of Coscus only breeds my just offence,   40
Whom time (which rots all, and makes botches pox,
And plodding on, must make a calf an ox)
Hath made a lawyer, which was (alas) of late
But a scarce poet; jollier of this state,
Than are new beneficed ministers, he throws
Like nets, or lime-twigs, wheresoe'er he goes,
His title of barrister, on every wench,
And woos in language of the Pleas, and Bench:
'A motion, Lady'. 'Speak Coscus'. 'I have been
In love, ever since *tricesimo* of the Queen,   50
Continual claims I have made, injunctions got
To stay my rival's suit, that he should not
Proceed'. 'Spare me'. 'In Hilary term I went,
You said, if I returned next 'size in Lent,
I should be in remitter of your grace;
In th' interim my letters should take place
Of affidavits'; words, words, which would tear
The tender labyrinth of a soft maid's ear,
More, more, than ten Sclavonians scolding, more
Than when winds in our ruined abbeys roar.   60
When sick with poetry, and possessed with Muse
Thou wast, and mad, I hoped; but men which choose
Law practice for mere gain, bold soul, repute
Worse than embrothelled strumpets prostitute.
Now like an owl-like watchman, he must walk
His hand still at a bill, now he must talk
Idly, like prisoners, which whole months will swear
That only suretyship hath brought them there,
And to every suitor lie in everything,
Like a king's favourite, yea like a king;   70
Like a wedge in a block, wring to the bar,
Bearing like asses, and more shameless far
Than carted whores, lie, to the grave judge; for
Bastardy abounds not in kings' titles, nor
Simony and sodomy in churchmen's lives,
As these things do in him; by these he thrives.
Shortly (as the sea) he will compass all our land;
From Scots, to Wight; from Mount, to Dover strand.

And spying heirs melting with luxury,
Satan will not joy at their sins, as he.   80
For as a thrifty wench scrapes kitchen stuff,
And barrelling the droppings, and the snuff,
Of wasting candles, which in thirty year
(Relic-like kept) perchance buys wedding gear;
Piecemeal he gets lands, and spends as much time
Wringing each acre, as men pulling prime.
In parchments then, large as his fields, he draws
Assurances, big, as glossed civil laws,
So huge, that men (in our time's forwardness)
Are Fathers of the Church for writing less.   90
These he writes not; nor for these written pays,
Therefore spares no length; as in those first days
When Luther was professed, he did desire
Short *Pater nosters*, saying as a friar
Each day his beads, but having left those laws,
Adds to Christ's prayer, the power and glory clause.
But when he sells or changes land, he impairs
His writings, and (unwatched) leaves out, *ses heires*,
As slily as any commenter goes by
Hard words, or sense; or in Divinity   100
As controverters, in vouched texts, leave out
Shrewd words, which might against them clear the doubt.
Where are those spread woods which clothed heretofore
Those bought lands? not built, nor burnt within door.
Where's th' old landlord's troops, and alms? In great halls
Carthusian fasts, and fulsome bacchanals
Equally I hate; means bless; in rich men's homes
I bid kill some beasts, but no hecatombs,
None starve, none surfeit so; but oh we allow,
Good works as good, but out of fashion now,   110
Like old rich wardrobes; but my words none draws
Within the vast reach of the huge statute laws.

Satire 3

Kind pity chokes my spleen; brave scorn forbids
Those tears to issue which swell my eye-lids,
I must not laugh, nor weep sins, and be wise,
Can railing then cure these worn maladies?

Is not our mistress fair religion,
As worthy of all our soul's devotion,
As virtue was to the first blinded age?
Are not heaven's joys as valiant to assuage
Lusts, as earth's honour was to them? Alas,
As we do them in means, shall they surpass   10
Us in the end, and shall thy father's spirit
Meet blind philosophers in heaven, whose merit
Of strict life may be imputed faith, and hear
Thee, whom he taught so easy ways and near
To follow, damned? O if thou dar'st, fear this;
This fear great courage, and high valour is.
Dar'st thou aid mutinous Dutch, and dar'st thou lay
Thee in ships' wooden sepulchres, a prey
To leaders' rage, to storms, to shot, to dearth?
Dar'st thou dive seas, and dungeons of the earth?   20
Hast thou courageous fire to thaw the ice
Of frozen north discoveries? and thrice
Colder than salamanders, like divine
Children in th'oven, fires of Spain, and the line,
Whose countries limbecks to our bodies be,
Canst thou for gain bear? and must every he
Which cries not, 'Goddess!' to thy mistress, draw,
Or eat thy poisonous words? courage of straw!
O desperate coward, wilt thou seem bold, and
To thy foes and his (who made thee to stand   30
Sentinel in his world's garrison) thus yield,
And for forbidden wars, leave th'appointed field?
Know thy foes: the foul Devil, he, whom thou
Strivest to please, for hate, not love, would allow
Thee fain, his whole realm to be quit; and as
The world's all parts wither away and pass,
So the world's self, thy other loved foe, is
In her decrepit wane, and thou loving this,
Dost love a withered and worn strumpet; last,
Flesh (itself 's death) and joys which flesh can taste,   40
Thou lovest; and thy fair goodly soul, which doth
Give this flesh power to taste joy, thou dost loathe.
  Seek true religion. O where? Mirreus
Thinking her unhoused here, and fled from us,
Seeks her at Rome; there, because he doth know
That she was there a thousand years ago,

He loves her rags so, as we here obey
The statecloth where the Prince sat yesterday.
Crants to such brave loves will not be enthralled,
But loves her only, who at Geneva is called   50
Religion, plain, simple, sullen, young,
Contemptuous, yet unhandsome; as among
Lecherous humours, there is one that judges
No wenches wholesome, but coarse country
    drudges.
Graius stays still at home here, and because
Some preachers, vile ambitious bawds, and laws
Still new like fashions, bid him think that she
Which dwells with us, is only perfect, he
Embraceth her, whom his godfathers will
Tender to him, being tender, as wards still   60
Take such wives as their guardians offer, or
Pay values. Careless Phrygius doth abhor
All, because all cannot be good, as one
Knowing some women whores, dares marry none.
Gracchus loves all as one, and thinks that so
As women do in divers countries go
In divers habits, yet are still one kind,
So doth, so is religion; and this blind-
ness too much light breeds; but unmoved thou
Of force must one, and forced but one allow;   70
And the right; ask thy father which is she,
Let him ask his; though truth and falsehood be
Near twins, yet truth a little elder is;
Be busy to seek her, believe me this,
He's not of none, nor worst, that seeks the best.
To adore, or scorn an image, or protest,
May all be bad; doubt wisely; in strange way
To stand inquiring right, is not to stray;
To sleep, or run wrong, is. On a huge hill,
Cragged, and steep, Truth stands, and he that will   80
Reach her, about must, and about must go;
And what the hill's suddenness resists, win so;
Yet strive so, that before age, death's twilight,
Thy soul rest, for none can work in that night.
To will, implies delay, therefore now do:
Hard deeds, the body's pains; hard knowledge too

The mind's endeavours reach, and mysteries
Are like the sun, dazzling, yet plain to all eyes.
Keep the truth which thou hast found; men do not stand
In so ill case here, that God hath with his hand   90
Signed kings blank-charters to kill whom they hate,
Nor are they vicars, but hangmen to Fate.
Fool and wretch, wilt thou let thy soul be tied
To man's laws, by which she shall not be tried
At the last day? Will it then boot thee
To say a Philip, or a Gregory,
A Harry, or a Martin taught thee this?
Is not this excuse for mere contraries,
Equally strong? cannot both sides say so?
That thou mayest rightly obey power, her bounds know;   100
Those past, her nature and name is changed; to be
Then humble to her is idolatry;
As streams are, power is; those blessed flowers that dwell
At the rough stream's calm head, thrive and prove well,
But having left their roots, and themselves given
To the streams's tyrannous rage, alas, are driven
Through mills, and rocks, and woods, and at last, almost
Consumed in going, in the sea are lost:
So perish souls, which more choose men's unjust
Power from God claimed, than God himself to trust.   110

Satire 4

Well; I may now receive, and die; my sin
Indeed is great, but I have been in
A purgatory, such as feared hell is
A recreation to, and scant map of this.
My mind, neither with pride's itch, nor yet hath been
Poisoned with love to see, or to be seen.
I had no suit there, nor new suit to show,
Yet went to Court; but as Glaze which did go
To a Mass in jest, catched, was fain to disburse
The hundred marks, which is the Statute's curse,   10
Before he 'scaped, so it pleased my destiny
(Guilty of my sin of going), to think me

As prone to all ill, and of good as forget-
ful, as proud, as lustful, and as much in debt,
As vain, as witless, and as false as they
Which dwell at Court, for once going that way.
Therefore I suffered this; towards me did run
A thing more strange, than on Nile's slime, the sun
E'er bred; or all which into Noah's Ark came;
A thing, which would have posed Adam to name;   20
Stranger than seven antiquaries' studies,
Than Afric's monsters, Guiana's rarities;
Stranger than strangers; one, who for a Dane,
In the Danes' Massacre had sure been slain,
If he had lived then; and without help dies,
When next the 'prentices 'gainst strangers rise.
One, whom the watch at noon lets scarce go by,
One, to whom the examining Justice sure would cry,
'Sir, by your priesthood tell me what you are.'
His clothes were strange, though coarse; and black, though   30
    bare;
Sleeveless his jerkin was, and it had been
Velvet, but 'twas now (so much ground was seen)
Become tufftaffaty; and our children shall
See it plain rash awhile, then naught at all.
This thing hath travelled, and saith, speaks all tongues
And only knoweth what to all states belongs;
Made of th' accents, and best phrase of all these,
He speaks one language; if strange meats displease,
Art can deceive, or hunger force my taste,
But pedant's motley tongue, soldier's bombast,   40
Mountebank's drugtongue, nor the terms of law
Are strong enough preparatives, to draw
Me to bear this: yet I must be content
With his tongue, in his tongue, called compliment:
In which he can win widows, and pay scores,
Make men speak treason, cozen subtlest whores,
Out-flatter favourites, or out-lie either
Jovius, or Surius, or both together.
He names me, and comes to me; I whisper, 'God!
How have I sinned, that thy wrath's furious rod,   50
This fellow, chooseth me?' He sayeth, 'Sir,
I love your judgment; whom do you prefer,

For the best linguist?' And I sillily
Said, that I thought Calepine's Dictionary;
'Nay but of men, most sweet Sir?' Beza then,
Some Jesuits, and two reverend men
Of our two Academies, I named; there
He stopped me, and said, 'Nay, your Apostles were
Good pretty linguists, and so Panurge was;
Yet a poor gentleman, all these may pass   60
By travail.' Then, as if he would have sold
His tongue, he praised it, and such wonders told
That I was fain to say, 'If you had lived, Sir,
Time enough to have been interpreter
To Babel's bricklayers, sure the Tower had stood.'
He adds, 'If of Court life you knew the good,
You would leave loneness.' I said, 'Not alone
My loneness is; but Spartans' fashion,
To teach by painting drunkards, doth not taste
Now; Aretine's pictures have made few chaste;   70
No more can princes' Courts, though there be few
Better pictures of vice, teach me virtue.'
He, like to a high stretched lute string squeaked,
    'O Sir,
'Tis sweet to talk of kings.' 'At Westminster,'
Said I, 'the man that keeps the Abbey tombs,
And for his price doth with whoever comes,
Of all our Harrys, and our Edwards talk,
From king to king and all their kin can walk:
Your ears shall hear naught, but kings; your eyes meet
Kings only; The way to it, is King Street.'   80
He smacked, and cried, 'He's base, mechanic, coarse,
So are all your Englishmen in their discourse.
Are not your Frenchmen neat?' 'Mine? as you see,
I have but one Frenchman, look, he follows me'
'Certes they are neatly clothed; I, of this mind am,
Your only wearing is your grogaram.'
'Not so Sir, I have more.' Under this pitch
He would not fly; I chaffed him; but as itch
Scratched into smart, and as blunt iron ground
Into an edge, hurts worse: so, I (fool) found,   90
Crossing hurt me; to fit my sullenness,
He to another key, his style doth address,

And asks, 'What news?' I tell him of new plays.
He takes my hand, and as a still, which stays
A semi-breve, 'twixt each drop, he niggardly,
As loth to enrich me, so tells many a lie,
More than ten Holinsheds, or Halls, or Stows,
Of trivial household trash he knows; he knows
When the Queen frowned, or smiled, and he knows what
A subtle statesman may gather of that;   100
He knows who loves; whom; and who by poison
Hastes to an office's reversion;
He knows who hath sold his land, and now doth beg
A licence, old iron, boots, shoes, and egg-
shells to transport; shortly boys shall not play
At span-counter, or blow-point, but they pay
Toll to some courtier; and wiser than all us,
He knows what lady is not painted; thus
He with home-meats tries me; I belch, spew, spit,
Look pale, and sickly, like a patient; yet   110
He thrusts on more; and as if he undertook
To say *Gallo-Belgicus* without book
Speaks of all states, and deeds, that have been since
The Spaniards came, to the loss of Amiens.
Like a big wife, at sight of loathed meat,
Ready to travail: so I sigh, and sweat
To hear this Macaron talk: in vain; for yet,
Either my humour, or his own to fit,
He like a privileged spy, whom nothing can
Discredit, libels now 'gainst each great man.   120
He names a price for every office paid;
He saith, our wars thrive ill, because delayed;
That offices are entailed, and that there are
Perpetuities of them, lasting as far
As the last day; and that great officers,
Do with the pirates share, and Dunkirkers.
Who wastes in meat, in clothes, in horse, he notes;
Who loves whores, who boys, and who goats.
I more amazed than Circe's prisoners, when
They felt themselves turn beasts, felt myself then   130
Becoming traitor, and methought I saw
One of our giant Statutes ope his jaw

To suck me in; for hearing him, I found
That as burnt venomed lechers do grow sound
By giving others their sores, I might grow
Guilty, and he free: therefore I did show
All signs of loathing; but since I am in,
I must pay mine, and my forefathers' sin
To the last farthing; therefore to my power
Toughly and stubbornly I bear this cross; but the hour   140
Of mercy now was come; he tries to bring
Me to pay a fine to 'scape his torturing,
And says, 'Sir, can you spare me?' I said, 'Willingly.'
'Nay, Sir, can you spare me a crown?' Thankfully I
Gave it, as ransom; but as fiddlers, still,
Though they be paid to be gone, yet needs will
Thrust one more jig upon you; so did he
With his long complimental thanks vex me.
But he is gone, thanks to his needy want,
And the prerogative of my crown: scant   150
His thanks were ended, when I, (which did see
All the Court filled with more strange things than he)
Ran from thence with such or more haste, than one
Who fears more actions, doth make from prison.
    At home in wholesome solitariness
My precious soul began, the wretchedness
Of suitors at Court to mourn, and a trance
Like his, who dreamed he saw hell, did advance
Itself on me; such men as he saw there,
I saw at Court, and worse, and more; low fear   160
Becomes the guilty, not the accuser; then,
Shall I, none's slave, of high-born, or raised men
Fear frowns? And, my mistress Truth, betray thee
To th' huffing braggart, puffed nobility?
No, no, thou which since yesterday hast been
Almost about the whole world, hast thou seen,
O sun, in all thy journey, vanity,
Such as swells the bladder of our Court? I
Think he which made your waxen garden, and
Transported it from Italy to stand   170
With us, at London, flouts our Presence, for
Just such gay painted things, which no sap, nor

Taste have in them, ours are; and natural
Some of the stocks are, their fruits, bastard all.
　'Tis ten a-clock and past; all whom the mews,
Balloon, tennis, diet, or the stews,
Had all the morning held, now the second
Time made ready, that day, in flocks, are found
In the Presence, and I, (God pardon me).
As fresh, and sweet their apparels be, as be   180
The fields they sold to buy them; 'For a King
Those hose are,' cry the flatterers; and bring
Them next week to the theatre to sell;
Wants reach all states; me seems they do as well
At stage, as Court; all are players; whoe'er looks
(For themselves dare not go) o'er Cheapside books,
Shall find their wardrobe's inventory. Now,
The ladies come; as pirates, which do know
That there came weak ships fraught with cochineal,
The men board them; and praise, as they think, well,   190
Their beauties; they the men's wits; both are bought.
Why good wits ne'er wear scarlet gowns, I thought
This cause: these men, men's wits for speeches buy,
And women buy all reds which scarlets dye.
He called her beauty lime-twigs, her hair net;
She fears her drugs ill laid, her hair loose set.
Would not Heraclitus laugh to see Macrine,
From hat, to shoe, himself at door refine,
As if the Presence were a moschite, and lift
His skirts and hose, and call his clothes to shrift,   200
Making them confess not only mortal
Great stains and holes in them, but venial
Feathers and dust, wherewith they fornicate;
And then by Dürer's rules survey the state
Of his each limb, and with strings the odds tries
Of his neck to his leg, and waist to thighs.
So in immaculate clothes, and symmetry
Perfect as circles, with such nicety
As a young preacher at his first time goes
To preach, he enters, and a lady which owes   210
Him not so much as good will, he arrests,
And unto her protests protests protests

So much as at Rome would serve to have thrown
Ten Cardinals into the Inquisition;
And whispered 'By Jesu', so often, that a
Pursuivant would have ravished him away
For saying of Our Lady's psalter; but 'tis fit
That they each other plague, they merit it.
But here comes Glorius that will plague them both,
Who, in the other extreme, only doth   220
Call a rough carelessness, good fashion;
Whose cloak his spurs tear; whom he spits on
He cares not; his ill words do no harm
To him; he rusheth in, as if 'Arm, arm',
He meant to cry; and though his face be as ill
As theirs which in old hangings whip Christ, yet still
He strives to look worse, he keeps all in awe;
Jests like a licensed fool, commands like law.

   Tired, now I leave this place, and but pleased so
As men which from gaols to execution go,   230
Go through the great chamber (why is it hung
With the seven deadly sins?). Being among
Those Ascaparts, men big enough to throw
Charing Cross for a bar, men that do know
No token of worth, but 'Queen's man', and fine
Living, barrels of beef, flagons of wine;
I shook like a spied spy. Preachers which are
Seas of wit and arts, you can, then dare,
Drown the sins of this place, for, for me
Which am but a scarce brook, it enough shall be   240
To wash the stains away; though I yet
With Maccabees' modesty, the known merit
Of my work lessen: yet some wise man shall,
I hope, esteem my writs canonical.

Satire 5

Thou shalt not laugh in this leaf, Muse, nor they
Whom any pity warms; he which did lay
Rules to make courtiers, (he being understood
May make good courtiers, but who courtiers good?)

Frees from the sting of jests all who in extreme
Are wretched or wicked: of these two a theme
Charity and liberty give me. What is he
Who officers' rage, and suitors' misery
Can write, and jest? If all things be in all,
As I think, since all, which were, are, and shall   10
Be, be made of the same elements:
Each thing, each thing implies or represents.
Then man is a world; in which, officers
Are the vast ravishing seas; and suitors,
Springs; now full, now shallow, now dry; which, to
That which drowns them, run: these self reasons do
Prove the world a man, in which, officers
Are the devouring stomach, and suitors
The excrements, which they void. All men are dust;
How much worse are suitors, who to men's lust   20
Are made preys? O worse than dust, or worm's meat,
For they do eat you now, whose selves worms shall eat.
They are the mills which grind you, yet you are
The wind which drives them; and a wasteful war
Is fought against you, and you fight it; they
Adulterate law, and you prepare their way
Like wittols; th' issue your own ruin is.
　　Greatest and fairest Empress, know you this?
Alas, no more than Thames' calm head doth know
Whose meads her arms drown, or whose corn o'er flow: 30
You Sir, whose righteousness she loves, whom I
By having leave to serve, am most richly
For service paid, authorized, now begin
To know and weed out this enormous sin.
　　O age of rusty iron! Some better wit
Call it some worse name, if aught equal it;
The Iron Age that was, when justice was sold; now
Injustice is sold dearer far. Allow
All demands, fees and duties—gamesters, anon
The money which you sweat, and swear for, is gone   40
Into other hands: so controverted lands
'Scape, like Angelica, the strivers' hands.
If law be in the judge's heart, and he
Have no heart to resist letter, or fee,

Where wilt thou appeal? power of the courts below
Flow from the first main head, and these can throw
Thee, if they suck thee in, to misery,
To fetters, halters; but if the injury
Steel thee to dare complain, alas, thou go'st
Against the stream, when upwards: when thou art most   50
Heavy and most faint; and in these labours they,
'Gainst whom thou shouldst complain, will in the way
Become great seas, o'er which, when thou shalt be
Forced to make golden bridges, thou shalt see
That all thy gold was drowned in them before;
All things follow their like, only who have may have more.
Judges are gods; he who made and said them so,
Meant not that men should be forced to them to go,
By means of angels; when supplications
We send to God, to Dominations,   60
Powers, Cherubins, and all heaven's courts, if we
Should pay fees as here, daily bread would be
Scarce to kings; so 'tis. Would it not anger
A stoic, a coward, yea a martyr,
To see a pursuivant come in, and call
All his clothes, copes; books, primers; and all
His plate, chalices; and mistake them away,
And ask a fee for coming? Oh, ne'er may
Fair Law's white reverend name be strumpeted,
To warrant thefts: she is established   70
Recorder to Destiny, on earth, and she
Speaks Fate's words, and but tells us who must be
Rich, who poor, who in chairs, who in gaols:
She is all fair, but yet hath foul long nails,
With which she scratcheth suitors; in bodies
Of men, so in law, nails are th' extremities,
So officers stretch to more than Law can do,
As our nails reach what no else part comes to.
Why barest thou to yon officer? Fool, hath he
Got those goods, for which erst men bared to thee?   80
Fool, twice, thrice, thou hast bought wrong, and now
     hungerly
Begg'st right; but that dole comes not till these die.
Thou hadst much, and law's Urim and Thummim try

Thou wouldst for more; and for all hast paper
Enough to clothe all the Great Carrack's pepper.
Sell that, and by that thou much more shalt leese,
Than Haman, when he sold his antiquities.
O wretch that thy fortunes should moralize
Aesop's fables, and make tales, prophecies.
Thou'rt the swimming dog whom shadows cozened,   90
And div'st, near drowning, for what vanished.

LOVE ELEGIES

Elegy 1: The Bracelet

UPON THE LOSS OF HIS MISTRESS' CHAIN, FOR WHICH
HE MADE SATISFACTION

Not that in colour it was like thy hair,
For armlets of that thou mayst let me wear,
Nor that thy hand it oft embraced and kissed,
For so it had that good, which oft I missed;
Nor for that silly old morality,
That as those links are tied, our love should be;
Mourn I that I thy sevenfold chain have lost,
Nor for the luck sake; but the bitter cost.
    Oh shall twelve righteous angels, which as yet
No leaven of vile solder did admit,   10
Nor yet by any way have strayed or gone
From the first state of their creation,
Angels, which heaven commanded to provide
All things to me, and be my faithful guide,
To gain new friends, to appease great enemies,
To comfort my soul, when I lie or rise;
Shall these twelve innocents, by thy severe
Sentence (dread judge) my sins' great burden bear?
Shall they be damned, and in the furnace thrown,
And punished for offences not their own?   20
They save not me, they do not ease my pains
When in that hell they are burnt and tied in chains.
    Were they but crowns of France, I cared not,
For, most of them their natural country rot
I think possesseth, they come here to us,
So lean, so pale, so lame, so ruinous,
And howsoe'er French kings most Christian be,
Their crowns are circumcised most Jewishly.
Or were they Spanish stamps, still travelling,
That are become as Catholic as their king,   30

Those unlicked bear-whelps, unfiled pistolets
That, more than cannon shot, avails or lets,
Which, negligently left unrounded, look
Like many-angled figures in the book
Of some great conjurer, which would enforce
Nature, as these do justice, from her course;
Which, as the soul quickens head, feet and heart,
As streams, like veins, run through th' earth's every part,
Visit all countries, and have slily made
Gorgeous France, ruined, ragged and decayed,   40
Scotland, which knew no State, proud in one day,
And mangled seventeen-headed Belgia;
Or were it such gold as that wherewithal
Almighty chemics from each mineral
Having by subtle fire a soul out-pulled,
Are dirtily and desperately gulled;
I would not spit to quench the fire they were in,
For they are guilty of much heinous sin,
But shall my harmless angels perish? Shall
I lose my guard, my ease, my food, my all?   50
Much hope, which they should nourish, will be dead,
Much of my able youth, and lustihead
Will vanish; if thou love, let them alone,
For thou wilt love me less when they are gone.
    Oh be content that some loud squeaking crier
Well-pleased with one lean threadbare groat for hire,
May like a devil roar through every street,
And gall the finder's conscience if they meet.
Or let me creep to some dread conjurer,
Which with fantastic schemes full-fills much paper,   60
Which hath divided heaven in tenements,
And with whores, thieves, and murderers stuffed his rents
So full, that though he pass them all in sin,
He leaves himself no room to enter in.
And if, when all his art and time is spent,
He say 'twill ne'er be found; oh be content;
Receive from him that doom ungrudgingly,
Because he is the mouth of destiny.
    Thou say'st (alas) the gold doth still remain,
Though it be changed, and put into a chain.   70

So in the first fall'n angels resteth still
Wisdom and knowledge, but 'tis turned to ill;
As these should do good works, and should provide
Necessities, but now must nurse thy pride.
And they are still bad angels; mine are none,
For form gives being, and their form is gone.
Pity these angels yet; their dignities
Pass Virtues, Powers, and Principalities.
   But thou art resolute; thy will be done.
Yet with such anguish as her only son   80
The mother in the hungry grave doth lay,
Unto the fire these martyrs I betray.
Good souls, for you give life to everything,
Good angels, for good messages you bring,
Destined you might have been to such a one
As would have loved and worshipped you alone,
One that would suffer hunger, nakedness,
Yea death, ere he would make your number less.
But I am guilty of your sad decay,
May your few fellows longer with me stay.   90
   But Oh thou wretched finder whom I hate
So much that I almost pity thy estate;
Gold being the heaviest metal amongst all,
May my most heavy curse upon thee fall.
Here fettered, manacled, and hanged in chains
First mayst thou be, then chained to hellish pains;
Or be with foreign gold bribed to betray
Thy country, and fail both of that and thy pay.
May the next thing thou stoop'st to reach, contain
Poison, whose nimble fume rot thy moist brain;   100
Or libels, or some interdicted thing,
Which negligently kept, thy ruin bring.
Lust-bred diseases rot thee; and dwell with thee
Itchy desire and no ability.
May all the hurt which ever gold hath wrought,
All mischiefs which all devils ever thought,
Want after plenty, poor and gouty age,
The plagues of travellers, love and marriage
Afflict thee; and at thy life's latest moment
May thy swoll'n sins themselves to thee present.   110

But I forgive; repent thou honest man:
Gold is restorative, restore it then,
Or if with it thou be'st loth to depart,
Because 'tis cordial, would 'twere at thy heart.

Elegy 2: To his Mistress Going to Bed

Come, Madam, come, all rest my powers defy,
Until I labour, I in labour lie.
The foe oft-times, having the foe in sight,
Is tired with standing though they never fight.
Off with that girdle, like heaven's zone glistering,
But a far fairer world encompassing.
Unpin that spangled breastplate, which you wear
That th' eyes of busy fools may be stopped there:
Unlace yourself, for that harmonious chime
Tells me from you that now 'tis your bed-time.   10
Off with that happy busk, which I envy,
That still can be, and still can stand so nigh.
Your gown going off, such beauteous state reveals,
As when from flowery meads th' hill's shadow steals.
Off with your wiry coronet and show
The hairy diadem which on you doth grow.
Off with those shoes: and then safely tread
In this love's hallowed temple, this soft bed.
In such white robes heaven's angels used to be
Received by men; thou angel bring'st with thee   20
A heaven like Mahomet's paradise; and though
Ill spirits walk in white, we easily know
By this these angels from an evil sprite,
They set our hairs, but these our flesh upright.
    Licence my roving hands, and let them go
Behind, before, above, between, below.
O my America, my new found land,
My kingdom, safeliest when with one man manned,
My mine of precious stones, my empery,
How blessed am I in this discovering thee.   30
To enter in these bonds is to be free,
Then where my hand is set my seal shall be.

Full nakedness, all joys are due to thee.
As souls unbodied, bodies unclothed must be,
To taste whole joys. Gems which you women use
Are like Atlanta's balls, cast in men's views,
That when a fool's eye lighteth on a gem
His earthly soul may covet theirs, not them.
Like pictures, or like books' gay coverings made
For laymen, are all women thus arrayed;   40
Themselves are mystic books, which only we
Whom their imputed grace will dignify
Must see revealed. Then since I may know,
As liberally as to a midwife show
Thyself; cast all, yea this white linen hence,
Here is no penance, much less innocence.
        To teach thee, I am naked first: why then
What needst thou have more covering than a man?

Elegy 3: Jealousy

Fond woman, which wouldst have thy husband die,
And yet complain'st of his great jealousy;
If swoll'n with poison, he lay in his last bed,
His body with a sere-bark covered,
Drawing his breath, as thick and short, as can
The nimblest crocheting musician,
Ready with loathsome vomiting to spew
His soul out of one hell, into a new,
Made deaf with his poor kindred's howling cries,
Begging with few feigned tears, great legacies,   10
Thou wouldst not weep, but jolly, and frolic be,
As a slave, which tomorrow should be free;
Yet weep'st thou, when thou seest him hungerly
Swallow his own death, heart's-bane jealousy.
O give him many thanks, he is courteous,
That in suspecting kindly warneth us.
We must not, as we used, flout openly,
In scoffing riddles, his deformity;
Nor at his board together being sat,
With words, nor touch, scarce looks adulterate.   20

Nor when he swoll'n, and pampered with great fare,
Sits down, and snorts, caged in his basket chair,
Must we usurp his own bed any more,
Nor kiss and play in his house, as before.
Now I see many dangers; for that is
His realm, his castle, and his diocese.
But if, as envious men, which would revile
Their prince, or coin his gold, themselves exile
Into another country, and do it there,
We play in another house, what should we fear?   30
There we will scorn his household policies,
His silly plots, and pensionary spies,
As the inhabitants of Thames' right side
Do London's Mayor; or Germans, the Pope's pride.

Elegy 4: The Anagram

Marry, and love thy Flavia, for, she
Hath all things, whereby others beauteous be,
For, though her eyes be small, her mouth is great,
Though they be ivory, yet her teeth are jet,
Though they be dim, yet she is light enough,
And though her harsh hair fall, her skin is rough;
What though her cheeks be yellow, her hair is red,
Give her thine, and she hath a maidenhead.
These things are beauty's elements, where these
Meet in one, that one must, as perfect, please.   10
If red and white and each good quality
Be in thy wench, ne'er ask where it doth lie.
In buying things perfumed, we ask, if there
Be musk and amber in it, but not where.
Though all her parts be not in th' usual place,
She hath yet an anagram of a good face.
If we might put the letters but one way,
In the lean dearth of words, what could we say?
When by the gamut some musicians make
A perfect song, others will undertake,   20
By the same gamut changed, to equal it.
Things simply good, can never be unfit.

She's fair as any, if all be like her,
And if none be, then she is singular.
All love is wonder; if we justly do
Account her wonderful, why not lovely too?
Love built on beauty, soon as beauty, dies,
Choose this face, changed by no deformities.
Women are all like angels; the fair be
Like those which fell to worse; but such as she,   30
Like to good angels, nothing can impair:
'Tis less grief to be foul, than to have been fair.
For one night's revels, silk and gold we choose,
But, in long journeys, cloth, and leather use.
Beauty is barren oft; best husbands say
There is best land, where there is foulest way.
Oh what a sovereign plaster will she be,
If thy past sins have taught thee jealousy!
Here needs no spies, nor eunuchs; her commit
Safe to thy foes; yea, to a marmoset.   40
When Belgia's cities, the round countries drown,
That dirty foulness guards, and arms the town:
So doth her face guard her; and so, for thee,
Which, forced by business, absent oft must be,
She, whose face, like clouds, turns the day to night,
Who, mightier than the sea, makes Moors seem white,
Who, though seven years, she in the stews had laid,
A nunnery durst receive, and think a maid,
And though in childbirth's labour she did lie,
Midwives would swear, 'twere but a tympany,   50
Whom, if she accuse herself, I credit less
Than witches, which impossibles confess,
Whom dildoes, bedstaves, and her velvet glass
Would be as loth to touch as Joseph was:
One like none, and liked of none, fittest were,
For, things in fashion every man will wear.

Elegy 5: Change

Although thy hand and faith, and good works too,
Have sealed thy love which nothing should undo,
Yea though thou fall back, that apostasy
Confirm thy love; yet much, much I fear thee.

Women are like the arts, forced unto none,
Open to all searchers, unprized, if unknown.
If I have caught a bird, and let him fly,
Another fowler using these means, as I,
May catch the same bird; and, as these things be,
Women are made for men, not him, nor me.   10
Foxes and goats, all beasts change when they please,
Shall women, more hot, wily, wild than these,
Be bound to one man, and did Nature then
Idly make them apter to endure than men?
They are our clogs, and their own; if a man be
Chained to a galley, yet the galley is free;
Who hath a plough-land, casts all his seed corn there,
And yet allows his ground more corn should bear;
Though Danuby into the sea must flow,
The sea receives the Rhine, Volga, and Po.   20
By nature, which gave it, this liberty
Thou lov'st, but Oh! canst thou love it and me?
Likeness glues love: then if so thou do,
To make us like and love, must I change too?
More than thy hate, I hate it, rather let me
Allow her change, than change as oft as she,
And so not teach, but force my opinion
To love not any one, nor every one.
To live in one land, is captivity,
To run all countries, a wild roguery;   30
Waters stink soon, if in one place they bide,
And in the vast sea are worse putrefied:
But when they kiss one bank, and leaving this
Never look back, but the next bank do kiss,
Then are they purest; change is the nursery
Of music, joy, life and eternity.

Elegy 6: The Perfume

Once, and but once found in thy company,
All thy supposed escapes are laid on me;
And as a thief at bar, is questioned there
By all the men, that have been robbed that year,

So am I, (by this traitorous means surprised)
By thy hydroptic father catechized.
Though he had wont to search with glazed eyes,
As though he came to kill a cockatrice,
Though he have oft sworn, that he would remove
Thy beauty's beauty, and food of our love,   10
Hope of his goods, if I with thee were seen,
Yet close and secret, as our souls, we have been.
Though thy immortal mother which doth lie
Still buried in her bed, yet will not die,
Take this advantage to sleep out day-light,
And watch thy entries, and returns all night,
And, when she takes thy hand, and would seem kind,
Doth search what rings, and armlets she can find,
And kissing notes the colour of thy face,
And fearing lest thou art swoll'n, doth thee embrace;   20
And to try if thou long, doth name strange meats,
And notes thy paleness, blushings, sighs, and sweats;
And politicly will to thee confess
The sins of her own youth's rank lustiness;
Yet love these sorceries did remove, and move
Thee to gull thine own mother for my love.
Thy little brethren, which like fairy sprites
Oft skipped into our chamber, those sweet nights,
And, kissed and ingled on thy father's knee,
Were bribed next day, to tell what they did see;   30
The grim eight-foot-high iron-bound serving-man,
That oft names God in oaths, and only then,
He that to bar the first gate, doth as wide
As the great Rhodian Colossus stride,
Which, if in hell no other pains there were,
Makes me fear hell, because he must be there:
Though by thy father he were hired for this,
Could never witness any touch or kiss.
But Oh, too common ill, I brought with me
That, which betrayed me to mine enemy: 40
A loud perfume, which at my entrance cried
Even at thy father's nose, so we were spied.
When, like a tyrant king, that in his bed
Smelt gunpowder, the pale wretch shivered.

Had it been some bad smell, he would have thought
That his own feet, or breath, that smell had wrought.
But as we in our isle imprisoned,
Where cattle only, and diverse dogs are bred,
The precious unicorns, strange monsters call,
So thought he good, strange, that had none at all.   50
I taught my silks, their whistling to forbear,
Even my oppressed shoes, dumb and speechless were,
Only, thou bitter sweet, whom I had laid
Next me, me traitorously hast betrayed,
And unsuspected hast invisibly
At once fled unto him, and stayed with me.
Base excrement of earth, which dost confound
Sense, from distinguishing the sick from sound;
By thee the silly amorous sucks his death
By drawing in a leprous harlot's breath;   60
By thee, the greatest stain to man's estate
Falls on us, to be called effeminate;
Though you be much loved in the prince's hall,
There, things that seem, exceed substantial.
Gods, when ye fumed on altars, were pleased well,
Because you were burnt, not that they liked your smell;
You are loathsome all, being taken simply alone,
Shall we love ill things joined, and hate each one?
If you were good, your good doth soon decay;
And you are rare, that takes the good away.   70
All my perfumes, I give most willingly
To embalm thy father's corse; What? will he die?

Elegy 7: His Picture

Here take my picture, though I bid farewell;
Thine, in my heart, where my soul dwells, shall dwell.
'Tis like me now, but I dead, 'twill be more
When we are shadows both, than 'twas before.
When weather-beaten I come back; my hand,
Perchance with rude oars torn, or sun-beams tanned,
My face and breast of haircloth, and my head
With care's rash sudden hoariness o'erspread,

My body a sack of bones, broken within,
And powder's blue stains scattered on my skin;   10
If rival fools tax thee to have loved a man,
So foul, and coarse, as oh, I may seem then,
This shall say what I was: and thou shalt say,
Do his hurts reach me? doth my worth decay?
Or do they reach his judging mind, that he
Should now love less, what he did love to see?
That which in him was fair and delicate,
Was but the milk, which in love's childish state
Did nurse it: who now is grown strong enough
To feed on that, which to disused tastes seems tough.   20

Elegy 8: On Sir Thomas Egerton

Sorrow, who to this house scarce knew the way,
Is, oh, heir of it, our all is his prey.
This strange chance claims strange wonder, and to us
Nothing can be so strange, as to weep thus.
'Tis well his life's loud speaking works deserve,
And give praise too, our cold tongues could not serve:
'Tis well, he kept tears from our eyes before,
That to fit this deep ill, we might have store.
Oh, if a sweet briar climb up by a tree,
If to a paradise that transplanted be,   10
Or felled, and burnt for holy sacrifice,
Yet, that must wither, which by it did rise,
As we for him dead: though no family
E'er rigged a soul for heaven's discovery
With whom more venturers more boldly dare
Venture their states, with him in joy to share.
We lose what all friends loved, him; he gains now
But life by death, which worst foes would allow,
If he could have foes, in whose practice grew
All virtues, whose names subtle schoolmen knew.   20
What ease can hope that we shall see'him, beget,
When we must die first, and cannot die yet?
His children are his pictures, oh they be
Pictures of him dead, senseless, cold as he.
Here needs no marble tomb, since he is gone,
He, and about him, his, are turned to stone.

Elegy 9

Oh, let me not serve so, as those men serve
Whom honours' smokes at once fatten and starve;
Poorly enriched with great men's words or looks;
Nor so write my name in thy loving books
As those idolatrous flatterers, which still
Their prince's styles, with many realms fulfil
Whence they no tribute have, and where no sway.
Such services I offer as shall pay
Themselves, I hate dead names: oh then let me
Favourite in ordinary, or no favourite be.   10
When my soul was in her own body sheathed,
Nor yet by oaths betrothed, nor kisses breathed
Into my purgatory, faithless thee,
Thy heart seemed wax, and steel thy constancy.
So, careless flowers strowed on the water's face,
The curled whirlpools suck, smack, and embrace,
Yet drown them; so, the taper's beamy eye
Amorously twinkling, beckons the giddy fly,
Yet burns his wing; and such the devil is,
Scarce visiting them, who are entirely his.   20
When I behold a stream, which, from the spring,
Doth with doubtful melodious murmuring,
Or in a speechless slumber, calmly ride
Her wedded channel's bosom, and then chide
And bend her brows, and swell if any bough
Do but stoop down, to kiss her upmost brow:
Yet, if her often gnawing kisses win
The traitorous bank to gape, and let her in,
She rusheth violently, and doth divorce
Her from her native, and her long-kept course,   30
And roars, and braves it, and in gallant scorn,
In flattering eddies promising return,
She flouts the channel, who thenceforth is dry;
Then say I: that is she, and this am I.
Yet let not thy deep bitterness beget
Careless despair in me, for that will whet
My mind to scorn; and Oh, love dulled with pain
Was ne'er so wise, nor well armed as disdain.

Then with new eyes I shall survey thee, and spy
Death in thy cheeks, and darkness in thine eye.   40
Though hope bred faith and love; thus taught, I shall
As nations do from Rome, from thy love fall.
My hate shall outgrow thine, and utterly
I will renounce thy dalliance: and when I
Am the recusant, in that resolute state,
What hurts it me to be excommunicate?

Elegy 10: Love's War

Till I have peace with thee, war other men,
And when I have peace, can I leave thee then?
All other wars are scrupulous; only thou,
O fair, free city, mayst thyself allow
To any one. In Flanders, who can tell
Whether the master press, or men rebel?
Only we know, that which all idiots say,
They bear most blows which come to part the fray.
France in her lunatic giddiness did hate
Ever our men, yea and our God of late,   10
Yet she relies upon our angels well,
Which ne'er return; no more than they which fell.
Sick Ireland is with a strange war possessed
Like to an ague, now raging, now at rest,
Which time will cure, yet it must do her good
If she were purged, and her head-vein let blood.
And Midas' joys our Spanish journeys give,
We touch all gold, but find no food to live;
And I should be in that hot parching clime,
To dust and ashes turned before my time.   20
To mew me in a ship, is to enthral
Me in a prison that were like to fall;
Or in a cloister, save that there men dwell
In a calm heaven, here in a swaggering hell.
Long voyages are long consumptions,
And ships are carts for executions.
Yea they are deaths; is't not all one to fly
Into another world as 'tis to die?

Here let me war; in these arms let me lie;
Here let me parley, batter, bleed, and die.   30
Thine arms imprison me, and mine arms thee,
Thy heart thy ransom is, take mine for me.
Other men war that they their rest may gain,
But we will rest that we may fight again.
Those wars the ignorant, these th' experienced love,
There we are always under, here above.
There engines far off breed a just true fear,
Near thrusts, pikes, stabs, yea bullets hurt not here.
There lies are wrongs, here safe uprightly lie;
There men kill men, we'will make one by and by.   40
Thou nothing; I not half so much shall do
In these wars as they may which from us two
Shall spring. Thousands we see which travel not
To wars, but stay, swords, arms, and shot
To make at home: and shall not I do then
More glorious service, staying to make men?

Elegy 11: On his Mistress

By our first strange and fatal interview,
By all desires which thereof did ensue,
By our long starving hopes, by that remorse
Which my words' masculine persuasive force
Begot in thee, and by the memory
Of hurts which spies and rivals threatened me,
I calmly beg; but by thy parents' wrath,
By all pains which want and divorcement hath,
I conjure thee; and all those oaths which I
And thou have sworn, to seal joint constancy,   10
Here I unswear, and overswear them thus:
Thou shalt not love by means so dangerous.
Temper, O fair love, love's impetuous rage,
Be my true mistress still, not my feigned page.
I'll go, and, by thy kind leave, leave behind
Thee, only worthy to nurse in my mind
Thirst to come back; oh, if thou die before,
From other lands my soul towards thee shall soar,

Thy (else almighty) beauty cannot move
Rage from the seas, nor thy love teach them love,   20
Nor tame wild Boreas' harshness; thou hast read
How roughly he in pieces shivered
Fair Orithea, whom he swore he loved.
Fall ill or good, 'tis madness to have proved
Dangers unurged; feed on this flattery,
That absent lovers one in th' other be.
Dissemble nothing, not a boy, nor change
Thy body's habit, nor mind's; be not strange
To thy self only; all will spy in thy face
A blushing womanly discovering grace.   30
Richly clothed apes are called apes, and as soon
Eclipsed as bright, we call the moon, the moon.
Men of France, changeable chameleons,
Spitals of diseases, shops of fashions,
Love's fuellers, and the rightest company
Of players which upon the world's stage be,
Will quickly know thee, and know thee; and alas
Th' indifferent Italian, as we pass
His warm land, well content to think thee page,
Will haunt thee, with such lust and hideous rage   40
As Lot's fair guests were vexed. But none of these
Nor spongy hydroptic Dutch, shall thee displease,
If thou stay here. Oh stay here, for, for thee
England is only a worthy gallery,
To walk in expectation, till from thence
Our great King call thee into his presence.
When I am gone, dream me some happiness,
Nor let thy looks our long-hid love confess,
Nor praise, nor dispraise me, nor bless nor curse
Openly love's force; nor in bed fright thy nurse   50
With midnight's startings, crying out, 'Oh, oh
Nurse, O my love is slain; I saw him go
O'er the white Alps, alone; I saw him, I,
Assailed, fight, taken, stabbed, bleed, fall, and die.'
Augur me better chance, except dread Jove
Think it enough for me, to have had thy love.

Elegy 12

Nature's lay idiot, I taught thee to love,
And in that sophistry, oh, thou dost prove
Too subtle: Fool, thou didst not understand
The mystic language of the eye nor hand:
Nor couldst thou judge the difference of the air
Of sighs, and say, this lies, this sounds despair:
Nor by the'eye's water call a malady
Desperately hot, or changing feverously.
I had not taught thee then, the alphabet
Of flowers, how they devisefully being set   10
And bound up, might with speechless secrecy
Deliver errands mutely, and mutually.
Remember since all thy words used to be
To every suitor, *Ay, if my friends agree*;
Since household charms, thy husband's name to teach,
Were all the love-tricks, that thy wit could reach;
And since an hour's discourse could scarce have made
One answer in thee, and that ill arrayed
In broken proverbs, and torn sentences.
Thou art not by so many duties his,   20
That from the world's common having severed thee,
Inlaid thee, neither to be seen, nor see,
As mine: who have with amorous delicacies
Refined thee into a blissful paradise.
Thy graces and good words my creatures be;
I planted knowledge and life's tree in thee,
Which oh, shall strangers taste? Must I alas
Frame and enamel plate, and drink in glass?
Chafe wax for others' seals? break a colt's force
And leave him then, being made a ready horse?   30

Elegy 13: Love's Progress

Whoever loves, if he do not propose
The right true end of love, he's one that goes
To sea for nothing but to make him sick.
And love's a bear-whelp born, if we o'er-lick

Our love, and force it new strange shapes to take,
We err, and of a lump a monster make.
Were not a calf a monster that were grown
Faced like a man, though better than his own?
Perfection is in unity: prefer
One woman first, and then one thing in her.   10
I, when I value gold, may think upon
The ductileness, the application,
The wholesomeness, the ingenuity,
From rust, from soil, from fire ever free,
But if I love it, 'tis because 'tis made
By our new nature, use, the soul of trade.
    All these in women we might think upon
(If women had them) and yet love but one.
Can men more injure women than to say
They love them for that by which they'are not they?   20
Makes virtue woman? Must I cool my blood
Till I both be, and find one, wise and good?
May barren angels love so. But if we
Make love to woman, virtue is not she,
As beauty's not, nor wealth. He that strays thus
From her to hers, is more adulterous
Than if he took her maid. Search every sphere
And firmament, our Cupid is not there.
He's an infernal god, and underground
With Pluto dwells, where gold and fire abound.   30
Men to such gods their sacrificing coals
Did not in altars lay, but pits and holes.
Although we see celestial bodies move
Above the earth, the earth we till and love:
So we her airs contemplate, words and heart,
And virtues; but we love the centric part.
    Nor is the soul more worthy, or more fit
For love than this, as infinite as it.
But in attaining this desired place
How much they stray, that set out at the face.   40
The hair a forest is of ambushes,
Of springs, snares, fetters and manacles.
The brow becalms us, when 'tis smooth and plain,
And when 'tis wrinkled, shipwrecks us again;
Smooth, 'tis a paradise where we would have
Immortal stay, and wrinkled 'tis our grave.

The nose like to the first meridian runs
Not 'twixt an east and west, but 'twixt two suns.
It leaves a cheek, a rosy hemisphere,
On either side, and then directs us where   50
Upon the Islands Fortunate we fall,
(Not faint Canary, but ambrosial)
Her swelling lips; to which when we are come
We anchor there, and think ourselves at home,
For they seem all: there sirens' songs, and there
Wise Delphic oracles do fill the ear;
There in a creek where chosen pearls do swell,
The remora, her cleaving tongue doth dwell.
These, and the glorious promontory, her chin
O'erpast; and the strait Hellespont between   60
The Sestos and Abydos of her breasts,
(Not of two lovers, but two loves the nests)
Succeeds a boundless sea, but that thine eye
Some island moles may scattered there descry;
And sailing towards her India, in that way
Shall at her fair Atlantic navel stay;
Though thence the current be thy pilot made,
Yet ere thou be where thou wouldst be embayed,
Thou shalt upon another forest set,
Where some do shipwreck, and no further get.   70
When thou art there, consider what this chase
Misspent, by thy beginning at the face.
    Rather set out below; practise my art,
Some symmetry the foot hath with that part
Which thou dost seek, and is thy map for that,
Lovely enough to stop, but not stay at;
Least subject to disguise and change it is;
Men say, the Devil never can change his.
It is the emblem that hath figured
Firmness; 'tis the first part that comes to bed.   80
Civility, we see, refined the kiss
Which at the face begun, transplanted is
Since to the hand, since to the imperial knee,
Now at the papal foot delights to be.
If kings think that the nearer way, and do
Rise from the foot, lovers may do so too.

For as free spheres move faster far than can
Birds, whom the air resists, so may that man
Which goes this empty and ethereal way,
Than if at beauty's elements he stay.   90
Rich Nature hath in women wisely made
Two purses, and their mouths aversely laid;
They then which to the lower tribute owe,
That way which that exchequer looks must go.
He which doth not, his error is as great,
As who by clyster gave the stomach meat.

Elegy 14: The Comparison

As the sweet sweat of roses in a still,
As that which from chafed musk cat's pores doth trill,
As the almighty balm of th' early east,
Such are the sweat drops on my mistress' breast,
And on her neck her skin such lustre sets,
They seem no sweat drops, but pearl carcanets.
Rank sweaty froth thy mistress' brow defiles,
Like spermatic issue of ripe menstruous boils,
Or like that scum, which, by need's lawless law
Enforced, Sanserra's starved men did draw   10
From parboiled shoes, and boots, and all the rest
Which were with any sovereign fatness blessed,
And like vile lying stones in saffroned tin,
Or warts, or weals, they hang upon her skin.
Round as the world's her head, on every side,
Like to the fatal ball which fell on Ide,
Or that whereof God had such jealousy,
As, for the ravishing thereof we die.
Thy head is like a rough-hewn statue of jet,
Where marks for eyes, nose, mouth, are yet scarce set;   20
Like the first Chaos, or flat seeming face
Of Cynthia, when th' earth's shadows her embrace.
Like Proserpine's white beauty-keeping chest,
Or Jove's best fortune's urn, is her fair breast.
Thine's like worm-eaten trunks, clothed in seal's skin,
Or grave, that's dirt without, and stink within.

And like that slender stalk, at whose end stands
The woodbine quivering, are her arms and hands.
Like rough-barked elmboughs, or the russet skin
Of men late scourged for madness, or for sin,   30
Like sun-parched quarters on the city gate,
Such is thy tanned skin's lamentable state.
And like a bunch of ragged carrots stand
The short swoll'n fingers of thy gouty hand.
Then like the chemic's masculine equal fire,
Which in the limbeck's warm womb doth inspire
Into th' earth's worthless dirt a soul of gold,
Such cherishing heat her best loved part doth hold.
Thine's like the dread mouth of a fired gun,
Or like hot liquid metals newly run   40
Into clay moulds, or like to that Etna
Where round about the grass is burnt away.
Are not your kisses then as filthy, and more,
As a worm sucking an envenomed sore?
Doth not thy fearful hand in feeling quake,
As one which gathering flowers, still fears a snake?
Is not your last act harsh, and violent,
As when a plough a stony ground doth rent?
So kiss good turtles, so devoutly nice
Are priests in handling reverent sacrifice,   50
And such in searching wounds the surgeon is
As we, when we embrace, or touch, or kiss.
Leave her, and I will leave comparing thus,
She, and comparisons are odious.

Elegy 15: The Autumnal

No spring, nor summer beauty hath such grace,
    As I have seen in one autumnal face.
Young beauties force your love, and that's a rape,
    This doth but counsel, yet you cannot scape.
If 'twere a shame to love, here 'twere no shame,
    Affection here takes reverence's name.
Were her first years the Golden Age; that's true,
    But now she's gold oft tried, and ever new.
That was her torrid and inflaming time,
    This is her tolerable tropic clime.   10

Fair eyes, who asks more heat than comes from hence,
  He in a fever wishes pestilence.
Call not these wrinkles, graves; if graves they were,
  They were Love's graves; for else he is nowhere.
Yet lies not Love dead here, but here doth sit
  Vowed to this trench, like an anachorit.
And here, till hers, which must be his death, come,
  He doth not dig a grave, but build a tomb.
Here dwells he, though he sojourn everywhere
  In Progress, yet his standing house is here.   20
Here, where still evening is; not noon, nor night;
  Where no voluptuousness, yet all delight.
In all her words, unto all hearers fit,
  You may at revels, you at council, sit.
This is Love's timber, youth his underwood;
  There he, as wine in June, enrages blood,
Which then comes seasonabliest, when our taste
  And appetite to other things, is past.
Xerxes' strange Lydian love, the platan tree,
  Was loved for age, none being so large as she,   30
Or else because, being young, nature did bless
  Her youth with age's glory, barrenness.
If we love things long sought, age is a thing
  Which we are fifty years in compassing.
If transitory things, which soon decay,
  Age must be loveliest at the latest day.
But name not winter-faces, whose skin's slack;
  Lank, as an unthrift's purse; but a soul's sack;
Whose eyes seek light within, for all here's shade;
  Whose mouths are holes, rather worn out, than made;   40
Whose every tooth to a several place is gone,
  To vex their souls at Resurrection;
Name not these living death's-heads unto me,
  For these, not ancient, but antiques be.
I hate extremes; yet I had rather stay
  With tombs, than cradles, to wear out a day.
Since such love's natural lation is, may still
  My love descend, and journey down the hill,
Not panting after growing beauties, so,
  I shall ebb out with them, who homeward go.   50

Sappho to Philaenis

Where is that holy fire, which verse is said
    To have? is that enchanting force decayed?
Verse, that draws Nature's works, from Nature's law,
    Thee, her best work, to her work cannot draw.
Have my tears quenched my old poetic fire;
    Why quenched they not as well, that of desire?
Thoughts, my mind's creatures, often are with thee,
    But I, their maker, want their liberty.
Only thine image, in my heart, doth sit,
    But that is wax, and fires environ it.   10
My fires have driven, thine have drawn it hence;
    And I am robbed of picture, heart, and sense.
Dwells with me still mine irksome memory,
    Which, both to keep, and lose, grieves equally.
That tells me how fair thou art: thou art so fair,
    As, gods, when gods to thee I do compare,
Are graced thereby; and to make blind men see,
    What things gods are, I say they are like to thee.
For, if we justly call each silly man
    A little world, what shall we call thee then?   20
Thou art not soft, and clear, and straight, and fair,
    As down, as stars, cedars, and lilies are,
But thy right hand, and cheek, and eye, only
    Are like thy other hand, and cheek, and eye.
Such was my Phao awhile, but shall be never,
    As thou wast, art, and, oh, mayst thou be ever.
Here lovers swear in their idolatry,
    That I am such; but grief discolours me.
And yet I grieve the less, lest grief remove
    My beauty, and make me unworthy of thy love.   30
Plays some soft boy with thee, oh there wants yet
    A mutual feeling which should sweeten it.
His chin, a thorny hairy unevenness
    Doth threaten, and some daily change possess.
Thy body is a natural paradise,
    In whose self, unmanured, all pleasure lies,
Nor needs perfection; why shouldst thou then
    Admit the tillage of a harsh rough man?

Men leave behind them that which their sin shows,
   And are as thieves traced, which rob when it snows.   40
But of our dalliance no more signs there are,
   Than fishes leave in streams, or birds in air.
And between us all sweetness may be had;
   All, all that Nature yields, or Art can add.
My two lips, eyes, thighs, differ from thy two,
   But so, as thine from one another do;
And, oh, no more; the likeness being such,
   Why should they not alike in all parts touch?
Hand to strange hand, lip to lip none denies;
   Why should they breast to breast, or thighs to thighs?   50
Likeness begets such strange self flattery,
   That touching myself, all seems done to thee.
Myself I embrace, and mine own hands I kiss,
   And amorously thank myself for this.
Me, in my glass, I call thee; but, alas,
   When I would kiss, tears dim mine eyes, and glass.
O cure this loving madness, and restore
   Me to me; thee, my half, my all, my more.
So may thy cheeks' red outwear scarlet dye,
   And their white, whiteness of the galaxy,   60
So may thy mighty, amazing beauty move
   Envy in all women, and in all men, love,
And so be change, and sickness, far from thee,
   As thou by coming near, keep'st them from me.

EPITHALAMIONS

Epithalamion Made at Lincoln's Inn

The sun-beams in the east are spread,
Leave, leave, fair bride, your solitary bed,
  No more shall you return to it alone,
It nurseth sadness, and your body's print,
Like to a grave, the yielding down doth dint;
    You and your other you meet there anon;
      Put forth, put forth that warm balm-breathing thigh,
Which when next time you in these sheets will smother
There it must meet another,
      Which never was, but must be, oft, more nigh;   10
Come glad from thence, go gladder than you came,
Today put on perfection, and a woman's name.

Daughters of London, you which be
Our golden mines, and furnished treasury,
  You which are angels, yet still bring with you
Thousands of angels on your marriage days,
Help with your presence, and device to praise
    These rites, which also unto you grow due;
      Conceitedly dress her, and be assigned,
By you, fit place for every flower and jewel,   20
Make her for love fit fuel,
      As gay as Flora, and as rich as Ind;
So may she fair, rich, glad, 'and in nothing lame,
Today put on perfection, and a woman's name.

And you frolic patricians,
Sons of these senators' wealth's deep oceans,
  Ye painted courtiers, barrels of others' wits,
Ye country men, who but your beasts love none,
Ye of those fellowships whereof he's one,

Of study and play made strange hermaphrodites,   30
     Here shine; this bridegroom to the temple bring.
Lo, in yon path, which store of strewed flowers graceth,
The sober virgin paceth;
     Except my sight fail, 'tis no other thing;
Weep not nor blush, here is no grief nor shame,
Today put on perfection, and a woman's name.

Thy two-leaved gates, fair temple, unfold,
And these two in thy sacred bosom hold,
     Till, mystically joined, but one they be;
Then may thy lean and hunger-starved womb   40
Long time expect their bodies and their tomb,
     Long after their own parents fatten thee;
     All elder claims, and all cold barrenness,
All yielding to new loves be far for ever,
Which might these two dissever,
     Always, all th'other may each one possess;
For, the best bride, best worthy of praise and fame,
Today puts on perfection, and a woman's name.

Oh winter days bring much delight,
Not for themselves, but for they soon bring night;   50
     Other sweets wait thee than these diverse meats,
Other disports than dancing jollities,
Other love tricks than glancing with the eyes,
     But that the sun still in our half sphere sweats;
     He flies in winter, but he now stands still,
Yet shadows turn; noon point he hath attained,
His steeds nill be restrained,
     But gallop lively down the western hill;
Thou shalt, when he hath run the world's half frame,
Tonight put on perfection, and a woman's name.   60

The amorous evening star is rose,
Why then should not our amorous star inclose
     Herself in her wished bed? Release your strings
Musicians, and dancers take some truce
With these your pleasing labours, for great use
     As much weariness as perfection brings;

You, and not only you, but all toiled beasts
Rest duly; at night all their toils are dispensed;
But in their beds commenced
      Are other labours, and more dainty feasts;   70
She goes a maid, who, lest she turn the same,
Tonight puts on perfection, and a woman's name.

Thy virgin's girdle now untie,
And in thy nuptial bed (love's altar) lie
   A pleasing sacrifice; now dispossess
Thee of these chains and robes which were put on
T'adorn the day, not thee; for thou, alone,
      Like virtue and truth, art best in nakedness;
         This bed is only to virginity
A grave, but, to a better state, a cradle;   80
Till now thou wast but able
      To be what now thou art; then that by thee
No more be said, I *may be*, but *I am*,
Tonight put on perfection, and a woman's name.

Even like a faithful man content,
That this life for a better should be spent,
   So, she a mother's rich style doth prefer,
And at the bridegroom's wished approach doth lie,
Like an appointed lamb, when tenderly
      The priest comes on his knees t'embowel her;   90
         Now sleep or watch with more joy; and O light
Of heaven, tomorrow rise thou hot, and early;
This sun will love so dearly
      Her rest, that long, long we shall want her sight;
Wonders are wrought, for she which had no maim,
Tonight puts on perfection, and a woman's name.

*An Epithalamion, or Marriage Song on the Lady Elizabeth
and Count Palatine being Married on St Valentine's Day*

            Hail Bishop Valentine, whose day this is,
                  All the air is thy diocese,
                  And all the chirping choristers
            And other birds are thy parishioners,
                  Thou marriest every year

The lyric lark, and the grave whispering dove,
The sparrow that neglects his life for love,
The household bird, with the red stomacher,
      Thou mak'st the blackbird speed as soon,
As doth the goldfinch, or the halcyon;   10
The husband cock looks out, and straight is sped,
And meets his wife, which brings her feather-bed.
This day more cheerfully than ever shine,
This day, which might enflame thyself, old Valentine.

Till now, thou warmed'st with multiplying loves
      Two larks, two sparrows, or two doves;
        All that is nothing unto this,
For thou this day couplest two phoenixes,
      Thou mak'st a taper see
What the sun never saw, and what the Ark   20
(Which was of fowls, and beasts, the cage, and park,)
Did not contain, one bed contains, through thee,
      Two phoenixes, whose joined breasts
Are unto one another mutual nests,
Where motion kindles such fires, as shall give
Young phoenixes, and yet the old shall live;
Whose love and courage never shall decline,
But make the whole year through, thy day, O Valentine.

Up then fair phoenix bride, frustrate the sun,
      Thyself from thine affection   30
        Tak'st warmth enough, and from thine eye
All lesser birds will take their jollity.
      Up, up, fair bride, and call,
Thy stars, from out their several boxes, take
Thy rubies, pearls, and diamonds forth, and make
Thyself a constellation, of them all,
      And by their blazing, signify,
That a great princess falls, but doth not die;
Be thou a new star, that to us portends
Ends of much wonder; and be thou those ends.   40
Since thou dost this day in new glory shine,
May all men date records, from this thy Valentine.

Come forth, come forth, and as one glorious flame
     Meeting another, grows the same,
     So meet thy Frederick, and so
To an unseparable union grow.
     Since separation
Falls not on such things as are infinite,
Nor things which are but one, can disunite.
You are twice inseparable, great, and one;   50
     Go then to where the Bishop stays,
To make you one, his way, which divers ways
Must be effected; and when all is past,
And that you are one, by hearts and hands made fast,
You two have one way left, yourselves to entwine,
Besides this Bishop's knot, or Bishop Valentine.

But oh, what ails the sun, that here he stays,
     Longer today, than other days?
     Stays he new light from these to get?
And finding here such store, is loth to set?   60
     And why do you two walk,
So slowly paced in this procession?
Is all your care but to be looked upon,
And be to others spectacle, and talk?
     The feast, with gluttonous delays,
Is eaten, and too long their meat they praise,
The masquers come late, and I think, will stay,
Like fairies, till the cock crow them away.
     Alas, did not antiquity assign
A night, as well as day, to thee, O Valentine?   70

They did, and night is come; and yet we see
     Formalities retarding thee.
     What mean these ladies, which (as though
They were to take a clock in pieces,) go
     So nicely about the bride;
A bride, before a good night could be said,
Should vanish from her clothes, into her bed,
As souls from bodies steal, and are not spied.
     But now she is laid; what though she be?
Yet there are more delays, for, where is he?   80

He comes, and passes through sphere after sphere:
First her sheets, then her arms, then anywhere.
Let not then this day, but this night be thine,
Thy day was but the eve to this, O Valentine.

Here lies a she sun, and a he moon here,
      She gives the best light to this sphere,
        Or each is both, and all, and so
They unto one another nothing owe,
          And yet they do, but are
So just and rich in that coin which they pay,   90
That neither would, nor needs forbear, nor stay;
Neither desires to be spared, nor to spare,
      They quickly pay their debt, and then
Take no acquittances, but pay again;
They pay, they give, they lend, and so let fall
No such occasion to be liberal.
More truth, more courage in these two do shine,
Than all thy turtles have, and sparrows, Valentine.

And by this act of these two phoenixes
      Nature again restored is,   100
      For since these two, are two no more,
There's but one phoenix still, as was before.
      Rest now at last, and we
As satyrs watch the sun's uprise, will stay
Waiting, when your eyes opened, let out day,
Only desired, because your face we see;
      Others near you shall whispering speak,
And wagers lay, at which side day will break,
And win by observing, then, whose hand it is
That opens first a curtain, hers or his;   110
This will be tried tomorrow after nine,
Till which hour, we thy day enlarge, O Valentine.

EARLY VERSE LETTERS

To Mr T. W.

Pregnant again with th' old twins hope, and fear,
Oft have I asked for thee, both how and where
Thou wert, and what my hopes of letters were;

As in our streets sly beggars narrowly
Watch motions of the giver's hand and eye,
And evermore conceive some hope thereby.

And now thine alms is given, thy letter is read,
The body risen again, the which was dead,
And thy poor starveling bountifully fed.

After this banquet my soul doth say grace,   10
And praise thee for it, and zealously embrace
Thy love, though I think thy love in this case
   To be as gluttons, which say 'midst their meat,
   They love that best of which they most do eat.

To Mr S. B.

O thou which to search out the secret parts
   Of the India, or rather paradise
   Of knowledge, hast with courage and advice
Lately launched into the vast sea of arts,
Disdain not in thy constant travailing
   To do as other voyagers, and make
   Some turns into less creeks, and wisely take
Fresh water at the Heliconian spring;
I sing not, siren like, to tempt; for I
   Am harsh; nor as those schismatics with you,   10
   Which draw all wits of good hope to their crew;
But seeing in you bright sparks of poetry,
   I, though I brought no fuel, had desire
With these articulate blasts to blow the fire.

To Mr T. W.

At once, from hence, my lines and I depart,
I to my soft still walks, they to my heart;
I to the nurse, they to the child of art;

Yet as a firm house, though the carpenter
Perish, doth stand: as an ambassador
Lies safe, howe'er his king be in danger:

So, though I languish, pressed with melancholy,
My verse, the strict map of my misery,
Shall live to see that, for whose want I die.

Therefore I envy them, and do repent,   10
That from unhappy me, things happy are sent;
Yet as a picture, or bare sacrament,
    Accept these lines, and if in them there be
    Merit of love, bestow that love on me.

To Mr E. G.

Even as lame things thirst their perfection, so
The slimy rhymes bred in our vale below,
Bearing with them much of my love and heart,
Fly unto that Parnassus, where thou art.
There thou o'erseest London: here I have been
By staying in London too much overseen.
Now pleasure's dearth our city doth possess,
Our theatres are filled with emptiness;
As lank and thin is every street and way
As a woman delivered yesterday.   10
Nothing whereat to laugh my spleen espies
But bearbaitings or law exercise.
Therefore I'll leave it, and in the country strive
Pleasures, now fled from London, to retrieve.
Do thou so too: and fill not like a bee
Thy thighs with honey, but as plenteously

As Russian merchants, thyself's whole vessel load,
And then at winter retail it here abroad.
Bless us with Suffolk's sweets; and as that is
Thy garden, make thy hive and warehouse this.

The Storm

TO MR CHRISTOPHER BROOKE

Thou which art I, ('tis nothing to be so)
Thou which art still thyself, by these shalt know
Part of our passage; and, a hand, or eye
By Hilliard drawn, is worth an history,
By a worse painter made; and (without pride)
When by thy judgement they are dignified,
My lines are such: 'tis the pre-eminence
Of friendship only to impute excellence.
England to whom we owe, what we be, and have,
Sad that her sons did seek a foreign grave   10
(For, Fate's, or Fortune's drifts non can soothsay,
Honour and misery have one face and way)
From out her pregnant entrails sighed a wind
Which at th' air's middle marble room did find
Such strong resistance, that itself it threw
Downward again; and so when it did view
How in the port, our fleet dear time did leese,
Withering like prisoners, which lie but for fees,
Mildly it kissed our sails, and, fresh and sweet,
As to a stomach starved, whose insides meet,   20
Meat comes, it came; and swole our sails, when we
So joyed, as Sara her swelling joyed to see.
But 'twas but so kind, as our countrymen,
Which bring friends one day's way, and leave them then.
Then like two mighty kings, which dwelling far
Asunder, meet against a third to war,
The south and west winds joined, and, as they blew,
Waves like a rolling trench before them threw.
Sooner than you read this line, did the gale,
Like shot, not feared till felt, our sails assail;   30

And what at first was called a gust, the same
Hath now a storm's, anon a tempest's name.
Jonas, I pity thee, and curse those men,
Who when the storm raged most, did wake thee then;
Sleep is pain's easiest salve, and doth fulfil
All offices of death, except to kill.
But when I waked, I saw, that I saw not.
I, and the sun, which should teach me had forgot
East, west, day, night, and I could only say,
If the world had lasted, now it had been day. 40
Thousands our noises were, yet we 'mongst all
Could none by his right name, but thunder call:
Lightning was all our light, and it rained more
Than if the sun had drunk the sea before.
Some coffined in their cabins lie, equally
Grieved that they are not dead, and yet must die.
And as sin-burdened souls from graves will creep,
At the last day, some forth their cabins peep:
And tremblingly ask what news, and do hear so,
Like jealous husbands, what they would not know. 50
Some sitting on the hatches, would seem there,
With hideous gazing to fear away fear.
Then note they the ship's sicknesses, the mast
Shaked with this ague, and the hold and waist
With a salt dropsy clogged, and all our tacklings
Snapping, like too high stretched treble strings.
And from our tottered sails, rags drop down so,
As from one hanged in chains, a year ago.
Even our ordnance placed for our defence,
Strive to break loose, and 'scape away from thence. 60
Pumping hath tired our men, and what's the gain?
Seas into seas thrown, we suck in again;
Hearing hath deafed our sailors; and if they
Knew how to hear, there's none knows what to say.
Compared to these storms, death is but a qualm,
Hell somewhat lightsome, and the Bermuda calm.
Darkness, light's elder brother, his birth-right
Claims o'er this world, and to heaven hath chased
    light.
All things are one, and that one none can be,
Since all forms, uniform deformity 70

Doth cover, so that we, except God say
Another *Fiat*, shall have no more day.
So violent, yet long these furies be,
That though thine absence starve me, I wish not thee.

The Calm

Our storm is past, and that storm's tyrannous rage,
A stupid calm, but nothing it, doth 'suage.
The fable is inverted, and far more
A block afflicts, now, than a stork before.
Storms chafe, and soon wear out themselves, or us;
In calms, heaven laughs to see us languish thus.
As steady as I can wish, that my thoughts were,
Smooth as thy mistress' glass, or what shines there,
The sea is now. And, as those Isles which we
Seek, when we can move, our ships rooted be.   10
As water did in storms, now pitch runs out
As lead, when a fired church becomes one spout.
And all our beauty, and our trim, decays,
Like courts removing, or like ended plays.
The fighting place now seamen's rags supply;
And all the tackling is a frippery.
No use of lanthorns; and in one place lay
Feathers and dust, today and yesterday.
Earth's hollownesses, which the world's lungs are,
Have no more wind than the upper vault of air.   20
We can nor lost friends, nor sought foes recover,
But meteor-like, save that we move not, hover.
Only the calenture together draws
Dear friends, which meet dead in great fishes' jaws:
And on the hatches as on altars lies
Each one, his own priest, and own sacrifice.
Who live, that miracle do multiply
Where walkers in hot ovens, do not die.
If in despite of these, we swim, that hath
No more refreshing, than our brimstone bath,   30
But from the sea, into the ship we turn,
Like parboiled wretches, on the coals to burn.

Like Bajazet encaged, the shepherd's scoff,
Or like slack-sinewed Samson, his hair off,
Languish our ships. Now, as a myriad
Of ants, durst th' Emperor's loved snake invade,
The crawling galleys, sea-goals, finny chips,
Might brave our Venice's, now bed-rid ships.
Whether a rotten state, and hope of gain,
Or to disuse me from the queasy pain   40
Of being beloved, and loving, or the thirst
Of honour, or fair death, out pushed me first,
I lose my end: for here as well as I
A desperate may live, and a coward die.
Stag, dog, and all which from, or towards flies,
Is paid with life, or prey, or doing dies.
Fate grudges us all, and doth subtly lay
A scourge, 'gainst which we all forget to pray,
He that at sea prays for more wind, as well
Under the poles may beg cold, heat in hell.   50
What are we then? How little more alas
Is man now, than before he was! he was
Nothing; for us, we are for nothing fit;
Chance, or ourselves still disproportion it.
We have no power, no will, no sense; I lie,
I should not then thus feel this misery.

To Mr Rowland Woodward

Like one who in her third widowhood doth profess
Herself a nun, tied to retiredness,
So affects my Muse now, a chaste fallowness,

Since she to few, yet to too many hath shown
How love-song weeds, and satiric thorns are grown
Where seeds of better arts, were early sown.

Though to use, and love poetry, to me,
Betrothed to no one art, be no adultery;
Omissions of good, ill, as ill deeds be.

For though to us it seem, and be light and thin,   10
Yet in those faithful scales, where God throws in
Men's works, vanity weighs as much as sin.

If our souls have stained their first white, yet we
May clothe them with faith, and dear honesty,
Which God imputes, as native purity.

There is no virtue, but religion:
Wise, valiant, sober, just, are names, which none
Want, which want not vice-covering discretion.

Seek we then ourselves in ourselves; for as
Men force the sun with much more force to pass,   20
By gathering his beams with a crystal glass;

So we, if we into ourselves will turn,
Blowing our sparks of virtue, may outburn
The straw, which doth about our hearts sojourn.

You know, physicians, when they would infuse
Into any oil, the soul of simples, use
Places, where they may lie still warm, to choose.

So works retiredness in us; to roam
Giddily, and be everywhere, but at home,
Such freedom doth a banishment become.   30

We are but farmers of ourselves, yet may,
If we can stock ourselves, and thrive, uplay
Much, much dear treasure for the great rent day.

Manure thyself then, to thyself be approved,
And with vain outward things be no more moved,
But to know, that I love thee and would be loved.

To Sir Henry Wotton

Here's no more news, than virtue, I may as well
Tell you Cadiz' or Saint Michael's tale for news, as tell
That vice doth here habitually dwell.

Yet, as to get stomachs, we walk up and down,
And toil to sweeten rest, so, may God frown,
If, but to loathe both, I haunt Court, or Town.

For here no one is from th' extremity
Of vice, by any other reason free,
But that the next to him, still, is worse than he.

In this world's warfare, they whom rugged Fate,   10
(God's commissary) doth so throughly hate,
As in the Court's squadron to marshal their state

If they stand armed with silly honesty,
With wishing prayers, and neat integrity,
Like Indian 'gainst Spanish hosts they be.

Suspicious boldness to this place belongs,
And to have as many ears as all have tongues;
Tender to know, tough to acknowledge wrongs.

Believe me Sir, in my youth's giddiest days,
When to be like the Court, was a play's praise,   20
Plays were not so like Courts, as Courts are like plays.

Then let us at these mimic antics jest,
Whose deepest projects, and egregious gests
Are but dull morals of a game at chests.

But now 'tis incongruity to smile,
Therefore I end; and bid farewell a while,
At court, though *From Court*, were the better style.

To Sir Henry Wotton, at his going Ambassador to Venice

After those reverend papers, whose soul is
    Our good and great King's loved hand and feared name,
By which to you he derives much of his,
    And (how he may) makes you almost the same,

A taper of his torch, a copy writ
    From his original, and a fair beam
Of the same warm, and dazzling sun, though it
    Must in another sphere his virtue stream:

After those learned papers which your hand
    Hath stored with notes of use and pleasure too,   10
From which rich treasury you may command
    Fit matter whether you will write or do:

After those loving papers, where friends send
    With glad grief, to your sea-ward steps, farewell,
Which thicken on you now, as prayers ascend
    To heaven in troops at a good man's passing bell:

Admit this honest paper, and allow
    It such an audience as yourself would ask;
What you must say at Venice this means now,
    And hath for nature, what you have for task.   20

To swear much love, not to be changed before
    Honour alone will to your fortune fit;
Nor shall I then honour your fortune, more
    Than I have done your honour wanting it.

But 'tis an easier load (though both oppress)
    To want, than govern greatness, for we are
In that, our own and only business,
    In this, we must for others' vices care;

'Tis therefore well your spirits now are placed
    In their last furnace, in activity;   30
Which fits them (schools and Courts and wars o'erpast)
    To touch and test in any best degree.

For me, (if there be such a thing as I)
   Fortune (if there be such a thing as she)
Spies that I bear so well her tyranny,
   That she thinks nothing else so fit for me;

But though she part us, to hear my oft prayers
   For your increase, God is as near me here;
And to send you what I shall beg, his stairs
   In length and ease are alike everywhere.   40

EPIGRAMS

Hero and Leander

Both robbed of air, we both lie in one ground,
Both whom one fire had burnt, one water drowned.

Pyramus and Thisbe

Two, by themselves, each other, love and fear
Slain, cruel friends, by parting have joined here.

Niobe

By children's birth, and death, I am become
So dry, that I am now made mine own tomb.

A Burnt Ship

Out of a fired ship, which, by no way
But drowning, could be rescued from the flame,
Some men leaped forth, and ever as they came
Near the foes' ships, did by their shot decay;
So all were lost, which in the ship were found,
  They in the sea being burnt, they in the burnt ship
    drowned.

Fall of a Wall

Under an undermined, and shot-bruised wall
A too-bold captain perished by the fall,
Whose brave misfortune, happiest men envied,
That had a town for tomb, his bones to hide.

A Lame Beggar

I am unable, yonder beggar cries,
  To stand, or move; if he say true, he *lies*.

Cales and Guiana

If you from spoil of th' old world's farthest end
To the new world your kindled valours bend,
What brave examples then do prove it true
That one thing's end doth still begin a new.

Sir John Wingfield

Beyond th' old Pillars many have travelled
Towards the sun's cradle, and his throne, and bed.
A fitter pillar our Earl did bestow
In that late island; for he well did know
Farther than Wingfield no man dares to go.

A Self-Accuser

Your mistress, that you follow whores, still taxeth you:
'Tis strange she should confess it, though it be true.

A Licentious Person

Thy sins and hairs may no man equal call,
For, as thy sins increase, thy hairs do fall.

Antiquary

If in his study he hath so much care
To hang all old strange things, let his wife beware.

The Juggler

Thou call'st me effeminate, for I love women's joys;
I call not thee manly, though thou follow boys.

Disinherited

Thy father all from thee, by his last will,
Gave to the poor; thou hast good title still.

The Liar

Thou in the fields walk'st out thy supping hours
  And yet thou swear'st thou hast supped like a king;
Like Nebuchadnezzar perchance with grass and
      flowers,
  A salad worse than Spanish dieting.

Mercurius Gallo-Belgicus

Like Aesop's fellow-slaves, O Mercury,
Which could do all things, thy faith is; and I
Like Aesop's self, which nothing; I confess
I should have had more faith, if thou hadst less;

Thy credit lost thy credit: 'tis sin to do,
In this case, as thou wouldst be done unto,
To believe all: change thy name: thou art like
Mercury in stealing, but liest like a Greek.

Phryne

Thy flattering picture, Phryne, is like thee,
Only in this, that you both painted be.

An Obscure Writer

Philo, with twelve years' study, hath been grieved
To be understood; when will he be believed?

Klockius

Klockius so deeply hath vowed, ne'er more to come
In bawdy house, that he dares not go home.

Raderus

Why this man gelded Martial I muse,
Except himself alone his tricks would use,
As Katherine, for the Court's sake, put down stews.

Ralphius

Compassion in the world again is bred:
Ralphius is sick, the broker keeps his bed.

The Progress of the Soul
Infinitati Sacrum

16 AUGUSTI 1601

Metempsychosis

POÊMA SATYRICON

EPISTLE

Others at the porches and entries of their buildings set their arms;
I, my picture; if any colours can deliver a mind so plain, and flat,
and through-light as mine. Naturally at a new author, I doubt, and
stick, and do not say quickly, good. I censure much and tax; and
this liberty costs me more than others, by how much my own
things are worse than others. Yet I would not be so rebellious
against myself, as not to do it, since I love it; nor so unjust to
others, as to do it *sine talione*. As long as I give them as good hold
upon me, they must pardon me my bitings. I forbid no repre-
hender, but him that like the Trent Council forbids not books, but 10
authors, damning whatever such a name hath or shall write. None
writes so ill, that he gives not something exemplary, to follow, or fly.
Now when I begin this book, I have no purpose to come into any
man's debt; how my stock will hold out I know not; perchance
waste, perchance increase in use; if I do borrow anything of anti-
quity, besides that I make account that I pay it to posterity, with as
much and as good: you shall still find me to acknowledge it, and to
thank not him only that hath digged out treasure for me, but that
hath lighted me a candle to the place. All which I will bid you
remember, (for I would have no such readers as I can teach) is, 20
that the Pythagorean doctrine doth not only carry one soul from
man to man, nor man to beast, but indifferently to plants also: and
therefore you must not grudge to find the same soul in an emperor,
in a post-horse, and in a mushroom, since no unreadiness in the
soul, but an indisposition in the organs works this. And therefore
though this soul could not move when it was a melon, yet it may
remember, and now tell me, at what lascivious banquet it was
served. And though it could not speak, when it was a spider, yet it
can remember, and now tell me, who used it for poison to attain
dignity. However the bodies have dulled her other faculties, her 30

memory hath ever been her own, which makes me so seriously
deliver you by her relation all her passages from her first making
when she was that apple which Eve eat, to this time when she is he,
whose life you shall find in the end of this book.

THE PROGRESS OF THE SOUL
FIRST SONG

I

I sing the progress of a deathless soul,
Whom Fate, which God made, but doth not control,
Placed in most shapes; all times before the law
Yoked us, and when, and since, in this I sing.
And the great world to his aged evening,
From infant morn, through manly noon I draw.
What the gold Chaldee, or silver Persian saw,
Greek brass, or Roman iron, is in this one;
A work to outwear Seth's pillars, brick and stone,
　　And (holy writ excepted) made to yield to none.　　10

2

Thee, eye of heaven, this great soul envies not,
By thy male force, is all we have, begot.
In the first east, thou now begin'st to shine,
Suck'st early balm, and island spices there,
And wilt anon in thy loose-reined career
At Tagus, Po, Seine, Thames, and Danow dine,
And see at night thy western land of mine,
Yet hast thou not more nations seen than she,
That before thee, one day began to be,
　　And thy frail light being quenched, shall long, long outlive
　　thee.　　20

3

Nor, holy Janus, in whose sovereign boat
The Church, and all the monarchies did float;
That swimming college, and free hospital
Of all mankind, that cage and vivary
Of fowls, and beasts, in whose womb, Destiny

Us, and our latest nephews did instal
(From thence are all derived, that fill this all),
Didst thou in that great stewardship embark
So diverse shapes into that floating park,
   As have been moved, and informed by this heavenly
     spark.   30

4

Great Destiny the commissary of God,
That hast marked out a path and period
For every thing; who, where we offspring took,
Our ways and ends seest at one instant; thou
Knot of all causes, thou whose changeless brow
Ne'er smiles nor frowns, O vouch thou safe to look
And show my story, in thy eternal book;
That (if my prayer be fit) I may understand
So much myself, as to know with what hand,
   How scant, or liberal this my life's race is spanned.   40

5

To my six lustres almost now outwore,
Except thy book owe me so many more,
Except my legend be free from the lets
Of steep ambition, sleepy poverty,
Spirit-quenching sickness, dull captivity,
Distracting business, and from beauty's nets,
And all that calls from this, and t'other whets,
O let me not launch out, but let me save
Th' expense of brain and spirit; that my grave
   His right and due, a whole unwasted man may have.   50

6

But if my days be long, and good enough,
In vain this sea shall enlarge, or enrough
Itself; for I will through the wave, and foam,
And shall in sad lone ways a lively sprite
Make my dark heavy poem light, and light.
For though through many straits, and lands I roam,
I launch at paradise, and I sail towards home;
The course I there began, shall here be stayed,
Sails hoisted there, struck here, and anchors laid
   In Thames, which were at Tigris, and Euphrates weighed.   60

7

For the great soul which here amongst us now
Doth dwell, and moves that hand, and tongue, and brow,
Which, as the moon the sea, moves us, to hear
Whose story, with long patience you will long;
(For 'tis the crown, and last strain of my song)
This soul to whom Luther and Mahomet were
Prisons of flesh; this soul which oft did tear,
And mend the wracks of th' Empire, and late Rome,
And lived where every great change did come,
Had first in paradise, a low, but fatal room.   70

8

Yet no low room, nor than the greatest, less,
If (as devout and sharp men fitly guess)
That Cross, our joy, and grief, where nails did tie
That all, which always was all, everywhere,
Which could not sin, and yet all sins did bear;
Which could not die, yet could not choose but die;
Stood in the self same room in Calvary,
Where first grew the forbidden learned tree,
For on that tree hung in security
This soul, made by the Maker's will from pulling free.   80

9

Prince of the orchard, fair as dawning morn,
Fenced with the law, and ripe as soon as born
That apple grew, which this soul did enlive,
Till the then climbing serpent, that now creeps
For that offence, for which all mankind weeps,
Took it, and to her whom the first man did wive
(Whom and her race, only forbiddings drive)
He gave it, she, to her husband, both did eat;
So perished the eaters, and the meat:
And we (for treason taints the blood) thence die and
sweat.   90

10

Man all at once was there by woman slain,
And one by one we're here slain o'er again
By them. The mother poisoned the well-head,
The daughters here corrupt us, rivulets,
No smallness 'scapes, no greatness breaks their nets,
She thrust us out, and by them we are led
Astray, from turning, to whence we are fled.
Were prisoners judges, 'twould seem rigorous,
She sinned, we bear; part of our pain is, thus
    To love them, whose fault to this painful love yoked us.   100

11

So fast in us doth this corruption grow,
That now we dare ask why we should be so.
Would God (disputes the curious rebel) make
A law, and would not have it kept? Or can
His creatures' will, cross his? Of every man
For one, will God (and be just) vengeance take?
Who sinned? 'twas not forbidden to the snake
Nor her, who was not then made; nor is 't writ
That Adam cropped, or knew the apple; yet
    The worm and she, and he, and we endure for it.   110

12

But snatch me heavenly Spirit from this vain
Reckoning their vanities, less is the gain
Than hazard still, to meditate on ill,
Though with good mind; their reasons, like those toys
Of glassy bubbles, which the gamesome boys
Stretch to so nice a thinness through a quill
That they themselves break, do themselves spill:
Arguing is heretics' game, and exercise
As wrestlers, perfects them; not liberties
    Of speech, but silence; hands, not tongues, end heresies.   120

13

Just in that instant when the serpent's gripe,
Broke the slight veins, and tender conduit-pipe,
Through which this soul from the tree's root did draw
Life, and growth to this apple, fled away
This loose soul, old, one and another day.
As lightning, which one scarce dares say, he saw,
'Tis so soon gone, (and better proof the law
Of sense, than faith requires) swiftly she flew
To a dark and foggy plot; her, her fate threw
   There through th'earth's pores, and in a plant housed
     her anew.   130

14

The plant thus abled, to itself did force
A place, where no place was; by nature's course
As air from water, water fleets away
From thicker bodies, but this root thronged so
His spongy confines gave him place to grow,
Just as in our streets, when the people stay
To see the Prince, and have so filled the way
That weasels scarce could pass, when she comes near
They throng and cleave up, and a passage clear,
   As if, for that time, their round bodies flattened were.   140

15

His right arm he thrust out towards the east,
Westward his left; th' ends did themselves digest
Into ten lesser strings, these fingers were:
And as a slumberer stretching on his bed,
This way he this, and that way scattered
His other leg, which feet with toes upbear;
Grew on his middle parts, the first day, hair,
To show, that in love's business he should still
A dealer be, and be used well, or ill:
   His apples kindle, his leaves, force of conception kill.   150

16

A mouth, but dumb, he hath; blind eyes, deaf ears,
And to his shoulders dangle subtle hairs;
A young Colossus there he stands upright,
And as that ground by him were conquered
A leafy garland wears he on his head
Enchased with little fruits, so red and bright
That for them you would call your love's lips white;
So, of a lone unhaunted place possessed,
Did this soul's second inn, built by the guest,
　This living buried man, this quiet mandrake, rest.　160

17

No lustful woman came this plant to grieve,
But 'twas because there was none yet but Eve:
And she (with other purpose) killed it quite;
Her sin had now brought in infirmities,
And so her cradled child, the moist red eyes
Had never shut, nor slept since it saw light,
Poppy she knew, she knew the mandrake's might,
And tore up both, and so cooled her child's blood;
Unvirtuous weeds might long unvexed have stood;
　But he's short-lived, that with his death can do most
　　good.　170

18

To an unfettered soul's quick nimble haste
Are falling stars, and heart's thoughts, but slow-paced:
Thinner than burnt air flies this soul, and she
Whom four new coming, and four parting suns
Had found, and left the mandrake's tenant, runs
Thoughtless of change, when her firm destiny
Confined, and enjailed her, that seemed so free
Into a small blue shell, the which a poor
Warm bird o'erspread, and sat still evermore,
　Till her enclosed child kicked, and pecked itself a door.　180

19

Out crept a sparrow, this soul's moving inn,
On whose raw arms stiff feathers now begin,
As children's teeth through gums, to break with pain,
His flesh is jelly yet, and his bones threads,
All a new downy mantle overspreads,
A mouth he opes, which would as much contain
As his late house, and the first hour speaks plain,
And chirps aloud for meat. Meat fit for men
His father steals for him, and so feeds then
    One, that within a month, will beat him from his hen.   190

20

In this world's youth wise nature did make haste,
Things ripened sooner, and did longer last;
Already this hot cock in bush and tree
In field and tent o'erflutters his next hen,
He asks her not, who did so last, nor when,
Nor if his sister, or his niece she be,
Nor doth she pule for his inconstancy
If in her sight he change, nor doth refuse
The next that calls; both liberty do use;
    Where store is of both kinds, both kinds may freely
      choose.   200

21

Men, till they took laws which made freedom less,
Their daughters, and their sisters did ingress;
Till now unlawful, therefore ill, 'twas not.
So jolly, that it can move, this soul is,
The body so free of his kindnesses,
That self-preserving it hath now forgot,
And slackeneth so the soul's, and body's knot
Which temperance straitens; freely on his she friends
He blood, and spirit, pith, and marrow spends,
    Ill steward of himself, himself in three years ends.   210

22

Else might he long have lived; man did not know
Of gummy blood, which doth in holly grow,
How to make bird-lime, nor how to deceive
With feigned calls, hid nets, or enwrapping snare,
The free inhabitants of the pliant air.
Man to beget, and woman to conceive
Asked not of roots, nor of cock-sparrows, leave:
Yet chooseth he, though none of these he fears,
Pleasantly three, than straitened twenty years
    To live, and to increase his race, himself outwears.   220

23

This coal with overblowing quenched and dead,
The soul from her too active organs fled
To a brook; a female fish's sandy roe
With the male's jelly, newly leavened was,
For they had intertouched as they did pass,
And one of those small bodies, fitted so,
This soul informed, and abled it to row
Itself with finny oars, which she did fit,
Her scales seemed yet of parchment, and as yet
    Perchance a fish, but by no name you could call it.   230

24

When goodly, like a ship in her full trim,
A swan, so white that you may unto him
Compare all whiteness, but himself to none,
Glided along, and as he glided watched,
And with his arched neck this poor fish catched.
It moved with state, as if to look upon
Low things it scorned, and yet before that one
Could think he sought it, he had swallowed clear
This, and much such, and unblamed devoured there
    All, but who too swift, too great, or well armed were.   240

25

Now swam a prison in a prison put,
And now this soul in double walls was shut,
Till melted with the swan's digestive fire,
She left her house the fish, and vapoured forth;
Fate not affording bodies of more worth
For her as yet, bids her again retire
To another fish, to any new desire
Made a new prey; for, he that can to none
Resistance make, nor complaint, sure is gone.
    Weakness invites, but silence feasts oppression.   250

26

Pace with her native stream, this fish doth keep,
And journeys with her, towards the glassy deep,
But oft retarded, once with a hidden net
Though with great windows, for when need first taught
These tricks to catch food, then they were not wrought
As now, with curious greediness to let
None 'scape, but few, and fit for use to get,
As, in this trap a ravenous pike was ta'en,
Who, though himself distressed, would fain have slain
    This wretch; so hardly are ill habits left again.   260

27

Here by her smallness she two deaths o'erpast,
Once innocence 'scaped, and left the oppressor fast;
The net through-swum, she keeps the liquid path,
And whether she leap up sometimes to breathe
And suck in air, or find it underneath,
Or working parts like mills or limbecks hath
To make the water thin and airlike, faith
Cares not, but safe the place she's come unto
Where fresh, with salt waves meet, and what to do
    She knows not, but between both makes a board or
      two.   270

28

So far from hiding her guests, water is
That she shows them in bigger quantities
Than they are. Thus doubtful of her way,
For game and not for hunger a sea pie
Spied through this traitorous spectacle, from high,
The silly fish where it disputing lay,
And to end her doubts and her, bears her away,
Exalted she is, but to the exalter's good,
As are by great ones, men which lowly stood.
    It's raised, to be the raiser's instrument and food.   280

29

Is any kind subject to rape like fish?
Ill unto man, they neither do, nor wish:
Fishers they kill not, nor with noise awake,
They do not hunt, nor strive to make a prey
Of beasts, nor their young sons to bear away;
Fowls they pursue not, nor do undertake
To spoil the nests industrious birds do make;
Yet them all these unkind kinds feed upon,
To kill them is an occupation,
    And laws make Fasts, and Lents for their destruction.   290

30

A sudden stiff land-wind in that self hour
To sea-ward forced this bird, that did devour
The fish; he cares not, for with ease he flies,
Fat gluttony's best orator: at last
So long he hath flown, and hath flown so fast
That many leagues at sea, now tired he lies,
And with his prey, that till then languished, dies:
The souls no longer foes, two ways did err,
The fish I follow, and keep no calendar
    Of the other; he lives yet in some great officer.   300

31

Into an embryon fish, our soul is thrown,
And in due time thrown out again, and grown
To such vastness as, if unmanacled
From Greece, Morea were, and that by some
Earthquake unrooted, loose Morea swum,
Or seas from Afric's body had severed
And torn the hopeful promontory's head,
This fish would seem these, and, when all hopes fail,
A great ship overset, or without sail
  Hulling, might (when this was a whelp) be like this
    whale.   310

32

At every stroke his brazen fins do take,
More circles in the broken sea they make
Than cannons' voices, when the air they tear:
His ribs are pillars, and his high arched roof
Of bark that blunts best steel, is thunder-proof:
Swim in him swallowed dolphins, without fear,
And feel no sides, as if his vast womb were
Some inland sea, and ever as he went
He spouted rivers up, as if he meant
  To join our seas, with seas above the firmament.   320

33

He hunts not fish, but as an officer
Stays in his court, as his own net, and there
All suitors of all sorts themselves enthral;
So on his back lies this whale wantoning,
And in his gulf-like throat, sucks everything
That passeth near. Fish chaseth fish, and all,
Flyer and follower, in this whirlpool fall;
O might not states of more equality
Consist? and is it of necessity
  That thousand guiltless smalls, to make one great,
    must die?   330

34

Now drinks he up seas, and he eats up flocks,
He jostles islands, and he shakes firm rocks.
Now in a roomful house this soul doth float,
And like a Prince she sends her faculties
To all her limbs, distant as provinces.
The sun hath twenty times both crab and goat
Parched, since first launched forth this living boat.
'Tis greatest now, and to destruction
Nearest; there's no pause at perfection.
    Greatness a period hath, but hath no station.   340

35

Two little fishes whom he never harmed,
Nor fed on their kind, two not throughly armed
With hope that they could kill him, nor could do
Good to themselves by his death (they do not eat
His flesh, nor suck those oils, which thence outstreat),
Conspired against him, and it might undo
The plot of all, that the plotters were two,
But that they fishes were, and could not speak.
How shall a tyrant wise strong projects break,
    If wretches can on them the common anger wreak?   350

36

The flail-finned thresher, and steel-beaked sword-fish
Only attempt to do, what all do wish.
The thresher backs him, and to beat begins;
The sluggard whale yields to oppression,
And to hide himself from shame and danger, down
Begins to sink; the swordfish upward spins,
And gores him with his beak; his staff-like fins,
So well the one, his sword the other plies,
That now a scoff, and prey, this tyrant dies,
    And (his own dole) feeds with himself all companies.   360

37

Who will revenge his death? or who will call
Those to account, that thought, and wrought his fall?
The heirs of slain kings, we see are often so
Transported with the joy of what they get,
That they, revenge and obsequies forget,
Nor will against such men the people go,
Because he's now dead, to whom they should show
Love in that act; Some kings by vice being grown
So needy of subjects' love, that of their own
   They think they lose, if love be to the dead Prince
     shown.   370

38

This soul, now free from prison, and passion,
Hath yet a little indignation
That so small hammers should so soon down beat
So great a castle. And having for her house
Got the strait cloister of a wretched mouse
(As basest men that have not what to eat,
Nor enjoy aught, do far more hate the great
Then they, who good reposed estates possess)
This soul, late taught that great things might by less
   Be slain, to gallant mischief doth herself address.   380

39

Nature's great masterpiece, an elephant,
The only harmless great thing; the giant
Of beasts; who thought, no more had gone, to make one
     wise
But to be just, and thankful, loth to offend,
(Yet nature hath given him no knees to bend)
Himself he up-props, on himself relies,
And foe to none, suspects no enemies,
Still sleeping stood; vexed not his fantasy
Black dreams; like an unbent bow, carelessly
   His sinewy proboscis did remissly lie: 390

40

In which as in a gallery this mouse
Walked, and surveyed the rooms of this vast house,
And to the brain, the soul's bedchamber, went,
And gnawed the life cords there; like a whole town
Clean undermined, the slain beast tumbled down;
With him the murderer dies, whom envy sent
To kill, not 'scape; for, only he that meant
To die, did ever kill a man of better room,
And thus he made his foe, his prey, and tomb:
   Who cares not to turn back, may any whither come.   400

41

Next, housed this soul a wolf's yet unborn whelp,
Till the best midwife, Nature, gave it help,
To issue. It could kill, as soon as go:
Abel, as white, and mild as his sheep were,
(Who in that trade of Church, and kingdoms, there
Was the first type) was still infested so
With this wolf, that it bred his loss and woe;
And yet his bitch, his sentinel attends
The flock so near, so well warns and defends,
   That the wolf, (hopeless else) to corrupt her, intends.   410

42

He took a course, which since, successfully,
Great men have often taken, to espy
The counsels, or to break the plots of foes,
To Abel's tent he stealeth in the dark,
On whose skirts the bitch slept; ere she could bark,
Attached her with strait grips, yet he called those,
Embracements of love; to love's work he goes,
Where deeds move more than words; nor doth she show
Now much resist, nor needs he straiten so
   His prey, for, were she loose, she would nor bark, nor
     go.   420

43

He hath engaged her; his, she wholly bides;
Who not her own, none other's secrets hides.
If to the flock he come, and Abel there,
She feigns hoarse barkings, but she biteth not,
Her faith is quite, but not her love forgot.
At last a trap, of which some everywhere
Abel had placed, ended his loss, and fear,
By the wolf's death; and now just time it was
That a quick soul should give life to that mass
    Of blood in Abel's bitch, and thither this did pass.   430

44

Some have their wives, their sisters some begot,
But in the lives of emperors you shall not
Read of a lust the which may equal this;
This wolf begot himself, and finished
What he began alive, when he was dead,
Son to himself, and father too, he is
A riddling lust, for which schoolmen would miss
A proper name. The whelp of both these lay
In Abel's tent, and with soft Moaba,
    His sister, being young, it used to sport and play.   440

45

He soon for her too harsh, and churlish grew,
And Abel (the dam dead) would use this new
For the field. Being of two kinds made,
He, as his dam, from sheep drove wolves away,
And as his sire, he made them his own prey.
Five years he lived, and cozened with his trade,
Then hopeless that his faults were hid, betrayed
Himself by flight, and by all followed,
From dogs, a wolf; from wolves, a dog he fled;
    And, like a spy to both sides false, he perished.   450

46

It quickened next a toyful ape, and so
Gamesome it was, that it might freely go
From tent to tent, and with the children play.
His organs now so like theirs he doth find,
That why he cannot laugh, and speak his mind,
He wonders. Much with all, most he doth stay
With Adam's fifth daughter Siphatecia,
Doth gaze on her, and, where she passeth, pass,
Gathers her fruits, and tumbles on the grass,
   And wisest of that kind, the first true lover was.   460

47

He was the first that more desired to have
One than another; first that e'er did crave
Love by mute signs, and had no power to speak;
First that could make love faces, or could do
The vaulter's somersaults, or used to woo
With hoiting gambols, his own bones to break
To make his mistress merry; or to wreak
Her anger on himself. Sins against kind
They easily do, that can let feed their mind
   With outward beauty, beauty they in boys and beasts
     do find.   470

48

By this misled, too low things men have proved,
And too high; beasts and angels have been loved;
This ape, though else through-vain, in this was wise,
He reached at things too high, but open way
There was, and he knew not she would say nay;
His toys prevail not, likelier means he tries,
He gazeth on her face with tear-shot eyes,
And up lifts subtly with his russet paw
Her kidskin apron without fear or awe
   Of Nature: Nature hath no gaol, though she have law.   480

49

First she was silly and knew not what he meant,
That virtue, by his touches, chafed and spent,
Succeeds an itchy warmth, that melts her quite,
She knew not first, now cares not what he doth,
And willing half and more, more than half loth,
She neither pulls nor pushes, but outright
Now cries, and now repents; when Tethlemite
Her brother, entered, and a great stone threw
After the ape, who, thus prevented, flew.
    This house thus battered down, the soul possessed
        a new.   490

50

And whether by this change she lose or win,
She comes out next, where the ape would have gone in.
Adam and Eve had mingled bloods, and now
Like chemics' equal fires, her temperate womb
Had stewed and formed it: and part did become
A spongy liver, that did richly allow,
Like a free conduit, on a high hill's brow,
Life-keeping moisture unto every part,
Part hardened itself to a thicker heart,
    Whose busy furnaces life's spirits do impart.   500

51

Another part became the well of sense,
The tender well-armed feeling brain, from whence,
Those sinewy strings which do our bodies tie,
Are ravelled out, and fast there by one end,
Did this soul limbs, these limbs a soul attend,
And now they joined: keeping some quality
Of every past shape, she knew treachery,
Rapine, deceit, and lust, and ills enow
To be a woman. Themech she is now,
    Sister and wife to Cain, Cain that first did plough.   510

52

Whoe'er thou be'st that read'st this sullen writ,
Which just so much courts thee, as thou dost it,
Let me arrest thy thoughts, wonder with me,
Why ploughing, building, ruling and the rest,
Or most of those arts, whence our lives are blessed,
By cursed Cain's race invented be,
And blessed Seth vexed us with astronomy.
There's nothing simply good, nor ill alone,
Of every quality comparison,
   The only measure is, and judge, opinion.   520

SONGS AND SONNETS

The Flea

Mark but this flea, and mark in this,
How little that which thou deny'st me is;
It sucked me first, and now sucks thee,
And in this flea, our two bloods mingled be;
Thou know'st that this cannot be said
A sin, or shame, or loss of maidenhead,
  Yet this enjoys before it woo,
  And pampered swells with one blood made of two,
  And this, alas, is more than we would do.

Oh stay, three lives in one flea spare,   10
Where we almost, nay more than married are.
This flea is you and I, and this
Our marriage bed, and marriage temple is;
Though parents grudge, and you, we'are met,
And cloistered in these living walls of jet.
  Though use make you apt to kill me,
  Let not to this, self murder added be,
  And sacrilege, three sins in killing three.

Cruel and sudden, hast thou since
Purpled thy nail, in blood of innocence?   20
In what could this flea guilty be,
Except in that drop which it sucked from thee?
Yet thou triumph'st, and say'st that thou
Find'st not thyself, nor me the weaker now;
  'Tis true, then learn how false fears be;
  Just so much honour, when thou yield'st to me,
  Will waste, as this flea's death took life from thee.

The Good Morrow

I wonder by my troth, what thou, and I
    Did, till we loved? were we not weaned till then,
But sucked on country pleasures, childishly?
    Or snorted we in the seven sleepers' den?
'Twas so; but this, all pleasures fancies be.
If ever any beauty I did see,
Which I desired, and got, 'twas but a dream of thee.

And now good morrow to our waking souls,
    Which watch not one another out of fear;
For love, all love of other sights controls,   10
    And makes one little room, an everywhere.
Let sea-discoverers to new worlds have gone,
Let maps to others, worlds on worlds have shown,
Let us possess one world, each hath one, and is one.

My face in thine eye, thine in mine appears,
    And true plain hearts do in the faces rest,
Where can we find two better hemispheres
    Without sharp north, without declining west?
Whatever dies, was not mixed equally;
If our two loves be one, or, thou and I   20
Love so alike, that none do slacken, none can die.

Song

Go, and catch a falling star,
    Get with child a mandrake root,
Tell me, where all past years are,
    Or who cleft the Devil's foot,
Teach me to hear mermaids singing,
Or to keep off envy's stinging,
        And find
        What wind
Serves to advance an honest mind.

If thou be'est born to strange sights,   10
   Things invisible to see,
Ride ten thousand days and nights,
   Till age snow white hairs on thee,
Thou, when thou return'st, wilt tell me
All strange wonders that befell thee,
       And swear
       Nowhere
Lives a woman true, and fair.

If thou find'st one, let me know,
   Such a pilgrimage were sweet,
Yet do not, I would not go,   20
   Though at next door we might meet,
Though she were true, when you met her,
And last, till you write your letter,
       Yet she
       Will be
False, ere I come, to two, or three.

Woman's Constancy

Now thou hast loved me one whole day,
Tomorrow when thou leav'st, what wilt thou say?
Wilt thou then antedate some new made vow?
       Or say that now
We are not just those persons, which we were?
Or, that oaths made in reverential fear
Of love, and his wrath, any may forswear?
Or, as true deaths, true marriages untie,
So lovers' contracts, images of those,
Bind but till sleep, death's image, them unloose?   10
       Or, your own end to justify,
For having purposed change, and falsehood, you
Can have no way but falsehood to be true?
Vain lunatic, against these 'scapes I could
       Dispute, and conquer, if I would,
       Which I abstain to do,
For by tomorrow, I may think so too.

The Undertaking

I have done one braver thing
   Than all the Worthies did,
And yet a braver thence doth spring,
   Which is, to keep that hid.

It were but madness now t'impart
   The skill of specular stone,
When he which can have learned the art
   To cut it, can find none.

So, if I now should utter this,
   Others (because no more   10
Such stuff to work upon, there is),
   Would love but as before.

But he who loveliness within
   Hath found, all outward loathes,
For he who colour loves, and skin,
   Loves but their oldest clothes.

If, as I have, you also do
   Virtue attired in woman see,
And dare love that, and say so too,
   And forget the He and She;   20

And if this love, though placed so,
   From profane men you hide,
Which will no faith on this bestow,
   Or, if they do, deride:

Then you have done a braver thing
   Than all the Worthies did,
And a braver thence will spring,
   Which is, to keep that hid.

The Sun Rising

Busy old fool, unruly sun,
    Why dost thou thus,
Through windows, and through curtains call on us?
Must to thy motions lovers' seasons run?
    Saucy pedantic wretch, go chide
    Late schoolboys, and sour prentices,
  Go tell court-huntsmen, that the King will ride,
  Call country ants to harvest offices;
Love, all alike, no season knows, nor clime,
Nor hours, days, months, which are the rags of time.   10

    Thy beams, so reverend, and strong
    Why shouldst thou think?
I could eclipse and cloud them with a wink,
But that I would not lose her sight so long:
    If her eyes have not blinded thine,
    Look, and tomorrow late, tell me,
  Whether both th'Indias of spice and mine
  Be where thou left'st them, or lie here with me.
Ask for those kings whom thou saw'st yesterday,
And thou shalt hear, All here in one bed lay.   20

    She'is all states, and all princes, I,
    Nothing else is.
Princes do but play us; compared to this,
All honour's mimic; all wealth alchemy.
    Thou sun art half as happy as we,
    In that the world's contracted thus;
  Thine age asks ease, and since thy duties be
  To warm the world, that's done in warming us.
Shine here to us, and thou art everywhere;
This bed thy centre is, these walls, thy sphere.   30

The Indifferent

I can love both fair and brown,
Her whom abundance melts, and her whom want betrays,
Her who loves loneness best, and her who masks and plays,
   Her whom the country formed, and whom the town,
      Her who believes, and her who tries,
      Her who still weeps with spongy eyes,
   And her who is dry cork, and never cries;
   I can love her, and her, and you and you,
   I can love any, so she be not true.

      Will no other vice content you?   10
Will it not serve your turn to do, as did your mothers?
Or have you all old vices spent, and now would find out
      others?
   Or doth a fear, that men are true, torment you?
      Oh we are not, be not you so,
      Let me, and do you, twenty know.
   Rob me, but bind me not, and let me go.
   Must I, who came to travel thorough you,
   Grow your fixed subject, because you are true?

      Venus heard me sigh this song,
And by love's sweetest part, variety, she swore,   20
She heard not this till now; and that it should be so no more.
   She went, examined, and returned ere long,
      And said, 'Alas, some two or three
      Poor heretics in love there be,
   Which think to stablish dangerous constancy.
   But I have told them, "Since you will be true,
   You shall be true to them, who are false to you."'

Love's Usury

   For every hour that thou wilt spare me now,
      I will allow,
   Usurious God of Love, twenty to thee,
   When with my brown, my grey hairs equal be;

Till then, Love, let my body reign, and let
Me travel, sojourn, snatch, plot, have, forget,
Resume my last year's relict: think that yet
    We had never met.

Let me think any rival's letter mine,
    And at next nine   10
Keep midnight's promise; mistake by the way
The maid, and tell the Lady of that delay;
Only let me love none, no, not the sport;
From country grass, to comfitures of Court,
Or city's quelque-choses, let report
    My mind transport.

This bargain's good; if when I am old, I be
    Inflamed by thee,
If thine own honour, or my shame, or pain,
Thou covet, most at that age thou shalt gain.   20
Do thy will then, then subject and degree,
And fruit of love, Love, I submit to thee,
Spare me till then, I'll bear it, though she be
    One that loves me.

The Canonization

For God's sake hold your tongue, and let me love,
  Or chide my palsy, or my gout,
My five grey hairs, or ruined fortune flout,
    With wealth your state, your mind with arts improve,
    Take you a course, get you a place,
    Observe his Honour, or his Grace,
Or the King's real, or his stamped face
  Contemplate; what you will, approve,
  So you will let me love.

Alas, alas, who's injured by my love?   10
  What merchant's ships have my sighs drowned?
Who says my tears have overflowed his ground?
  When did my colds a forward spring remove?

When did the heats which my veins fill
  Add one more to the plaguy bill?
Soldiers find wars, and lawyers find out still
  Litigious men, which quarrels move,
  Though she and I do love.

Call us what you will, we are made such by love;
  Call her one, me another fly,   20
We are tapers too, and at our own cost die,
  And we in us find the eagle and the dove;
    The phoenix riddle hath more wit
    By us; we two being one, are it.
So, to one neutral thing both sexes fit.
  We die and rise the same, and prove
  Mysterious by this love.

We can die by it, if not live by love,
  And if unfit for tombs and hearse
Our legend be, it will be fit for verse;   30
  And if no piece of chronicle we prove,
    We'll build in sonnets pretty rooms;
    As well a well wrought urn becomes
The greatest ashes, as half-acre tombs,
  And by these hymns, all shall approve
  Us canonized for love.

And thus invoke us; 'You whom reverend love
  Made one another's hermitage;
You, to whom love was peace, that now is rage;
  Who did the whole world's soul extract, and drove,   40
    Into the glasses of your eyes,
    So made such mirrors, and such spies,
That they did all to you epitomize,
  Countries, towns, courts: beg from above
  A pattern of your love!'

The Triple Fool

I am two fools, I know,
For loving, and for saying so
   In whining poetry;
But where's that wiseman, that would not be I,
   If she would not deny?
Then as th'earth's inward narrow crooked lanes
Do purge sea water's fretful salt away,
   I thought, if I could draw my pains
Through rhyme's vexation, I should them allay.
Grief brought to numbers cannot be so fierce,   10
For, he tames it, that fetters it in verse.

   But when I have done so,
Some man, his art and voice to show,
   Doth set and sing my pain,
And by delighting many, frees again
   Grief, which verse did restrain.
To love and grief tribute of verse belongs,
But not of such as pleases when 'tis read,
   Both are increased by such songs:
For both their triumphs so are published,   20
And I, which was two fools, do so grow three;
Who are a little wise, the best fools be.

Lovers' Infiniteness

If yet I have not all thy love,
Dear, I shall never have it all;
I cannot breathe one other sigh, to move,
Nor can entreat one other tear to fall.
And all my treasure, which should purchase thee,
Sighs, tears, and oaths, and letters I have spent,
Yet no more can be due to me,
Than at the bargain made was meant.
If then thy gift of love were partial,
That some to me, some should to others fall,   10
   Dear, I shall never have thee all.

Or if then thou gavest me all,
All was but all, which thou hadst then;
But if in thy heart, since, there be or shall
New love created be, by other men,
Which have their stocks entire, and can in tears,
In sighs, in oaths, and letters outbid me,
This new love may beget new fears,
For, this love was not vowed by thee.
And yet it was, thy gift being general,   20
The ground, thy heart is mine; whatever shall
    Grow there, dear, I should have it all.

Yet I would not have all yet,
He that hath all can have no more,
And since my love doth every day admit
New growth, thou shouldst have new rewards in store;
Thou canst not every day give me thy heart,
If thou canst give it, then thou never gav'st it:
Love's riddles are, that though thy heart depart,
It stays at home, and thou with losing sav'st it: 30
But we will have a way more liberal,
Than changing hearts, to join them, so we shall
    Be one, and one another's all.

Song

Sweetest love, I do not go,
    For weariness of thee,
Nor in hope the world can show
    A fitter love for me;
        But since that I
Must die at last, 'tis best,
To use my self in jest
    Thus by feigned deaths to die.

Yesternight the sun went hence,
    And yet is here today,   10
He hath no desire nor sense,
    Nor half so short a way:

Then fear not me,
But believe that I shall make
Speedier journeys, since I take
    More wings and spurs than he.

O how feeble is man's power,
    That if good fortune fall,
Cannot add another hour,
    Nor a lost hour recall!   20
        But come bad chance,
And we join to it our strength,
And we teach it art and length,
    Itself o'er us to advance.

When thou sigh'st, thou sigh'st not wind,
    But sigh'st my soul away,
When thou weep'st, unkindly kind,
    My life's blood doth decay.
        It cannot be
That thou lov'st me, as thou say'st,   30
If in thine my life thou waste,
    Thou art the best of me.

Let not thy divining heart
    Forethink me any ill,
Destiny may take thy part,
    And may thy fears fulfil;
        But think that we
Are but turned aside to sleep;
They who one another keep
    Alive, ne'er parted be.   40

The Legacy

When I died last, and, dear, I die
    As often as from thee I go,
    Though it be an hour ago,
And lovers' hours be full eternity,

I can remember yet, that I
  Something did say, and something did bestow;
Though I be dead, which sent me, I should be
Mine own executor and legacy.

I heard me say, Tell her anon,
  That my self, that is you, not I,   10
    Did kill me, and when I felt me die,
I bid me send my heart, when I was gone;
But I alas could there find none,
  When I had ripped me, and searched where hearts should
    lie;
It killed me again that I who still was true,
In life, in my last will should cozen you.

Yet I found something like a heart,
  But colours it, and corners had,
  It was not good, it was not bad,
It was entire to none, and few had part.   20
As good as could be made by art
  It seemed, and therefore for our losses sad,
I meant to send this heart instead of mine,
But oh, no man could hold it, for 'twas thine.

A Fever

Oh do not die, for I shall hate
  All women so, when thou art gone,
That thee I shall not celebrate,
  When I remember, thou wast one.

But yet thou canst not die, I know;
  To leave this world behind, is death,
But when thou from this world wilt go,
  The whole world vapours with thy breath.

Or if, when thou, the world's soul, go'st,
  It stay, 'tis but thy carcase then,   10
The fairest woman, but thy ghost,
  But corrupt worms, the worthiest men.

Oh wrangling schools, that search what fire
   Shall burn this world, had none the wit
Unto this knowledge to aspire,
   That this her fever might be it?

And yet she cannot waste by this,
   Nor long bear this torturing wrong,
For much corruption needful is
   To fuel such a fever long.   20

These burning fits but meteors be,
   Whose matter in thee is soon spent.
Thy beauty, and all parts, which are thee,
   Are unchangeable firmament.

Yet 'twas of my mind, seizing thee,
   Though it in thee cannot persever.
For I had rather owner be
   Of thee one hour, than all else ever.

Air and Angels

Twice or thrice had I loved thee,
Before I knew thy face or name;
So in a voice, so in a shapeless flame,
Angels affect us oft, and worshipped be;
   Still when, to where thou wert, I came,
Some lovely glorious nothing I did see.
   But since my soul, whose child love is,
Takes limbs of flesh, and else could nothing do,
   More subtle than the parent is
Love must not be, but take a body too,   10
   And therefore what thou wert, and who
     I bid love ask, and now
That it assume thy body, I allow,
And fix itself in thy lip, eye, and brow.

Whilst thus to ballast love, I thought,
And so more steadily to have gone,
With wares which would sink admiration,
I saw, I had love's pinnace overfraught,
    Every thy hair for love to work upon
Is much too much, some fitter must be sought;   20
    For, nor in nothing, nor in things
Extreme, and scatt'ring bright, can love inhere;
    Then as an angel, face and wings
Of air, not pure as it, yet pure doth wear,
    So thy love may be my love's sphere;
       Just such disparity
As is 'twixt air and angels' purity,
'Twixt women's love, and men's will ever be.

Break of Day

'Tis true, 'tis day, what though it be?
O wilt thou therefore rise from me?
Why should we rise, because 'tis light?
Did we lie down, because 'twas night?
Love which in spite of darkness brought us hither,
Should in despite of light keep us together.

Light hath no tongue, but is all eye;
If it could speak as well as spy,
This were the worst, that it could say,
That being well, I fain would stay,   10
And that I loved my heart and honour so,
That I would not from him, that had them, go.

Must business thee from hence remove?
Oh, that's the worst disease of love,
The poor, the foul, the false, love can
Admit, but not the busied man.
He which hath business, and makes love, doth do
Such wrong, as when a married man doth woo.

The Anniversary

All kings, and all their favourites,
   All glory of honours, beauties, wits,
The sun itself, which makes times, as they pass,
Is elder by a year, now, than it was
When thou and I first one another saw:
All other things, to their destruction draw,
   Only our love hath no decay;
This, no tomorrow hath, nor yesterday,
Running it never runs from us away,
But truly keeps his first, last, everlasting day.   10

Two graves must hide thine and my corse,
   If one might, death were no divorce,
Alas, as well as other princes, we,
(Who prince enough in one another be),
Must leave at last in death, these eyes, and ears,
Oft fed with true oaths, and with sweet salt tears;
   But souls where nothing dwells but love
(All other thoughts being inmates) then shall prove
This, or a love increased there above,
When bodies to their graves, souls from their graves
    remove.   20

And then we shall be throughly blessed,
   But we no more, than all the rest.
Here upon earth, we are kings, and none but we
Can be such kings, nor of such subjects be;
Who is so safe as we? where none can do
Treason to us, except one of us two.
   True and false fears let us refrain,
Let us love nobly, and live, and add again
Years and years unto years, till we attain
To write threescore, this is the second of our reign.   30

A Valediction: of my Name in the Window

My name engraved herein,
Doth contribute my firmness to this glass,
    Which, ever since that charm, hath been
    As hard, as that which graved it, was;
Thine eye will give it price enough, to mock
        The diamonds of either rock.

    'Tis much that glass should be
As all confessing, and through-shine as I,
    'Tis more, that it shows thee to thee,
    And clear reflects thee to thine eye.   10
But all such rules, love's magic can undo,
        Here you see me, and I am you.

    As no one point, nor dash,
Which are but accessory to this name,
    The showers and tempests can outwash,
    So shall all times find me the same;
You this entireness better may fulfil,
        Who have the pattern with you still.

    Or if too hard and deep
This learning be, for a scratched name to teach,   20
    It, as a given death's head keep
    Lovers' mortality to preach,
Or think this ragged bony name to be
        My ruinous anatomy.

    Then, as all my souls be
Emparadised in you, (in whom alone
    I understand, and grow and see,)
    The rafters of my body, bone
Being still with you, the muscle, sinew, and vein,
        Which tile this house, will come again.   30

    Till my return repair
And recompact my scattered body so,
   As all the virtuous powers which are
   Fixed in the stars, are said to flow
Into such characters, as graved be
     When these stars have supremacy,

    So since this name was cut
When love and grief their exaltation had,
   No door 'gainst this name's influence shut;
   As much more loving, as more sad,   40
'Twill make thee; and thou shouldst, till I return,
     Since I die daily, daily mourn.

    When thy inconsiderate hand
Flings ope this casement, with my trembling name,
   To look on one, whose wit or land,
   New battery to thy heart may frame,
Then think this name alive, and that thou thus
     In it offend'st my Genius.

    And when thy melted maid,
Corrupted by thy lover's gold, and page,   50
   His letter at thy pillow hath laid,
   Disputed it, and tamed thy rage,
And thou begin'st to thaw towards him, for this,
     May my name step in, and hide his.

    And if this treason go
To an overt act, and that thou write again;
   In superscribing, this name flow
   Into thy fancy, from the pane.
So, in forgetting thou rememberest right,
     And unaware to me shalt write.   60

    But glass, and lines must be
No means our firm substantial love to keep;
   Near death inflicts this lethargy,
   And this I murmur in my sleep;
Impute this idle talk, to that I go,
     For dying men talk often so.

Twickenham Garden

Blasted with sighs, and surrounded with tears,
    Hither I come to seek the spring,
    And at mine eyes, and at mine ears,
Receive such balms, as else cure everything;
    But O, self traitor, I do bring
The spider love, which transubstantiates all,
    And can convert manna to gall,
And that this place may thoroughly be thought
    True paradise, I have the serpent brought.

'Twere wholesomer for me, that winter did   10
    Benight the glory of this place,
    And that a grave frost did forbid
These trees to laugh, and mock me to my face;
    But that I may not this disgrace
Endure, nor yet leave loving, Love, let me
    Some senseless piece of this place be;
Make me a mandrake, so I may groan here,
    Or a stone fountain weeping out my year.

Hither with crystal vials, lovers come,
    And take my tears, which are love's wine,   20
And try your mistress' tears at home,
For all are false, that taste not just like mine;
    Alas, hearts do not in eyes shine,
Nor can you more judge woman's thoughts by tears,
    Than by her shadow, what she wears.
O perverse sex, where none is true but she,
    Who's therefore true, because her truth kills me.

A Valediction: of the Book

I'll tell thee now (dear love) what thou shalt do
    To anger destiny, as she doth us,
    How I shall stay, though she esloign me thus,
And how posterity shall know it too;

How thine may out-endure
  Sibyl's glory, and obscure
  Her who from Pindar could allure,
And her, through whose help Lucan is not lame,
And her, whose book (they say) Homer did find, and name.

Study our manuscripts, those myriads   10
  Of letters, which have passed 'twixt thee and me,
  Thence write our annals, and in them will be
To all whom love's subliming fire invades,
    Rule and example found;
    There, the faith of any ground
    No schismatic will dare to wound,
  That sees, how Love this grace to us affords,
To make, to keep, to use, to be these his records.

This book, as long lived as the elements,
  Or as the world's form, this all-graved tome   20
  In cypher write, or new made idiom;
We for Love's clergy only are instruments,
    When this book is made thus,
    Should again the ravenous
    Vandals and Goths inundate us,
  Learning were safe; in this our universe
Schools might learn sciences, spheres music, angels verse.

Here Love's divines (since all divinity
  Is love or wonder) may find all they seek,
  Whether abstract spiritual love they like,   30
Their souls exhaled with what they do not see,
    Or, loth so to amuse
    Faith's infirmity, they choose
    Something which they may see and use;
  For, though mind be the heaven, where love doth sit,
Beauty a convenient type may be to figure it.

Here more than in their books may lawyers find,
  Both by what titles mistresses are ours,
  And how prerogative these states devours,
Transferred from Love himself, to womankind,   40

Who though from heart, and eyes,
  They exact great subsidies,
  Forsake him who on them relies,
And for the cause, honour, or conscience give,
Chimeras, vain as they, or their prerogative.

Here statesmen, (or of them, they which can read),
  May of their occupation find the grounds,
  Love and their art alike it deadly wounds,
If to consider what 'tis, one proceed,
    In both they do excel   50
    Who the present govern well,
    Whose weakness none doth, or dares tell;
In this thy book, such will their nothing see,
As in the Bible some can find out alchemy.

Thus vent thy thoughts; abroad I'll study thee,
  As he removes far off, that great heights takes;
  How great love is, presence best trial makes,
But absence tries how long this love will be;
    To take a latitude
    Sun, or stars, are fitliest viewed   60
    At their brightest, but to conclude
Of longitudes, what other way have we,
But to mark when, and where the dark eclipses be?

Community

Good we must love, and must hate ill,
For ill is ill, and good good still,
  But there are things indifferent,
Which we may neither hate, nor love,
But one, and then another prove,
  As we shall find our fancy bent.

If then at first wise Nature had
Made women either good or bad,
  Then some we might hate, and some choose,
But since she did them so create,   10
That we may neither love, nor hate,
  Only this rests, All, all may use.

If they were good it would be seen,
Good is as visible as green,
   And to all eyes itself betrays:
If they were bad, they could not last,
Bad doth itself, and others waste,
   So, they deserve nor blame, nor praise.

But they are ours as fruits are ours,
He that but tastes, he that devours,   20
   And he that leaves all, doth as well:
Changed loves are but changed sorts of meat,
And when he hath the kernel eat,
   Who doth not fling away the shell?

Love's Growth

I scarce believe my love to be so pure
   As I had thought it was,
   Because it doth endure
Vicissitude, and season, as the grass;
Methinks I lied all winter, when I swore,
My love was infinite, if spring make it more.
But if this medicine, love, which cures all sorrow
With more, not only be no quintessence,
But mixed of all stuffs, paining soul, or sense,
And of the sun his working vigour borrow,   10
Love's not so pure, and abstract, as they use
To say, which have no mistress but their Muse,
But as all else, being elemented too,
Love sometimes would contemplate, sometimes do.

And yet not greater, but more eminent,
   Love by the spring is grown;
   As, in the firmament,
Stars by the sun are not enlarged, but shown,
Gentle love deeds, as blossoms on a bough,
From love's awakened root do bud out now.   20

If, as in water stirred more circles be
Produced by one, love such additions take,
Those like so many spheres, but one heaven make,
For, they are all concentric unto thee;
And though each spring do add to love new heat,
As princes do in times of action get
New taxes, and remit them not in peace,
No winter shall abate the spring's increase.

Love's Exchange

Love, any devil else but you,
Would for a given soul give something too.
   At Court your fellows every day,
Give th' art of rhyming, huntsmanship, and play,
   For them who were their own before;
   Only I have nothing which gave more,
But am, alas, by being lowly, lower.

   I ask not dispensation now
To falsify a tear, or sigh, or vow,
   I do not sue from thee to draw   10
A *non obstante* on nature's law,
   These are prerogatives, they inhere
   In thee and thine; none should forswear
Except that he Love's minion were.

   Give me thy weakness, make me blind,
Both ways, as thou and thine, in eyes and mind;
   Love, let me never know that this
Is love, or, that love childish is.
   Let me not know that others know
   That she knows my pain, lest that so   20
A tender shame make me mine own new woe.

   If thou give nothing, yet thou' art just,
Because I would not thy first motions trust;
   Small towns which stand stiff, till great shot
Enforce them, by war's law condition not.
   Such in love's warfare is my case,
   I may not article for grace,
Having put Love at last to show this face.

This face, by which he could command
And change the idolatry of any land,   30
    This face, which wheresoe'er it comes,
Can call vowed men from cloisters, dead from tombs,
    And melt both poles at once, and store
    Deserts with cities, and make more
Mines in the earth, than quarries were before.

    For this Love is enraged with me,
Yet kills not. If I must example be
    To future rebels; if th' unborn
Must learn, by my being cut up, and torn:
    Kill, and dissect me, Love; for this   40
    Torture against thine own end is,
Racked carcases make ill anatomies.

Confined Love

    Some man unworthy to be possessor
Of old or new love, himself being false or weak,
    Thought his pain and shame would be lesser,
If on womankind he might his anger wreak,
        And thence a law did grow,
        One should but one man know;
        But are other creatures so?

    Are sun, moon, or stars by law forbidden,
To smile where they list, or lend away their light?
    Are birds divorced, or are they chidden   10
If they leave their mate, or lie abroad a-night?
        Beasts do no jointures lose
        Though they new lovers choose,
        But we are made worse than those.

    Who e'er rigged fair ship to lie in harbours,
And not to seek new lands, or not to deal withal?
    Or built fair houses, set trees, and arbours,
Only to lock up, or else to let them fall?
        Good is not good, unless
        A thousand it possess,   20
        But doth waste with greediness.

The Dream

Dear love, for nothing less than thee
Would I have broke this happy dream,
　　　　It was a theme
For reason, much too strong for fantasy,
Therefore thou waked'st me wisely; yet
My dream thou brok'st not, but continued'st it,
Thou art so true, that thoughts of thee suffice,
To make dreams truths, and fables histories;
Enter these arms, for since thou thought'st it best,
Not to dream all my dream, let's act the rest.　　　　　10

As lightning, or a taper's light,
Thine eyes, and not thy noise waked me;
　　　　Yet I thought thee
(For thou lov'st truth) an angel, at first sight,
But when I saw thou saw'st my heart,
And knew'st my thoughts, beyond an angel's art,
When thou knew'st what I dreamed, when thou knew'st
　　　when
Excess of joy would wake me, and cam'st then,
I must confess, it could not choose but be
Profane, to think thee anything but thee.　　　　　20

Coming and staying showed thee, thee,
But rising makes me doubt, that now,
　　　　Thou art not thou.
That love is weak, where fear's as strong as he;
'Tis not all spirit, pure, and brave,
If mixture it of fear, shame, honour, have.
Perchance as torches which must ready be,
Men light and put out, so thou deal'st with me,
Thou cam'st to kindle, goest to come; then I
Will dream that hope again, but else would die.　　　　　30

A Valediction: of Weeping

    Let me pour forth
My tears before thy face, whilst I stay here,
For thy face coins them, and thy stamp they bear,
And by this mintage they are something worth,
    For thus they be
    Pregnant of thee;
Fruits of much grief they are, emblems of more,
When a tear falls, that thou falls which it bore,
So thou and I are nothing then, when on a divers shore.

    On a round ball   10
A workman that hath copies by, can lay
An Europe, Afric, and an Asia,
And quickly make that, which was nothing, all,
    So doth each tear,
    Which thee doth wear,
A globe, yea world by that impression grow,
Till thy tears mixed with mine do overflow
This world, by waters sent from thee, my heaven dissolved so.

    O more than moon,
Draw not up seas to drown me in thy sphere,   20
Weep me not dead, in thine arms, but forbear
To teach the sea, what it may do too soon;
    Let not the wind
    Example find,
To do me more harm, than it purposeth;
Since thou and I sigh one another's breath,
Whoe'er sighs most, is cruellest, and hastes the other's death.

Love's Alchemy

Some that have deeper digged love's mine than I,
Say, where his centric happiness doth lie:
    I have loved, and got, and told,
But should I love, get, tell, till I were old,

I should not find that hidden mystery;
      Oh, 'tis imposture all:
And as no chemic yet the elixir got,
      But glorifies his pregnant pot,
      If by the way to him befall
Some odoriferous thing, or medicinal,   10
  So, lovers dream a rich and long delight,
  But get a winter-seeming summer's night.

Our ease, our thrift, our honour, and our day,
Shall we, for this vain bubble's shadow pay?
      Ends love in this, that my man,
Can be as happy as I can; if he can
Endure the short scorn of a bridegroom's play?
      That loving wretch that swears,
'Tis not the bodies marry, but the minds,
      Which he in her angelic finds,   20
      Would swear as justly, that he hears,
In that day's rude hoarse minstrelsy, the spheres.
  Hope not for mind in women; at their best
  Sweetness and wit, they are but mummy, possessed.

The Curse

Whoever guesses, thinks, or dreams he knows
Who is my mistress, wither by this curse;
      His only, and only his purse
      May some dull heart to love dispose,
And she yield then to all that are his foes;
  May he be scorned by one, whom all else scorn,
  Forswear to others, what to her he hath sworn,
  With fear of missing, shame of getting, torn:

Madness his sorrow, gout his cramps, may be
Make, by but thinking, who hath made him such: 10
      And may he feel no touch
      Of conscience, but of fame, and be
Anguished, not that 'twas sin, but that 'twas she:
  In early and long scarceness may he rot,
  For land which had been his, if he had not
  Himself incestuously an heir begot:

May he dream treason, and believe, that he
Meant to perform it, and confess, and die,
   And no record tell why:
   His sons, which none of his may be,   20
Inherit nothing but his infamy:
 Or may he so long parasites have fed,
 That he would fain be theirs, whom he hath bred,
 And at the last be circumcised for bread:

The venom of all stepdames, gamesters' gall,
What tyrants, and their subjects interwish,
   What plants, mines, beasts, fowl, fish,
   Can contribute, all ill which all
Prophets, or poets spake; and all which shall
 Be annexed in schedules unto this by me,   30
Fall on that man; for if it be a she
Nature beforehand hath out-cursed me.

The Message

Send home my long strayed eyes to me,
Which (oh) too long have dwelt on thee,
Yet since there they have learned such ill,
   Such forced fashions,
   And false passions,
    That they be
    Made by thee
Fit for no good sight, keep them still.

Send home my harmless heart again,
Which no unworthy thought could stain,   10
But if it be taught by thine
   To make jestings
   Of protestings,
    And cross both
    Word and oath,
Keep it, for then 'tis none of mine.

Yet send me back my heart and eyes,
That I may know, and see thy lies,
And may laugh and joy, when thou
    Art in anguish   20
    And dost languish
      For some one
      That will none,
Or prove as false as thou art now.

A Nocturnal upon St Lucy's Day,
being the shortest day

'Tis the year's midnight, and it is the day's,
Lucy's, who scarce seven hours herself unmasks,
  The sun is spent, and now his flasks
  Send forth light squibs, no constant rays;
    The world's whole sap is sunk:
The general balm th' hydroptic earth hath drunk,
Whither, as to the bed's-feet, life is shrunk,
Dead and interred; yet all these seem to laugh,
Compared with me, who am their epitaph.

Study me then, you who shall lovers be   10
At the next world, that is, at the next spring:
  For I am every dead thing,
  In whom love wrought new alchemy.
    For his art did express
A quintessence even from nothingness,
From dull privations, and lean emptiness
He ruined me, and I am re-begot
Of absence, darkness, death; things which are not.

All others, from all things, draw all that's good,
Life, soul, form, spirit, whence they being have;   20
  I, by love's limbeck, am the grave
  Of all, that's nothing. Oft a flood

Have we two wept, and so
Drowned the whole world, us two; oft did we grow
To be two chaoses, when we did show
Care to aught else; and often absences
Withdrew our souls, and made us carcases.

But I am by her death (which word wrongs her)
Of the first nothing, the elixir grown;
Were I a man, that I were one,   30
I needs must know; I should prefer,
If I were any beast,
Some ends, some means; yea plants, yea stones detest,
And love; all, all some properties invest;
If I an ordinary nothing were,
As shadow, a light, and body must be here.

But I am none; nor will my sun renew.
You lovers, for whose sake, the lesser sun
At this time to the Goat is run
To fetch new lust, and give it you,   40
Enjoy your summer all;
Since she enjoys her long night's festival,
Let me prepare towards her, and let me call
This hour her vigil, and her eve, since this
Both the year's, and the day's deep midnight is.

Witchcraft by a Picture

I fix mine eye on thine, and there
Pity my picture burning in thine eye,
My picture drowned in a transparent tear,
When I look lower I espy;
Hadst thou the wicked skill
By pictures made and marred, to kill,
How many ways mightst thou perform thy will?

But now I have drunk thy sweet salt tears,
  And though thou pour more I'll depart;
My picture vanished, vanish fears,   10
That I can be endamaged by that art;
  Though thou retain of me
One picture more, yet that will be,
Being in thine own heart, from all malice free.

The Bait

Come live with me, and be my love,
And we will some new pleasures prove
Of golden sands, and crystal brooks,
With silken lines, and silver hooks.

There will the river whispering run
Warmed by thy eyes, more than the sun.
And there the'enamoured fish will stay,
Begging themselves they may betray.

When thou wilt swim in that live bath,
Each fish, which every channel hath,   10
Will amorously to thee swim,
Gladder to catch thee, than thou him.

If thou, to be so seen, be'st loth,
By sun, or moon, thou darkenest both,
And if myself have leave to see,
I need not their light, having thee.

Let others freeze with angling reeds,
And cut their legs, with shells and weeds,
Or treacherously poor fish beset,
With strangling snare, or windowy net: 20

Let coarse bold hands, from slimy nest
The bedded fish in banks out-wrest,
Or curious traitors, sleavesilk flies
Bewitch poor fishes' wandering eyes.

For thee, thou need'st no such deceit,
For thou thyself art thine own bait,
That fish, that is not catched thereby,
Alas, is wiser far than I.

The Apparition

When by thy scorn, O murderess, I am dead,
And that thou think'st thee free
From all solicitation from me,
Then shall my ghost come to thy bed,
And thee, feigned vestal, in worse arms shall see;
Then thy sick taper will begin to wink,
And he, whose thou art then, being tired before,
Will, if thou stir, or pinch to wake him, think
    Thou call'st for more,
And in false sleep will from thee shrink,   10
And then poor aspen wretch, neglected thou
Bathed in a cold quicksilver sweat wilt lie
  A verier ghost than I;
What I will say, I will not tell thee now,
Lest that preserve thee; and since my love is spent,
I had rather thou shouldst painfully repent,
Than by my threatenings rest still innocent.

The Broken Heart

He is stark mad, who ever says,
    That he hath been in love an hour,
Yet not that love so soon decays,
    But that it can ten in less space devour;
Who will believe me, if I swear
That I have had the plague a year?
    Who would not laugh at me, if I should say,
    I saw a flask of powder burn a day?

Ah, what a trifle is a heart,
  If once into Love's hands it come!   10
All other griefs allow a part
  To other griefs, and ask themselves but some,
They come to us, but us Love draws,
He swallows us, and never chaws:
  By him, as by chain-shot, whole ranks do die,
  He is the tyrant pike, our hearts the fry.

If 'twere not so, what did become
  Of my heart, when I first saw thee?
I brought a heart into the room,
  But from the room, I carried none with me;   20
If it had gone to thee, I know
Mine would have taught thy heart to show
  More pity unto me: but Love, alas,
  At one first blow did shiver it as glass.

Yet nothing can to nothing fall,
  Nor any place be empty quite,
Therefore I think my breast hath all
  Those pieces still, though they be not unite;
And now as broken glasses show
A hundred lesser faces, so   30
My rags of heart can like, wish, and adore,
But after one such love, can love no more.

A Valediction: forbidding Mourning

As virtuous men pass mildly away,
  And whisper to their souls, to go,
Whilst some of their sad friends do say,
  The breath goes now, and some say, no:

So let us melt, and make no noise,
  No tear-floods, nor sigh-tempests move,
'Twere profanation of our joys
  To tell the laity our love.

Moving of th' earth brings harms and fears,
  Men reckon what it did and meant,   10
But trepidation of the spheres,
  Though greater far, is innocent.

Dull sublunary lovers' love
  (Whose soul is sense) cannot admit
Absence, because it doth remove
  Those things which elemented it.

But we by a love, so much refined,
  That ourselves know not what it is,
Inter-assured of the mind,
  Care less, eyes, lips, and hands to miss.   20

Our two souls therefore, which are one,
  Though I must go, endure not yet
A breach, but an expansion,
  Like gold to airy thinness beat.

If they be two, they are two so
  As stiff twin compasses are two,
Thy soul the fixed foot, makes no show
  To move, but doth, if th'other do.

And though it in the centre sit,
  Yet when the other far doth roam,   30
It leans, and hearkens after it,
  And grows erect, as that comes home.

Such wilt thou be to me, who must
  Like th' other foot, obliquely run;
Thy firmness makes my circle just,
  And makes me end, where I begun.

The Ecstasy

Where, like a pillow on a bed,
  A pregnant bank swelled up, to rest
The violet's reclining head,
  Sat we two, one another's best;

Our hands were firmly cemented
　　With a fast balm, which thence did spring,
Our eye-beams twisted, and did thread
　　Our eyes, upon one double string;

So to' intergraft our hands, as yet
　　Was all the means to make us one,　　　　　10
And pictures in our eyes to get
　　Was all our propagation.

As 'twixt two equal armies, Fate
　　Suspends uncertain victory,
Our souls, (which to advance their state,
　　Were gone out), hung 'twixt her, and me.

And whilst our souls negotiate there,
　　We like sepulchral statues lay;
All day, the same our postures were,
　　And we said nothing, all the day.　　　　　20

If any, so by love refined,
　　That he soul's language understood,
And by good love were grown all mind,
　　Within convenient distance stood,

He (though he knew not which soul spake
　　Because both meant, both spake the same)
Might thence a new concoction take,
　　And part far purer than he came.

This ecstasy doth unperplex
　　(We said) and tell us what we love,　　　　　30
We see by this, it was not sex,
　　We see, we saw not what did move:

But as all several souls contain
　　Mixture of things, they know not what,
Love, these mixed souls doth mix again,
　　And makes both one, each this and that.

A single violet transplant,
   The strength, the colour, and the size,
(All which before was poor, and scant),
   Redoubles still, and multiplies.   40

When love, with one another so
   Interinanimates two souls,
That abler soul, which thence doth flow,
   Defects of loneliness controls.

We then, who are this new soul, know,
   Of what we are composed, and made,
For, th' atomies of which we grow,
   Are souls, whom no change can invade.

But O alas, so long, so far
   Our bodies why do we forbear?   50
They are ours, though they are not we, we are
   The intelligences, they the sphere.

We owe them thanks, because they thus,
   Did us, to us, at first convey,
Yielded their forces, sense, to us,
   Nor are dross to us, but allay.

On man heaven's influence works not so,
   But that it first imprints the air,
So soul into the soul may flow,
   Though it to body first repair.   60

As our blood labours to beget
   Spirits, as like souls as it can,
Because such fingers need to knit
   That subtle knot, which makes us man:

So must pure lovers' souls descend
   T' affections, and to faculties,
Which sense may reach and apprehend,
   Else a great prince in prison lies.

To our bodies turn we then, that so
    Weak men on love revealed may look;   70
Love's mysteries in souls do grow,
    But yet the body is his book.

And if some lover, such as we,
    Have heard this dialogue of one,
Let him still mark us, he shall see
    Small change, when we'are to bodies gone.

Love's Deity

I long to talk with some old lover's ghost,
    Who died before the god of love was born:
I cannot think that he, who then loved most,
    Sunk so low, as to love one which did scorn.
But since this god produced a destiny,
And that vice-nature, custom, lets it be;
    I must love her, that loves not me.

Sure, they which made him god, meant not so much,
    Nor he, in his young godhead practised it.
But when an even flame two hearts did touch,   10
    His office was indulgently to fit
Actives to passives. Correspondency
Only his subject was. It cannot be
    Love, till I love her, that loves me.

But every modern god will now extend
    His vast prerogative, as far as Jove.
To rage, to lust, to write to, to commend,
    All is the purlieu of the god of love.
Oh were we wakened by this tyranny
To ungod this child again, it could not be   20
    I should love her, who loves not me.

Rebel and atheist too, why murmur I,
    As though I felt the worst that love could do?
Love might make me leave loving, or might try
    A deeper plague, to make her love me too,
Which, since she loves before, I am loth to see;
Falsehood is worse than hate; and that must be,
    If she whom I love, should love me.

Love's Diet

To what a cumbersome unwieldiness
And burdenous corpulence my love had grown,
    But that I did, to make it less,
    And keep it in proportion,
Give it a diet, made it feed upon
That which love worst endures, discretion.

Above one sigh a day I allowed him not,
Of which my fortune, and my faults had part;
    And if sometimes by stealth he got
    A she sigh from my mistress' heart,
And thought to feast on that, I let him see
'Twas neither very sound, nor meant to me.

If he wrung from me a tear, I brined it so
With scorn or shame, that him it nourished not;
    If he sucked hers, I let him know
    'Twas not a tear, which he had got,
His drink was counterfeit, as was his meat;
For, eyes which roll towards all, weep not, but sweat.

Whatever he would dictate, I writ that,
But burnt my letters; when she writ to me,
    And that that favour made him fat,
    I said, 'If any title be
Conveyed by this, ah, what doth it avail,
To be the fortieth name in an entail?'

Thus I reclaimed by buzzard love, to fly
At what, and when, and how, and where I choose;
   Now negligent of sport I lie,
   And now as other falconers use,
I spring a mistress, swear, write, sigh and weep:
And the game killed, or lost, go talk, and sleep.   30

The Will

Before I sigh my last gasp, let me breathe,
Great Love, some legacies; here I bequeath
Mine eyes to Argus, if mine eyes can see,
If they be blind, then Love, I give them thee;
My tongue to fame; to ambassadors mine ears; —
   To women or the sea, my tears.
Thou, Love, hast taught me heretofore
By making me serve her who had twenty more,
That I should give to none, but such, as had too much before.

My constancy I to the planets give;   10
My truth to them, who at the Court do live;
Mine ingenuity and openness,
To Jesuits; to buffoons my pensiveness;
My silence to any, who abroad hath been;
   My money to a Capuchin.
Thou Love taught'st me, by appointing me
To love there, where no love received can be,
Only to give to such as have an incapacity.

My faith I give to Roman Catholics;
All my good works unto the schismatics   20
Of Amsterdam; my best civility
And courtship, to an university;
My modesty I give to soldiers bare;
   My patience let gamesters share.
Thou Love taught'st me, by making me
Love her that holds my love disparity,
Only to give to those that count my gifts indignity.

I give my reputation to those
Which were my friends; mine industry to foes;
To schoolmen I bequeath my doubtfulness;   30
My sickness to physicians, or excess;
To Nature, all that I in rhyme have writ;
   And to my company my wit.
Thou Love, by making me adore
 Her, who begot this love in me before,
Taught'st me to make, as though I gave, when I did but
   restore.

To him for whom the passing bell next tolls,
I give my physic books; my written rolls
Of moral counsels, I to Bedlam give;
My brazen medals, unto them which live   40
In want of bread; to them which pass among
   All foreigners, mine English tongue.
Thou, Love, by making me love one
 Who thinks her friendship a fit portion
For younger lovers, dost my gifts thus disproportion.

Therefore I'll give no more; but I'll undo
The world by dying; because love dies too.
Then all your beauties will be no more worth
Than gold in mines, where none doth draw it forth;
And all your graces no more use shall have   50
   Than a sundial in a grave.
Thou Love taught'st me, by making me
 Love her, who doth neglect both me and thee,
To invent, and practise this one way, to annihilate all three.

The Funeral

Whoever comes to shroud me, do not harm
   Nor question much
That subtle wreath of hair, which crowns my arm;
The mystery, the sign you must not touch,
   For 'tis my outward soul,
Viceroy to that, which then to heaven being gone,
   Will leave this to control,
And keep these limbs, her provinces, from dissolution.

For if the sinewy thread my brain lets fall
      Through every part,   10
Can tie those parts, and make me one of all;
These hairs which upward grew, and strength and art
      Have from a better brain,
Can better do it; except she meant that I
      By this should know my pain,
As prisoners then are manacled, when they are condemned
      to die.

Whate'er she meant by it, bury it with me,
      For since I am
Love's martyr, it might breed idolatry,
If into others' hands these relics came;   20
      As 'twas humility
To afford to it all that a soul can do,
      So, 'tis some bravery,
That since you would save none of me, I bury some of you.

The Blossom

    Little think'st thou, poor flower,
     Whom I have watched six or seven days,
And seen thy birth, and seen what every hour
Gave to thy growth, thee to this height to raise,
And now dost laugh and triumph on this bough,
      Little think'st thou
That it will freeze anon, and that I shall
Tomorrow find thee fall'n, or not at all.

    Little think'st thou, poor heart
     That labour'st yet to nestle thee,   10
And think'st by hovering here to get a part
In a forbidden or forbidding tree,
And hop'st her stiffness by long siege to bow:
      Little think'st thou,
That thou tomorrow, ere that sun doth wake,
Must with this sun, and me a journey take.

But thou which lov'st to be
   Subtle to plague thyself, wilt say,
Alas, if you must go, what's that to me?
Here lies my business, and here I will stay: 20
You go to friends, whose love and means present
      Various content
To your eyes, ears, and tongue, and every part.
If then your body go, what need you a heart?

   Well then, stay here; but know,
     When thou hast stayed and done thy most;
A naked thinking heart, that makes no show,
Is to a woman, but a kind of ghost;
How shall she know my heart; or having none,
      Know thee for one?   30
Practice may make her know some other part,
But take my word, she doth not know a heart.

   Meet me at London, then,
     Twenty days hence, and thou shalt see
Me fresher, and more fat, by being with men,
Than if I had stayed still with her and thee.
For God's sake, if you can, be you so too:
     I would give you
There, to another friend, whom we shall find
As glad to have my body, as my mind.   40

The Primrose

   Upon this primrose hill,
     Where, if heaven would distil
A shower of rain, each several drop might go
To his own primrose, and grow manna so;
And where their form, and their infinity
     Make a terrestrial galaxy,
     As the small stars do in the sky:
I walk to find a true love; and I see
That 'tis not a mere woman, that is she,
But must, or more, or less than woman be.   10

Yet know I not, which flower
    I wish; a six, or four;
For should my true love less than woman be,
She were scarce anything; and then, should she
Be more than woman, she would get above
    All thought of sex, and think to move
    My heart to study her and not to love;
Both these were monsters; since there must reside
Falsehood in woman, I could more abide,
She were by art, than nature falsified.   20

    Live primrose then, and thrive
    With thy true number, five;
And women, whom this flower doth represent,
With this mysterious number be content;
Ten is the farthest number; if half ten
    Belong unto each woman, then
    Each woman may take half us men;
Or if this will not serve their turn, since all
Numbers are odd, or even, and they fall
First into this, five, women may take us all.   30

The Relic

    When my grave is broke up again
    Some second guest to entertain,
    (For graves have learned that woman-head
    To be to more than one a bed)
    And he that digs it, spies
A bracelet of bright hair about the bone,
    Will he not let us alone,
And think that there a loving couple lies,
Who thought that this device might be some way
To make their souls, at the last busy day,   10
Meet at this grave, and make a little stay?

    If this fall in a time, or land,
    Where mis-devotion doth command,
    Then, he that digs us up, will bring
    Us, to the Bishop, and the King,

To make us relics; then
Thou shalt be a Mary Magdalen, and I
A something else thereby;
All women shall adore us, and some men;
And since at such time, miracles are sought,   20
I would have that age by this paper taught
What miracles we harmless lovers wrought.

First, we loved well and faithfully,
Yet knew not what we loved, nor why,
Difference of sex no more we knew,
Than our guardian angels do;
Coming and going, we
Perchance might kiss, but not between those meals;
Our hands ne'er touched the seals,
Which nature, injured by late law, sets free: 30
These miracles we did; but now alas,
All measure, and all language, I should pass,
Should I tell what a miracle she was.

The Damp

When I am dead, and doctors know not why,
And my friends' curiosity
Will have me cut up to survey each part,
When they shall find your picture in my heart,
You think a sudden damp of love
Will through all their senses move,
And work on them as me, and so prefer
Your murder, to the name of massacre.

Poor victories; but if you dare be brave,
And pleasure in your conquest have,   10
First kill th' enormous giant, your Disdain,
And let th' enchantress Honour, next be slain,
And like a Goth and Vandal rise,
Deface records, and histories
Of your own arts and triumphs over men,
And without such advantage kill me then.

For I could muster up as well as you
     My giants, and my witches too,
Which are vast Constancy, and Secretness,
But these I neither look for, nor profess;   20
     Kill me as woman, let me die
     As a mere man; do you but try
Your passive valour, and you shall find then,
Naked you have odds enough of any man.

The Dissolution

She is dead; and all which die
   To their first elements resolve;
And we were mutual elements to us,
     And made of one another.
   My body then doth hers involve,
And those things whereof I consist, hereby
In me abundant grow, and burdenous,
     And nourish not, but smother.
   My fire of passion, sighs of air,
Water of tears, and earthly sad despair,   10
     Which my materials be,
But near worn out by love's security,
She, to my loss, doth by her death repair,
   And I might live long wretched so
But that my fire doth with my fuel grow.
     Now as those active kings
   Whose foreign conquest treasure brings,
Receive more, and spend more, and soonest break:
This (which I am amazed that I can speak)
     This death, hath with my store   20
      My use increased.
And so my soul more earnestly released,
Will outstrip hers; as bullets flown before
A latter bullet may o'ertake, the powder being more.

A Jet Ring Sent

Thou art not so black, as my heart,
  Nor half so brittle, as her heart, thou art;
What wouldst thou say? Shall both our properties by thee be
    spoke,
  Nothing more endless, nothing sooner broke?

  Marriage rings are not of this stuff;
  Oh, why should aught less precious, or less tough
Figure our loves? Except in thy name thou have bid it say,
  I am cheap, and naught but fashion, fling me away.

  Yet stay with me since thou art come,
  Circle this finger's top, which didst her thumb.   10
Be justly proud, and gladly safe, that thou dost dwell with
    me,
  She that, oh, broke her faith, would soon break thee.

Negative Love

I never stooped so low, as they
Which on an eye, cheek, lip, can prey,
  Seldom to them, which soar no higher
  Than virtue or the mind to admire,
For sense, and understanding may
  Know, what gives fuel to their fire:
My love, though silly, is more brave,
For may I miss, whene'er I crave,
If I know yet what I would have.

If that be simply perfectest   10
Which can by no way be expressed
  But negatives, my love is so.
  To all, which all love, I say no.
If any who decipher best,
  What we know not, ourselves, can know,
Let him teach me that nothing; this
As yet my ease, and comfort is,
Though I speed not, I cannot miss.

The Prohibition

Take heed of loving me,
At least remember, I forbade it thee;
    Not that I shall repair my unthrifty waste
Of breath and blood, upon thy sighs, and tears,
    By being to thee then what to me thou wast;
But, so great joy, our life at once outwears,
    Then, lest thy love, by my death, frustrate be,
    If thou love me, take heed of loving me.

Take heed of hating me,
Or too much triumph in the victory.   10
    Not that I shall be mine own officer,
And hate with hate again retaliate;
    But thou wilt lose the style of conqueror,
If I, thy conquest, perish by thy hate.
    Then, lest my being nothing lessen thee,
    If thou hate me, take heed of hating me.

Yet, love and hate me too,
So, these extremes shall neither's office do;
    Love me, that I may die the gentler way;
Hate me, because thy love's too great for me;   20
    Or let these two, themselves, not me decay;
So shall I live thy stage, not triumph be;
    Lest thou thy love and hate and me undo,
    To let me live, Oh love and hate me too.

The Expiration

So, so, break off this last lamenting kiss,
    Which sucks two souls, and vapours both away,
Turn thou ghost that way, and let me turn this,
    And let ourselves benight our happiest day,
We asked none leave to love; nor will we owe
    Any, so cheap a death, as saying, Go;

Go; and if that word have not quite killed thee,
   Ease me with death, by bidding me go too.
Oh, if it have, let my word work on me,
   And a just office on a murderer do.   10
Except it be too late, to kill me so,
   Being double dead, going, and bidding, go.

The Computation

For the first twenty years, since yesterday,
   I scarce believed, thou couldst be gone away,
For forty more, I fed on favours past,
   And forty on hopes, that thou wouldst, they might last.
Tears drowned one hundred, and sighs blew out two,
   A thousand, I did neither think, nor do,
   Or not divide, all being one thought of you;
   Or in a thousand more, forgot that too.
Yet call not this long life; but think that I
Am, by being dead, immortal; can ghosts die?   10

The Paradox

No lover saith, I love, nor any other
   Can judge a perfect lover;
He thinks that else none can, nor will agree
   That any loves but he:
I cannot say I loved, for who can say
   He was killed yesterday?
Love with excess of heat, more young than old,
   Death kills with too much cold;
We die but once, and who loved last did die,
   He that saith twice, doth lie: 10
For though he seem to move, and stir a while,
   It doth the sense beguile.
Such life is like the light which bideth yet
   When the light's life is set,

Or like the heat, which fire in solid matter
    Leaves behind, two hours after.
Once I loved and died; and am now become
    Mine epitaph and tomb.
Here dead men speak their last, and so do I;
    Love-slain, lo, here I lie.   20

Farewell to Love

    Whilst yet to prove,
I thought there was some deity in love
    So did I reverence, and gave
Worship, as atheists at their dying hour
Call, what they cannot name, an unknown power,
    As ignorantly did I crave:
        Thus when
Things not yet known are coveted by men,
    Our desires give them fashion, and so
As they wax lesser, fall, as they size, grow.   10

    But, from late fair
His highness sitting in a golden chair,
    Is not less cared for after three days
By children, than the thing which lovers so
Blindly admire, and with such worship woo;
    Being had, enjoying it decays:
        And thence,
What before pleased them all, takes but one sense,
    And that so lamely, as it leaves behind
A kind of sorrowing dullness to the mind.   20

    Ah cannot we,
As well as cocks and lions jocund be,
    After such pleasures? Unless wise
Nature decreed (since each such act, they say,
Diminisheth the length of life a day)
    This; as she would man should despise
        The sport,
Because that other curse of being short,
    And only for a minute made to be
Eager, desires to raise posterity.   30

Since so, my mind
Shall not desire what no man else can find,
  I'll no more dote and run
To pursue things which had, endamaged me.
And when I come where moving beauties be,
  As men do when the summer's sun
      Grows great,
Though I admire their greatness, shun their heat;
  Each place can afford shadow. If all fail,
'Tis but applying worm-seed to the tail.   40

A Lecture upon the Shadow

Stand still, and I will read to thee
A lecture, love, in love's philosophy.
    These three hours that we have spent,
    Walking here, two shadows went
Along with us, which we ourselves produced;
But, now the sun is just above our head,
    We do those shadows tread;
    And to brave clearness all things are reduced.
  So whilst our infant loves did grow,
  Disguises did, and shadows, flow,   10
  From us, and our care; but, now 'tis not so.

That love hath not attained the high'st degree,
Which is still diligent lest others see.

Except our loves at this noon stay,
We shall new shadows make the other way.
    As the first were made to blind
    Others; these which come behind
Will work upon ourselves, and blind our eyes.
If our loves faint, and westwardly decline;
    To me thou, falsely, thine,   20
    And I to thee mine actions shall disguise.
  The morning shadows wear away,
  But these grow longer all the day,
  But oh, love's day is short, if love decay.

Love is a growing, or full constant light;
And his first minute, after noon, is night.

The Dream ('Image of her . . .')

Image of her whom I love, more than she,
   Whose fair impression in my faithful heart,
Makes me her medal, and makes her love me,
   As kings do coins, to which their stamps impart
The value: go, and take my heart from hence,
   Which now is grown too great and good for me:
Honours oppress weak spirits, and our sense
   Strong objects dull; the more, the less we see.

When you are gone, and reason gone with you,
   Then fantasy is queen and soul, and all;   10
She can present joys meaner than you do;
   Convenient, and more proportional.
So, if I dream I have you, I have you,
   For, all our joys are but fantastical.
And so I 'scape the pain, for pain is true;
   And sleep which locks up sense, doth lock out all.

After a such fruition I shall wake,
   And, but the waking, nothing shall repent;
And shall to love more thankful sonnets make,
   Than if more honour, tears, and pains were spent.   20
But dearest heart, and dearer image stay;
   Alas, true joys at best are dream enough;
Though you stay here you pass too fast away:
   For even at first life's taper is a snuff.

Filled with her love, may I be rather grown
Mad with much heart, than idiot with none.

To Sir Henry Goodyer

Who makes the past, a pattern for next year,
  Turns no new leaf, but still the same things reads,
Seen things, he sees again, heard things doth hear,
  And makes his life but like a pair of beads.

A palace, when 'tis that, which it should be,
  Leaves growing, and stands such, or else decays:
But he which dwells there is not so; for he
  Strives to urge upward, and his fortune raise;

So had your body her morning, hath her noon,
  And shall not better; her next change is night: 10
But her fair larger guest, to whom sun and moon
  Are sparks, and short-lived, claims another right.

The noble soul by age grows lustier,
  Her appetite and her digestion mend,
We must not starve, nor hope to pamper her
  With women's milk, and pap unto the end.

Provide you manlier diet; you have seen
  All libraries, which are schools, camps, and courts;
But ask your garners if you have not been
  In harvests, too indulgent to your sports. 20

Would you redeem it? then yourself transplant
  A while from hence. Perchance outlandish ground
Bears no more wit, than ours, but yet more scant
  Are those diversions there, which here abound.

To be a stranger hath that benefit,
  We can beginnings, but not habits choke.
Go; whither? Hence; you get, if you forget;
  New faults, till they prescribe in us, are smoke.

Our soul, whose country's heaven, and God her father,
    Into this world, corruption's sink, is sent,   30
Yet, so much in her travail she doth gather,
    That she returns home, wiser than she went;

It pays you well, if it teach you to spare,
    And make you ashamed, to make your hawk's praise yours,
Which when herself she lessens in the air,
    You then first say, that high enough she towers.

Howsoever, keep the lively taste you hold
    Of God, love him as now, but fear him more,
And in your afternoons think what you told
    And promised him, at morning prayer before.   40

Let falsehood like a discord anger you,
    Else be not froward. But why do I touch
Things, of which none is in your practice new,
    And fables, or fruit-trenchers teach as much;

But thus I make you keep your promise Sir,
    Riding I had you, though you still stayed there,
And in these thoughts, although you never stir,
    You came with me to Mitcham, and are here.

To the Countess of Bedford

Madam,
Reason is our soul's left hand, Faith her right,
    By these we reach divinity, that's you;
Their loves, who have the blessing of your sight,
    Grew from their reason, mine from far faith grew.

But as, although a squint lefthandedness
    Be ungracious, yet we cannot want that hand,
So would I, not to increase, but to express
    My faith, as I believe, so understand.

Therefore I study you first in your Saints,
   Those friends, whom your election glorifies,   10
Then in your deeds, accesses, and restraints,
   And what you read, and what yourself devise.

But soon, the reasons why you are loved by all,
   Grow infinite, and so pass reason's reach,
Then back again to implicit faith I fall,
   And rest on what the catholic voice doth teach;

That you are good: and not one heretic
   Denies it: if he did, yet you are so.
For, rocks, which high-topped and deep-rooted stick,
   Waves wash, not undermine, nor overthrow.   20

In everything there naturally grows
   A balsamum to keep it fresh, and new,
If 'twere not injured by extrinsic blows;
   Your birth and beauty are this balm in you.

But you of learning and religion,
   And virtue, and such ingredients, have made
A mithridate, whose operation
   Keeps off, or cures what can be done or said.

Yet, this is not your physic, but your food,
   A diet fit for you; for you are here   30
The first good angel, since the world's frame stood,
   That ever did in woman's shape appear.

Since you are then God's masterpiece, and so
   His factor for our loves; do as you do,
Make your return home gracious; and bestow
   This life on that; so make one life of two.
      For so God help me, I would not miss you there
      For all the good which you can do me here.

To the Countess of Bedford

Madam,
You have refined me, and to worthiest things
  (Virtue, art, beauty, fortune,) now I see
Rareness, or use, not nature value brings;
    And such, as they are circumstanced, they be.
      Two ills can ne'er perplex us, sin to excuse;
      But of two good things, we may leave and choose.

Therefore at Court, which is not virtue's clime,
  (Where a transcendent height, (as, lowness me)
Makes her not be, or not show) all my rhyme
    Your virtues challenge, which there rarest be;   10
      For, as dark texts need notes: there some must be
      To usher virtue, and say, *This is she*.

So in the country is beauty; to this place
  You are the season (Madam) you the day,
'Tis but a grave of spices, till your face
    Exhale them, and a thick close bud display.
      Widowed and reclused else, her sweets she enshrines
      As China, when the sun at Brazil dines.

Out from your chariot, morning breaks at night,
  And falsifies both computations so;   20
Since a new world doth rise here from your light,
    We your new creatures, by new reckonings go.
      This shows that you from nature loathly stray,
      That suffer not an artificial day.

In this you have made the Court the antipodes,
  And willed your delegate, the vulgar sun,
To do profane autumnal offices,
    Whilst here to you, we sacrificers run;
      And whether priests, or organs, you we obey,
      We sound your influence, and your dictates say.   30

Yet to that deity which dwells in you,
   Your virtuous soul, I now not sacrifice;
These are petitions and not hymns; they sue
   But that I may survey the edifice.
      In all religions as much care hath been
      Of temples' frames, and beauty, as rites within.

As all which go to Rome, do not thereby
   Esteem religions, and hold fast the best,
But serve discourse, and curiosity,
   With that which doth religion but invest,   40
      And shun th' entangling labyrinths of schools,
      And make it wit, to think the wiser fools:

So in this pilgrimage I would behold
   You as you' are virtue's temple, not as she,
What walls of tender crystal her enfold,
   What eyes, hands, bosom, her pure altars be;
      And after this survey, oppose to all
      Babblers of chapels, you th' Escurial.

Yet not as consecrate, but merely as fair,
   On these I cast a lay and country eye.   50
Of past and future stories, which are rare,
   I find you all record, all prophecy.
      Purge but the book of Fate, that it admit
      No sad nor guilty legends, you are it.

If good and lovely were not one, of both
   You were the transcript, and original,
The elements, the parent, and the growth,
   And every piece of you, is both their all:
      So entire are all your deeds, and you, that you
      Must do the same thing still: you cannot two.   60

But these (as nice thin school divinity
   Serves heresy to further or repress)
Taste of poetic rage, or flattery,
   And need not, where all hearts one truth profess;
      Oft from new proofs, and new phrase, new doubts grow,
      As strange attire aliens the men we know.

Leaving then busy praise, and all appeal
    To higher courts, sense's decree is true,
The mine, the magazine, the commonweal,
    The story of beauty, in Twickenham is, and you.   70
        Who hath seen one, would both; as, who had been
        In Paradise, would seek the cherubin.

To Mrs M. H.

Mad paper stay, and grudge not here to burn
    With all those sons whom my brain did create,
At least lie hid with me, till thou return
    To rags again, which is thy native state.

What though thou have enough unworthiness
    To come unto great place as others do,
That's much; emboldens, pulls, thrusts I confess,
    But 'tis not all, thou shouldst be wicked too.

And, that thou canst not learn, or not of me;
    Yet thou wilt go; go, since thou goest to her   10
Who lacks but faults to be a prince, for she,
    Truth, whom they dare not pardon, dares prefer.

But when thou com'st to that perplexing eye
    Which equally claims love and reverence,
Thou wilt not long dispute it, thou wilt die;
    And, having little now, have then no sense.

Yet when her warm redeeming hand, which is
    A miracle; and made such to work more,
Doth touch thee, sapless leaf, thou grow'st by this
    Her creature; glorified more than before.   20

Then as a mother which delights to hear
    Her early child mis-speak half-uttered words,
Or, because majesty doth never fear
    Ill or bold speech, she audience affords.

And then, cold speechless wretch, thou diest again,
    And wisely; what discourse is left for thee?
From speech of ill, and her, thou must abstain,
    And is there any good which is not she?

Yet mayst thou praise her servants, though not her,
    And wit, and virtue, and honour her attend,   30
And since they are but her clothes, thou shalt not err
    If thou her shape and beauty and grace commend.

Who knows thy destiny? when thou hast done,
    Perchance her cabinet may harbour thee,
Whither all noble ambitious wits do run,
    A nest almost as full of good as she.

When thou art there, if any, whom we know,
    Were saved before, and did that heaven partake,
When she revolves his papers, mark what show
    Of favour, she, alone, to them doth make.   40

Mark, if to get them, she o'erskip the rest,
    Mark, if she read them twice, or kiss the name;
Mark, if she do the same that they protest,
    Mark, if she mark whether her woman came.

Mark, if slight things be objected, and o'erblown.
    Mark, if her oaths against him be not still
Reserved, and that she grieves she's not her own,
    And chides the doctrine that denies freewill.

I bid thee not do this to be my spy;
    Nor to make myself her familiar;   50
But so much I do love her choice, that I
    Would fain love him that shall be loved of her.

To the Countess of Bedford at New Year's Tide

This twilight of two years, not past nor next,
    Some emblem is of me, or I of this,
Who meteor-like, of stuff, and form perplexed,
    Whose what, and where, in disputation is,
    If I should call me anything, should miss.

I sum the years, and me, and find me not
   Debtor to th' old, nor creditor to the new,
That cannot say, my thanks I have forgot,
   Nor trust I this with hopes, and yet scarce true
   This bravery is, since these times showed me you.   10

In recompense I would show future times
   What you were, and teach them to urge towards such,
Verse embalms virtue; and tombs, or thrones of rhymes,
   Preserve frail transitory fame, as much
   As spice doth bodies from corrupt air's touch.

Mine are short-lived; the tincture of your name
   Creates in them, but dissipates as fast
New spirits; for, strong agents with the same
   Force that doth warm and cherish, us do waste;
   Kept hot with strong extracts, no bodies last: 20

So, my verse built of your just praise, might want
   Reason and likelihood, the firmest base,
And made of miracle, now faith is scant,
   Will vanish soon, and so possess no place,
   And you, and it, too much grace might disgrace.

When all (as truth commands assent) confess
   All truth of you, yet they will doubt how I
One corn of one low anthill's dust, and less,
   Should name, know, or express a thing so high,
   And not an inch, measure infinity.   30

I cannot tell them, nor myself, nor you,
   But leave, lest truth be endangered by my praise,
And turn to God, who knows I think this true,
   And useth oft, when such a heart mis-says,
   To make it good, for, such a praiser prays.

He will best teach you, how you should lay out
   His stock of beauty, learning, favour, blood,
He will perplex security with doubt,
   And clear those doubts; hide from you, and show you
     good,
   And so increase your appetite and food;   40

He will teach you, that good and bad have not
  One latitude in cloisters, and in Court,
Indifferent there the greatest space hath got,
  Some pity is not good there, some vain disport,
  On this side sin, with that place may comport.

Yet he, as he bounds seas, will fix your hours,
  Which pleasure, and delight may not ingress,
And though what none else lost, be truliest yours,
  He will make you, what you did not, possess,
  By using others', not vice, but weakness.   50

He will make you speak truths, and credibly,
  And make you doubt, that others do not so:
He will provide you keys, and locks, to spy,
  And 'scape spies, to good ends, and he will show
  What you may not acknowledge, what not know.

For your own conscience, he gives innocence,
  But for your fame, a discreet wariness,
And though to 'scape, than to revenge offence
  Be better, he shows both, and to repress
  Joy, when your state swells, sadness when 'tis less. 60

From need of tears he will defend your soul,
  Or make a rebaptizing of one tear;
He cannot, (that's, he will not) dis-enrol
  Your name; and when with active joy we hear
  This private gospel, then 'tis our New Year.

To the Countess of Bedford

Honour is so sublime perfection,
And so refined; that when God was alone
And creatureless at first, himself had none;

But as of the elements, these which we tread,
Produce all things with which we'are joyed or fed,
And, those are barren both above our head:

So from low persons doth all honour flow:
Kings, whom they would have honoured, to us show,
And but direct our honour, not bestow.

For when from herbs the pure parts must be won   10
From gross, by stilling, this is better done
By despised dung, than by the fire or sun.

Care not then, Madam, how low your praisers lie;
In labourers' ballads oft more piety
God finds, than in *Te Deum*'s melody.

And, ordnance raised on towers so many mile
Send not their voice, nor last so long a while
As fires from th' earth's low vaults in Sicil Isle.

Should I say I lived darker than were true,
Your radiation can all clouds subdue;   20
But one, 'tis best light to contemplate you.

You, for whose body God made better clay,
Or took soul's stuff such as shall late decay,
Or such as needs small change at the last day.

This, as an amber drop enwraps a bee,
Covering discovers your quick soul; that we
May in your through-shine front your heart's thoughts see.

You teach (though we learn not) a thing unknown
To our late times, the use of specular stone,
Through which all things within without were shown.   30

Of such were temples; so and of such you are;
Being and seeming is your equal care,
And virtue's whole sum is but know and dare.

But as our souls of growth and souls of sense
Have birthright of our reason's soul, yet hence
They fly not from that, nor seek precedence:

Nature's first lesson, so, discretion,
Must not grudge zeal a place, nor yet keep none,
Not banish itself, nor religion.

Discretion is a wise man's soul, and so   40
Religion is a Christian's, and you know
How these are one, her *yea*, is not her *no*.

Nor may we hope to solder still and knit
These two, and dare to break them; nor must wit
Be colleague to religion, but be it.

In those poor types of God (round circles) so
Religions' types, the pieceless centres flow,
And are in all the lines which all ways go.

If either ever wrought in you alone
Or principally, then religion   50
Wrought your ends, and your ways discretion.

Go thither still, go the same way you went,
Who so would change, do covet or repent;
Neither can reach you, great and innocent.

To the Countess of Huntingdon

Madam,
Man to God's image, Eve, to man's was made,
   Nor find we that God breathed a soul in her,
Canons will not Church functions you invade,
   Nor laws to civil office you prefer.

Who vagrant transitory comets sees,
   Wonders, because they are rare; but a new star
Whose motion with the firmament agrees,
   Is miracle; for, there no new things are;

In woman so perchance mild innocence
   A seldom comet is, but active good   10
A miracle, which reason 'scapes, and sense;
   For, art and nature this in them withstood.

As such a star, the Magi led to view
   The manger-cradled infant, God below:
By virtue's beams by fame derived from you,
   May apt souls, and the worst may, virtue know.

If the world's age, and death be argued well
   By the sun's fall, which now towards earth doth bend,
Then we might fear that virtue, since she fell
   So low as woman, should be near her end.   20

But she's not stooped, but raised; exiled by men
   She fled to heaven, that's heavenly things, that's you,
She was in all men, thinly scattered then,
   But now amassed, contracted in a few.

She gilded us: but you are gold, and she;
   Us she informed, but transubstantiates you;
Soft dispositions which ductile be,
   Elixir-like, she makes not clean, but new.

Though you a wife's and mother's name retain,
   'Tis not as woman, for all are not so,   30
But virtue having made you virtue, is fain
   To adhere in these names, her and you to show,

Else, being alike pure, we should neither see,
   As, water being into air rarefied,
Neither appear, till in one cloud they be,
   So, for our sakes you do low names abide;

Taught by great constellations, which being framed
   Of the most stars, take low names, Crab, and Bull,
When single planets by the gods are named,
   You covet not great names, of great things full.   40

So you, as woman, one doth comprehend,
　And in the veil of kindred others see;
To some you are revealed, as in a friend,
　And as a virtuous prince far off, to me:

To whom, because from you all virtues flow,
　And 'tis not none, to dare contemplate you,
I, which do so, as your true subject owe
　Some tribute for that, so these lines are due.

If you can think these flatteries, they are,
　For then your judgement is below my praise, 50
If they were so, oft, flatteries work as far,
　As counsels, and as far th' endeavour raise.

So my ill reaching you might there grow good,
　But I remain a poisoned fountain still;
But not your beauty, virtue, knowledge, blood
　Are more above all flattery, than my will.

And if I flatter any, 'tis not you
　But my own judgement, who did long ago
Pronounce, that all these praises should be true,
　And virtue should your beauty, and birth outgrow. 60

Now that my prophecies are all fulfilled,
　Rather than God should not be honoured too,
And all these gifts confessed, which he instilled,
　Yourself were bound to say that which I do.

So I, but your recorder am in this,
　Or mouth, or speaker of the universe,
A ministerial notary, for 'tis
　Not I, but you and fame, that make this verse;

I was your prophet in your younger days,
And now your chaplain, God in you to praise. 70

To Sir Edward Herbert, at Juliers

Man is a lump, where all beasts kneaded be,
    Wisdom makes him an ark where all agree;
The fool, in whom these beasts do live at jar,
    Is sport to others, and a theatre,
Nor 'scapes he so, but is himself their prey;
    All which was man in him, is eat away,
And now his beasts on one another feed,
    Yet couple in anger, and new monsters breed;
How happy is he, which hath due place assigned
    To his beasts, and disafforested his mind!   10
Empaled himself to keep them out, not in;
    Can sow, and dares trust corn, where they have been;
Can use his horse, goat, wolf, and every beast,
    And is not ass himself to all the rest.
Else, man not only is the herd of swine,
    But he's those devils too, which did incline
Them to a headlong rage, and made them worse:
    For man can add weight to heaven's heaviest curse.
As souls (they say) by our first touch, take in
    The poisonous tincture of original sin,   20
So, to the punishments which God doth fling,
    Our apprehension contributes the sting.
To us, as to his chickens, he doth cast
    Hemlock, and we as men, his hemlock taste.
We do infuse to what he meant for meat,
    Corrosiveness, or intense cold or heat.
For, God no such specific poison hath
    As kills we know not how; his fiercest wrath
Hath no antipathy, but may be good
    At least for physic, if not for our food.   30
Thus man, that might be his pleasure, is his rod,
    And is his devil, that might be his God.
Since then our business is, to rectify
    Nature, to what she was, we are led awry
By them, who man to us in little show,
    Greater than due, no form we can bestow
On him; for man into himself can draw
    All, all his faith can swallow, or reason chaw,

All that is filled, and all that which doth fill,
  All the round world, to man is but a pill; 40
In all it works not, but it is in all
  Poisonous, or purgative, or cordial,
For, knowledge kindles calentures in some,
  And is to others icy opium.
As brave as true, is that profession then
  Which you do use to make; that you know man.
This makes it credible, you have dwelt upon
  All worthy books, and now are such a one.
Actions are authors, and of those in you
  Your friends find every day a mart of new. 50

To the Countess of Bedford

BEGUN IN FRANCE BUT NEVER PERFECTED

Though I be dead, and buried, yet I have
  (Living in you), Court enough in my grave,
As oft as there I think myself to be,
  So many resurrections waken me.
That thankfulness your favours have begot
  In me, embalms me, that I do not rot.
This season as 'tis Easter, as 'tis spring,
  Must both to growth and to confession bring
My thoughts disposed unto your influence, so,
  These verses bud, so these confessions grow; 10
First I confess I have to others lent
  Your stock, and over prodigally spent
Your treasure, for since I had never known
  Virtue or beauty, but as they are grown
In you, I should not think or say they shine,
  (So as I have) in any other mine;
Next I confess this my confession,
  For, 'tis some fault thus much to touch upon
Your praise to you, where half rights seem too much,
  And make your mind's sincere complexion blush. 20
Next I confess my impenitence, for I
  Can scarce repent my first fault, since thereby

Remote low spirits, which shall ne'er read you,
  May in less lessons find enough to do,
By studying copies, not originals,
  Desunt caetera.

Epitaph on Himself

TO THE COUNTESS OF BEDFORD

Madam,
  That I might make your cabinet my tomb,
    And for my fame which I love next my soul,
  Next to my soul provide the happiest room,
    Admit to that place this last funeral scroll.
      Others by wills give legacies, but I
      Dying, of you do beg a legacy.

OMNIBUS

My fortune and my choice this custom break,
When we are speechless grown, to make stones speak,
Though no stone tell thee what I was, yet thou
In my grave's inside seest what thou art now: 10
Yet thou'art not yet so good, till death us lay
To ripe and mellow here, we are stubborn clay.
Parents make us earth, and souls dignify
Us to be glass; here to grow gold we lie.
Whilst in our souls sin bred and pampered is,
Our souls become worm-eaten carcases;
So we ourselves miraculously destroy.
Here bodies with less miracle enjoy
Such privileges, enabled here to scale
Heaven, when the trumpet's air shall them exhale.   20
Hear this, and mend thyself, and thou mend'st me,
By making me being dead, do good to thee,
  And think me well composed, that I could now
  A last-sick hour to syllables allow.

POEMS ABOUT DEATHS

Elegy on the Lady Markham

Man is the world, and death the ocean,
   To which God gives the lower parts of man.
This sea environs all, and though as yet
   God hath set marks, and bounds, 'twixt us and it,
Yet doth it roar, and gnaw, and still pretend,
   And breaks our banks, whene'er it takes a friend.
Then our land waters (tears of passion) vent;
   Our waters, then, above our firmament,
(Tears which our soul doth for her sins let fall)
   Take all a brackish taste, and funeral.   10
And even these tears, which should wash sin, are sin.
   We, after God's 'No', drown our world again.
Nothing but man of all envenomed things
   Doth work upon itself, with inborn stings.
Tears are false spectacles, we cannot see
   Through passion's mist, what we are, or what she.
In her, this sea of death hath made no breach,
   But as the tide doth wash the slimy beach,
And leaves embroidered works upon the sand,
   So is her flesh refined by death's cold hand.   20
As men of China, after an age's stay
   Do take up porcelain, where they buried clay;
So at this grave, her limbeck, which refines
   The diamonds, rubies, sapphires, pearls, and mines,
Of which this flesh was, her soul shall inspire
   Flesh of such stuff, as God, when his last fire
Annuls this world, to recompense it, shall,
   Make and name then, th' elixir of this all.
They say, the sea, when it gains, loseth too;
   If carnal death (the younger brother) do   30
Usurp the body, our soul, which subject is
   To th' elder death, by sin, is freed by this;

They perish both, when they attempt the just;
 For, graves our trophies are, and both deaths' dust.
So, unobnoxious now, she hath buried both;
 For, none to death sins, that to sin is loth.
Nor do they die, which are not loth to die,
 So hath she this, and that virginity.
Grace was in her extremely diligent,
 That kept her from sin, yet made her repent.   40
Of what small spots pure white complains! Alas,
 How little poison cracks a crystal glass!
She sinned, but just enough to let us see
 That God's word must be true, all, sinners be.
So much did zeal her conscience rarefy,
 That, extreme truth lacked little of a lie,
Making omissions, acts; laying the touch
 Of sin, on things that sometimes may be such.
As Moses' cherubins, whose natures do
 Surpass all speed, by him are winged too: 50
So would her soul, already in heaven, seem then,
 To climb by tears, the common stairs of men.
How fit she was for God, I am content
 To speak, that death his vain haste may repent.
How fit for us, how even and how sweet,
 How good in all her titles, and how meet,
To have reformed this forward heresy,
 That women can no parts of friendship be;
How moral, how divine shall not be told,
 Lest they that hear her virtues, think her old,   60
And lest we take death's part, and make him glad
 Of such a prey, and to his triumph add.

To the Lady Bedford

You that are she and you, that's double she,
 In her dead face, half of yourself shall see;
She was the other part, for so they do
 Which build them friendships, become one of two;
So two, that but themselves no third can fit,
 Which were to be so, when they were not yet.

Twins, though their birth Cusco, and Musco take,
    As divers stars one constellation make,
Paired like two eyes, have equal motion, so
    Both but one means to see, one way to go;   10
Had you died first, a carcase she had been;
    And we your rich tomb in her face had seen;
She like the soul is gone, and you here stay,
    Not a live friend; but th' other half of clay;
And since you act that part, as men say, 'Here
    Lies such a Prince', when but one part is there,
And do all honour and devotion due
    Unto the whole, so we all reverence you;
For such a friendship who would not adore
    In you, who are all what both was before,   20
Not all, as if some perished by this,
    But so, as all in you contracted is;
As of this all, though many parts decay,
    The pure which elemented them shall stay;
And though diffused, and spread in infinite,
    Shall recollect, and in one all unite:
So madam, as her soul to heaven is fled,
    Her flesh rests in the earth, as in a bed;
Her virtues do, as to their proper sphere,
    Return to dwell with you, of whom they were;   30
As perfect motions are all circular,
    So they to you, their sea, whence less streams are;
She was all spices, you all metals; so
    In you two we did both rich Indies know;
And as no fire, nor rust can spend or waste
    One dram of gold, but what was first shall last,
Though it be forced in water, earth, salt, air,
    Expansed in infinite, none will impair;
So, to yourself you may additions take,
    But nothing can you less, or changed make.   40
Seek not in seeking new, to seem to doubt,
    That you can match her, or not be without;
But let some faithful book in her room be,
    Yet but of Judith no such book as she.

Elegy on Mistress Bulstrode

Death I recant, and say, unsaid by me
  Whate'er hath slipped, that might diminish thee.
Spiritual treason, atheism 'tis, to say,
  That any can thy summons disobey.
Th' earth's face is but thy table; there are set
  Plants, cattle, men, dishes for Death to eat.
In a rude hunger now he millions draws
  Into his bloody, or plaguey, or starved jaws.
Now he will seem to spare, and doth more waste,
  Eating the best first, well preserved to last.   10
Now wantonly he spoils, and eats us not,
  But breaks off friends, and lets us piecemeal rot.
Nor will this earth serve him; he sinks the deep
  Where harmless fish monastic silence keep,
Who (were Death dead) by roes of living sand,
  Might sponge that element, and make it land.
He rounds the air, and breaks the hymnic notes
  In birds', heaven's choristers, organic throats,
Which (if they did not die) might seem to be
  A tenth rank in the heavenly hierarchy.   20
O strong and long-lived death, how cam'st thou in?
  And how without creation didst begin?
Thou hast, and shalt see dead, before thou diest,
  All the four monarchies, and antichrist.
How could I think thee nothing, that see now
  In all this all, nothing else is, but thou.
Our births and lives, vices, and virtues, be
  Wasteful consumptions, and degrees of thee.
For, we to live, our bellows wear, and breath,
  Nor are we mortal, dying, dead, but death.   30
And though thou be'st, O mighty bird of prey,
  So much reclaimed by God, that thou must lay
All that thou kill'st at his feet, yet doth he
  Reserve but few, and leaves the most to thee.
And of those few, now thou hast overthrown
  One whom thy blow makes, not ours, nor thine own.
She was more storeys high: hopeless to come
  To her soul, thou hast offered at her lower room.

Her soul and body was a king and court:
   But thou hast both of captain missed and fort.   40
As houses fall not, though the king remove,
   Bodies of saints rest for their souls above.
Death gets 'twixt souls and bodies such a place
   As sin insinuates 'twixt just men and grace,
Both work a separation, no divorce.
   Her soul is gone to usher up her corse,
Which shall be almost another soul, for there
   Bodies are purer, than best souls are here.
Because in her, her virtues did outgo
   Her years, wouldst thou, O emulous death, do so?   50
And kill her young to thy loss? must the cost
   Of beauty, and wit, apt to do harm, be lost?
What though thou found'st her proof 'gainst sins of youth?
   Oh, every age a diverse sin pursueth.
Thou shouldst have stayed, and taken better hold,
   Shortly ambitious, covetous, when old,
She might have proved: and such devotion
   Might once have strayed to superstition.
If all her virtues must have grown, yet might
   Abundant virtue' have bred a proud delight.   60
Had she persevered just, there would have been
   Some that would sin, mis-thinking she did sin.
Such as would call her friendship, love, and feign
   To sociableness, a name profane;
Or sin, by tempting, or, not daring that,
   By wishing, though they never told her what.
Thus mightst thou' have slain more souls, hadst thou not
     crossed
   Thyself, and to triumph, thine army lost.
Yet though these ways be lost, thou hast left one,
   Which is, immoderate grief that she is gone.   70
But we may 'scape that sin, yet weep as much,
   Our tears are due, because we are not such.
Some tears, that knot of friends, her death must cost,
   Because the chain is broke, though no link lost.

An Elegy upon the Death of Mistress Bulstrode

Language thou art too narrow, and too weak
   To ease us now; great sorrow cannot speak;
If we could sigh out accents, and weep words,
   Grief wears, and lessens, that tears breath affords.
Sad hearts, the less they seem, the more they are,
   (So guiltiest men stand mutest at the bar)
Not that they know not, feel not their estate,
   But extreme sense hath made them desperate;
Sorrow, to whom we owe all that we be,
   Tyrant, in the fifth and greatest monarchy,   10
Was't, that she did possess all hearts before,
   Thou hast killed her, to make thy empire more?
Knew'st thou some would, that knew her not, lament,
   As in a deluge perish th' innocent?
Was't not enough to have that palace won,
   But thou must raze it too, that was undone?
Hadst thou stayed there, and looked out at her eyes,
   All had adored thee that now from thee flies,
For they let out more light, than they took in,
   They told not when, but did the day begin;   20
She was too sapphirine, and clear for thee;
   Clay, flint, and jet now thy fit dwellings be;
Alas, she was too pure, but not too weak;
   Whoe'er saw crystal ordinance but would break?
And if we be thy conquest, by her fall
   Thou'hast lost thy end, for in her perish all;
Or if we live, we live but to rebel,
   They know her better now, that knew her well.
If we should vapour out, or pine, and die,
   Since she first went, that were not misery;   30
She changed our world with hers; now she is gone,
   Mirth and prosperity is oppression;
For of all mortal virtues she was all
   The ethics speak of virtues cardinal.
Her soul was paradise; the cherubin
   Set to keep it was grace, that kept out sin;
She had no more than let in death, for we
   All reap consumption from one fruitful tree;

God took her hence, lest some of us should love
    Her, like that plant, him and his laws above,   40
And when we tears, he mercy shed in this,
    To raise our minds to heaven where now she is;
Who if her virtues would have let her stay
    We'had had a saint, have now a holiday;
Her heart was that strange bush, where, sacred fire,
    Religion, did not consume, but inspire
Such piety, so chaste use of God's day,
    That what we turn to feast, she turned to pray,
And did prefigure here, in devout taste,
    The rest of her high Sabaoth, which shall last.   50
Angels did hand her up, who next God dwell,
    (For she was of that order whence most fell)
Her body left with us, lest some had said,
    She could not die, except they saw her dead;
For from less virtue, and less beauteousness,
    The gentiles framed them gods and goddesses.
The ravenous earth that now woos her to be
    Earth too, will be lemnia; and the tree
That wraps that crystal in a wooden tomb,
    Shall be took up spruce, filled with diamond;   60
And we her sad glad friends all bear a part
    Of grief, for all would waste a stoic's heart.

To the Countess of Bedford

To have written then, when you writ, seemed to me
    Worst of spiritual vices, simony,
And not to have written then, seems little less
    Than worst of civil vices, thanklessness.
In this, my debt I seemed loth to confess,
    In that, I seemed to shun beholdingness.
But 'tis not so, nothings, as I am, may
    Pay all they have, and yet have all to pay.
Such borrow in their payments, and owe more
    By having leave to write so, than before.   10
Yet since rich mines in barren grounds are shown,
    May not I yield (not gold) but coal or stone?

Temples were not demolished, though profane:
   Here Peter Jove's, there Paul hath Dian's fane.
So whether my hymns you admit or choose,
   In me you have hallowed a pagan Muse,
And denizened a stranger, who mistaught
   By blamers of the times they marred, hath sought
Virtues in corners, which now bravely do
   Shine in the world's best part, or all it; you.   20
I have been told, that virtue in courtiers' hearts
   Suffers an ostracism, and departs.
Profit, ease, fitness, plenty, bid it go,
   But whither, only knowing you, I know;
Your (or you) virtue, two vast uses serves,
   It ransoms one sex, and one Court preserves;
There's nothing but your worth, which being true,
   Is known to any other, not to you:
And you can never know it; to admit
   No knowledge of your worth, is some of it.   30
But since to you, your praises discords be,
   Stoop others' ills to meditate with me.
Oh! to confess we know not what we should,
   Is half excuse; we know not what we would.
Lightness depresseth us, emptiness fills,
   We sweat and faint, yet still go down the hills;
As new philosophy arrests the sun,
   And bids the passive earth about it run,
So we have dulled our mind, it hath no ends;
   Only the body's busy, and pretends;   40
As dead low earth eclipses and controls
   The quick high moon: so doth the body, souls.
In none but us, are such mixed engines found,
   As hands of double office: for, the ground
We till with them; and them to heaven we raise;
   Who prayerless labours, or, without this, prays,
Doth but one half, that's none; he which said, *Plough*
   And look not back, to look up doth allow.
Good seed degenerates, and oft obeys
   The soil's disease, and into cockle strays.   50
Let the mind's thoughts be but transplanted so,
   Into the body, and bastardly they grow.

What hate could hurt our bodies like our love?
  We, but no foreign tyrants could, remove
These not engraved, but inborn dignities
  Caskets of souls; temples, and palaces:
For, bodies shall from death redeemed be,
  Souls but preserved, not naturally free.
As men to our prisons, new souls to us are sent,
  Which learn vice there, and come in innocent.   60
First seeds of every creature are in us,
  Whate'er the world hath bad, or precious,
Man's body can produce, hence hath it been
  That stones, worms, frogs, and snakes in man are seen:
But who e'er saw, though nature can work so,
  That pearl, or gold, or corn in man did grow?
We' have added to the world Virginia, and sent
  Two new stars lately to the firmament;
Why grudge we us (not heaven) the dignity
  T' increase with ours, those fair souls' company?   70
But I must end this letter, though it do
  Stand on two truths, neither is true to you.
Virtue hath some perverseness; for she will
  Neither believe her good, nor others' ill.
Even in you, virtue's best paradise,
  Virtue hath some, but wise degrees of vice.
Too many virtues, or too much of one
  Begets in you unjust suspicion.
And ignorance of vice, makes virtue less,
  Quenching compassion of our wretchedness.   80
But these are riddles; some aspersion
  Of vice becomes well some complexion.
Statesmen purge vice with vice, and may corrode
  The bad with bad, a spider with a toad:
For so, ill thralls not them, but they tame ill
  And make her do much good against her will,
But in your commonwealth, or world in you,
  Vice hath no office, or good work to do.
Take then no vicious purge, but be content
  With cordial virtue, your known nourishment.   90

A Funeral Elegy

'Tis lost, to trust a tomb with such a guest,
  Or to confine her in a marble chest.
Alas, what's marble, jet, or porphyry,
  Prized with the chrysolite of either eye,
Or with those pearls, and rubies which she was?
  Join the two Indies in one tomb, 'tis glass;
And so is all to her materials,
  Though every inch were ten Escurials,
Yet she's demolished: can we keep her then
  In works of hands, or of the wits of men?   10
Can these memorials, rags of paper, give
  Life to that name, by which name they must live?
Sickly, alas, short-lived, aborted be
  Those carcase verses, whose soul is not she.
And can she, who no longer would be she,
  Being such a tabernacle, stoop to be
In paper wrapped; or, when she would not lie
  In such a house, dwell in an elegy?
But 'tis no matter; we may well allow
  Verse to live so long as the world will now.   20
For her death wounded it. The world contains
  Princes for arms, and counsellors for brains,
Lawyers for tongues, divines for hearts, and more,
  The rich for stomachs, and for backs, the poor;
The officers for hands, merchants for feet
  By which remote and distant countries meet.
But those fine spirits which do tune and set
  This organ, are those pieces which beget
Wonder and love; and these were she; and she
  Being spent, the world must needs decrepit be.   30
For since death will proceed to triumph still,
  He can find nothing, after her, to kill,
Except the world itself, so great as she.
  Thus brave and confident may Nature be,
Death cannot give her such another blow,
  Because she cannot such another show.
But must we say she 's dead? May 't not be said
  That as a sundered clock is piecemeal laid,

Not to be lost, but by the maker's hand
　　Repolished, without error then to stand,   40
Or as the Afric Niger stream enwombs
　　Itself into the earth, and after comes
(Having first made a natural bridge, to pass
　　For many leagues) far greater than it was,
May 't not be said, that her grave shall restore
　　Her, greater, purer, firmer, than before?
Heaven may say this, and joy in 't; but can we
　　Who live, and lack her, here this vantage see?
What is 't to us, alas, if there have been
　　An Angel made a Throne, or Cherubin?   50
We lose by 't: and as aged men are glad
　　Being tasteless grown, to joy in joys they had,
So now the sick starved world must feed upon
　　This joy, that we had her, who now is gone.
Rejoice then Nature, and this world, that you,
　　Fearing the last fires hastening to subdue
Your force and vigour, ere it were near gone,
　　Wisely bestowed and laid it all on one.
One, whose clear body was so pure, and thin,
　　Because it need disguise no thought within.   60
'Twas but a through-light scarf, her mind to enrol,
　　Or exhalation breathed out from her soul.
One, whom all men who durst no more, admired,
　　And whom, whoe'er had worth enough, desired;
As when a temple's built, saints emulate
　　To which of them it shall be consecrate.
But as when heaven looks on us with new eyes,
　　Those new stars every artist exercise,
What place they should assign to them they doubt,
　　Argue, and agree not, till those stars go out: 70
So the world studied whose this piece should be,
　　Till she can be nobody's else, nor she:
But like a lamp of balsamum, desired
　　Rather to 'adorn, than last, she soon expired,
Clothed in her virgin white integrity;
　　For marriage, though it do not stain, doth dye.
To 'scape th' infirmities which wait upon
　　Woman, she went away, before she was one.

And the world's busy noise to overcome,
  Took so much death, as served for opium.   80
For though she could not, nor could choose to die,
  She hath yielded to too long an ecstasy.
He which not knowing her sad history,
  Should come to read the book of destiny,
How fair and chaste, humble and high she had been,
  Much promised, much performed, at not fifteen,
And measuring future things by things before,
  Should turn the leaf to read, and read no more,
Would think that either destiny mistook,
  Or that some leaves were torn out of the book.   90
But 'tis not so; Fate did but usher her
  To years of reason's use, and then infer
Her destiny to herself; which liberty
  She took but for thus much, thus much to die.
Her modesty not suffering her to be
  Fellow-commissioner with Destiny,
She did no more but die; if after her
  Any shall live, which dare true good prefer,
Every such person is her delegate,
  T' accomplish that which should have been her fate.   100
They shall make up that book, and shall have thanks
  Of Fate, and her, for filling up their blanks.
For future virtuous deeds are legacies,
  Which from the gift of her example rise.
And 'tis in heaven part of spiritual mirth,
  To see how well the good play her, on earth.

An Anatomy of the World

THE FIRST ANNIVERSARY

When that rich soul which to her heaven is gone,   *The entry*
Whom all they celebrate, who know they have one,   *into the*
(For who is sure he hath a soul, unless   *work*
It see, and judge, and follow worthiness,
And by deeds praise it? He who doth not this,
May lodge an inmate soul, but 'tis not his.)

When that Queen ended here her progress time,
And, as to'her standing house, to heaven did climb,
Where, loth to make the saints attend her long,
She's now a part both of the choir, and song,   10
This world, in that great earthquake languished;
For in a common bath of tears it bled,
Which drew the strongest vital spirits out:
But succoured then with a perplexed doubt,
Whether the world did lose, or gain in this,
(Because since now no other way there is
But goodness, to see her, whom all would see,
All must endeavour to be good as she),
This great consumption to a fever turned,
And so the world had fits; it joyed, it mourned.   20
And, as men think, that agues physics are,
And th'ague being spent, give over care,
So thou, sick world, mistak'st thyself to be
Well, when alas, thou 'rt in a lethargy.
Her death did wound and tame thee then, and then
Thou mightst have better spared the sun, or man;
That wound was deep, but 'tis more misery,
That thou hast lost thy sense and memory.
'Twas heavy then to hear thy voice of moan,
But this is worse, that thou art speechless grown.   30
Thou hast forgot thy name, thou hadst; thou wast
Nothing but she, and her thou hast o'erpast.
For as a child kept from the font, until
A prince, expected long, come to fulfil
The ceremonies, thou unnamed hadst laid,
Had not her coming, thee her palace made:
Her name defined thee, gave thee form and frame,
And thou forget'st to celebrate thy name.
Some months she hath been dead (but being dead,
Measures of times are all determined)   40
But long she'hath been away, long, long, yet none
Offers to tell us who it is that's gone.
But as in states doubtful of future heirs,
When sickness without remedy impairs
The present prince, they're loth it should be said,
The prince doth languish, or the prince is dead:
So mankind feeling now a general thaw,

A strong example gone, equal to law,
The cement which did faithfully compact
And glue all virtues, now resolved, and slacked,   50
Thought it some blasphemy to say she'was dead;
Or that our weakness was discovered
In that confession; therefore spoke no more
Than tongues, the soul being gone, the loss deplore.
But though it be too late to succour thee,
Sick world, yea dead, yea putrefied, since she
Thy'instrinsic balm, and thy preservative,
Can never be renewed, thou never live,
I (since no man can make thee live) will try,
What we may gain by thy anatomy.   60
Her death hath taught us dearly, that thou art
Corrupt and mortal in thy purest part.
Let no man say, the world itself being dead,
'Tis labour lost to have discovered
The world's infirmities, since there is none   *What life*
Alive to study this dissection;   *the world*
For there's a kind of world remaining still,   *hath still*
Though she which did inanimate and fill
The world, be gone, yet in this last long night,
Her ghost doth walk; that is, a glimmering light,   70
A faint weak love of virtue and of good
Reflects from her, on them which understood
Her worth; and though she have shut in all day,
The twilight of her memory doth stay;
Which, from the carcase of the old world, free,
Creates a new world; and new creatures be
Produced: the matter and the stuff of this,
Her virtue, and the form our practice is.
And though to be thus elemented, arm
These creatures, from home-born intrinsic harm,   80
(For all assumed unto this dignity,
So many weedless paradises be,
Which of themselves produce no venomous sin,
Except some foreign serpent bring it in)
Yet, because outward storms the strongest break,
And strength itself by confidence grows weak,
This new world may be safer, being told

The dangers and diseases of the old:
For with due temper men do then forgo,
Or covet things, when they their true worth know.
There is no health; physicians say that we
At best, enjoy but a neutrality.
And can there be worse sickness, than to know
That we are never well, nor can be so?
We are born ruinous: poor mothers cry,
That children come not right, nor orderly,
Except they headlong come, and fall upon
An ominous precipitation.
How witty's ruin! how importunate
Upon mankind! it laboured to frustrate
Even God's purpose; and made woman, sent
For man's relief, cause of his languishment,
They were to good ends, and they are so still,
But accessory, and principal in ill.
For that first marriage was our funeral:
One woman at one blow, then killed us all,
And singly, one by one, they kill us now.
We do delightfully ourselves allow
To that consumption; and profusely blind,
We kill ourselves, to propagate our kind.
And yet we do not that; we are not men:
There is not now that mankind, which was then,
When as the sun, and man, did seem to strive,
(Joint tenants of the world) who should survive.
When stag, and raven, and the long-lived tree,
Compared with man, died in minority.
When, if a slow-paced star had stol'n away
From the observer's marking, he might stay
Two or three hundred years to see'it again,
And then make up his observation plain;
When, as the age was long, the size was great:
Man's growth confessed, and recompensed the meat:
So spacious and large, that every soul
Did a fair kingdom, and large realm control:
And when the very stature thus erect,
Did that soul a good way towards heaven direct.
Where is this mankind now? who lives to age,
Fit to be made Methusalem his page?

*The
sicknesses
of the world* 90

*Impossibility
of health*

100

*Shortness
of life*

120

Alas, we scarce live long enough to try
Whether a new made clock run right, or lie.   130
Old grandsires talk of yesterday with sorrow,
And for our children we reserve tomorrow.
So short is life, that every peasant strives,
In a torn house, or field, to have three lives.
And as in lasting, so in length is man
Contracted to an inch, who was a span.   *Smallness of*
stature
For had a man at first, in forests strayed,
Or shipwrecked in the sea, one would have laid
A wager that an elephant, or whale
That met him, would not hastily assail   140
A thing so equal to him: now alas,
The fairies, and the pygmies well may pass
As credible; mankind decays so soon,
We'are scarce our fathers' shadows cast at noon.
Only death adds to'our length: nor are we grown
In stature to be men, till we are none.
But this were light, did our less volume hold
All the old text; or had we changed to gold
Their silver; or disposed into less glass
Spirits of virtue, which then scattered was.   150
But 'tis not so: we' are not retired, but damped;
And as our bodies, so our minds are cramped:
'Tis shrinking, not close weaving, that hath thus,
In mind and body both bedwarfed us.
We seem ambitious, God's whole work to undo;
Of nothing he made us, and we strive too,
To bring ourselves to nothing back; and we
Do what we can, to do 't so soon as he.
With new diseases on ourselves we war,
And with new physic, a worse engine far.   160
Thus man, this world's vice-emperor, in whom
All faculties, all graces are at home;
And if in other creatures they appear,
They're but man's ministers, and legates there,
To work on their rebellions, and reduce
Them to civility, and to man's use:
This man, whom God did woo, and loth t' attend
Till man came up, did down to man descend,
This man, so great, that all that is, is his,

Oh what a trifle, and poor thing he is! 170
If man were anything, he's nothing now:
Help, or at least some time to waste, allow
T' his other wants, yet when he did depart
With her whom we lament, he lost his heart.
She, of whom th' ancients seemed to prophesy,
When they called virtues by the name of *she*,
She in whom virtue was so much refined,
That for allay unto so pure a mind
She took the weaker sex, she that could drive
The poisonous tincture, and the stain of Eve, 180
Out of her thoughts, and deeds; and purify
All, by a true religious alchemy;
She, she is dead; she's dead; when thou know'st this,
Thou know'st how poor a trifling thing man is.
And learn'st thus much by our anatomy,
The heart being perished, no part can be free.
And that except thou feed (not banquet) on
The supernatural food, religion,
Thy better growth grows withered, and scant;
Be more than man, or thou'art less than an ant. 190
Then, as mankind, so is the world's whole frame
Quite out of joint, almost created lame:
For, before God had made up all the rest,
Corruption entered, and depraved the best:
It seized the angels, and then first of all
The world did in her cradle take a fall,
And turned her brains, and took a general maim
Wronging each joint of th' universal frame.
The noblest part, man, felt it first; and then *Decay of*
Both beasts and plants, cursed in the curse of man. *nature in* 200
other parts
So did the world from the first hour decay,
That evening was beginning of the day,
And now the springs and summers which we see,
Like sons of women after fifty be.
And new philosophy calls all in doubt,
The element of fire is quite put out;
The sun is lost, and th' earth, and no man's wit
Can well direct him, where to look for it.
And freely men confess, that this world's spent,
When in the planets, and the firmament 210

They seek so many new; they see that this
Is crumbled out again to his atomies.
'Tis all in pieces, all coherence gone;
All just supply, and all relation:
Prince, subject, father, son, are things forgot,
For every man alone thinks he hath got
To be a phoenix, and that there can be
None of that kind, of which he is, but he.
This is the world's condition now, and now
She that should all parts to reunion bow,   220
She that had all magnetic force alone,
To draw, and fasten sundered parts in one;
She whom wise nature had invented then
When she observed that every sort of men
Did in their voyage in this world's sea stray,
And needed a new compass for their way;
She that was best, and first original
Of all fair copies; and the general
Steward to Fate; she whose rich eyes, and breast,
Gilt the West Indies, and perfumed the East;   230
Whose having breathed in this world, did bestow
Spice on those Isles, and bade them still smell so,
And that rich Indy which doth gold inter,
Is but as single money, coined from her:
She to whom this world must itself refer,
As suburbs, or the microcosm of her,
She, she is dead; she's dead: when thou know'st this,
Thou know'st how lame a cripple this world is.
And learn'st thus much by our anatomy,
That this world's general sickness doth not lie   240
In any humour, or one certain part;
But, as thou saw'st it rotten at the heart,
Thou seest a hectic fever hath got hold
Of the whole substance, not to be controlled,
And that thou hast but one way, not to admit
The world's infection, to be none of it.
For the world's subtlest immaterial parts
Feel this consuming wound, and age's darts.
For the world's beauty is decayed, or gone,   *Disformity*
Beauty, that's colour, and proportion.   *of parts*   250
We think the heavens enjoy their spherical,

Their round proportion embracing all.
But yet their various and perplexed course,
Observed in divers ages, doth enforce
Men to find out so many eccentric parts,
Such divers down-right lines, such overthwarts,
As disproportion that pure form. It tears
The firmament in eight and forty shares,
And in these constellations there arise
New stars, and old do vanish from our eyes: 260
As though heaven suffered earthquakes, peace or war,
When new towns rise, and old demolished are.
They have impaled within a zodiac
The free-born sun, and keep twelve signs awake
To watch his steps; the goat and crab control,
And fright him back, who else to either pole
(Did not these tropics fetter him) might run:
For his course is not round; nor can the sun
Perfect a circle, or maintain his way
One inch direct; but where he rose today   270
He comes no more, but with a cozening line,
Steals by that point, and so is serpentine:
And seeming weary with his reeling thus,
He means to sleep, being now fall'n nearer us.
So, of the stars which boast that they do run
In circle still, none ends where he begun.
All their proportion's lame, it sinks, it swells.
For of meridians, and parallels,
Man hath weaved out a net, and this net thrown
Upon the heavens, and now they are his own.   280
Loth to go up the hill, or labour thus
To go to heaven, we make heaven come to us.
We spur, we rein the stars, and in their race
They're diversely content t' obey our pace.
But keeps the earth her round proportion still?
Doth not a Tenerife, or higher hill
Rise so high like a rock, that one might think
The floating moon would shipwreck there, and sink?
Seas are so deep, that whales being struck today,
Perchance tomorrow, scarce at middle way   290
Of their wished journey's end, the bottom, die.
And men, to sound depths, so much line untie,

As one might justly think, that there would rise
At end thereof, one of th' Antipodes:
If under all, a vault infernal be,
(Which sure is spacious, except that we
Invent another torment, that there must
Millions into a strait hot room be thrust)
Then solidness, and roundness have no place.
Are these but warts, and pock-holes in the face   300
Of th' earth? Think so: but yet confess, in this
The world's proportion disfigured is,
That those two legs whereon it doth rely,   *Disorder*
Reward and punishment are bent awry.   *in the*
And, oh, it can no more be questioned,   *world*
That beauty's best, proportion, is dead,
Since even grief itself, which now alone
Is left us, is without proportion.
She by whose lines proportion should be
Examined, measure of all symmetry,
Whom had that ancient seen, who thought souls made   310
Of harmony, he would at next have said
That harmony was she, and thence infer,
That souls were but resultances from her,
And did from her into our bodies go,
As to our eyes, the forms from objects flow:
She, who if those great Doctors truly said
That the Ark to man's proportions was made,
Had been a type for that, as that might be
A type of her in this, that contrary   320
Both elements, and passions lived at peace
In her, who caused all civil war to cease.
She, after whom, what form soe'er we see,
Is discord, and rude incongruity;
She, she is dead, she's dead; when thou know'st this
Thou know'st how ugly a monster this world is:
And learn'st thus much by our anatomy,
That here is nothing to enamour thee:
And that, not only faults in inward parts,
Corruptions in our brains, or in our hearts,   330
Poisoning the fountains, whence our actions spring,
Endanger us: but that if everything
Be not done fitly'and in proportion,

To satisfy wise, and good lookers on,
(Since most men be such as most think they be)
They're loathsome too, by this deformity.
For good, and well, must in our actions meet:
Wicked is not much worse than indiscreet.
But beauty's other second element,
Colour, and lustre now, is as near spent. 340
And had the world his just proportion,
Were it a ring still, yet the stone is gone.
As a compassionate turquoise which doth tell
By looking pale, the wearer is not well,
As gold falls sick being stung with mercury,
All the world's parts of such complexion be.
When nature was most busy, the first week,
Swaddling the new born earth, God seemed to like
That she should sport herself sometimes, and play,
To mingle, and vary colours every day: 350
And then, as though she could not make enow,
Himself his various rainbow did allow.
Sight is the noblest sense of any one,
Yet sight hath only colour to feed on,
And colour is decayed: summer's robe grows
Dusky, and like an oft dyed garment shows.
Our blushing red, which used in cheeks to spread,
Is inward sunk, and only our souls are red.
Perchance the world might have recovered,
If she whom we lament had not been dead: 360
But she, in whom all white, and red, and blue
(Beauty's ingredients) voluntary grew,
As in an unvexed paradise; from whom
Did all things' verdure, and their lustre come,
Whose composition was miraculous,
Being all colour, all diaphanous,
(For air, and fire but thick gross bodies were,
And liveliest stones but drowsy, and pale to her),
She, she, is dead; she's dead: when thou know'st this,
Thou know'st how wan a ghost this our world is: 370
And learn'st thus much by our anatomy,
That it should more affright, than pleasure thee.
And that, since all fair colour then did sink,
'Tis now but wicked vanity, to think

To colour vicious deeds with good pretence,   *Weakness in*
Or with bought colours to illude men's sense.   *the want of*
Nor in aught more this world's decay appears,   *correspondence*
Than that her influence the heaven forbears,   *of heaven*
Or that the elements do not feel this,   *and earth*
The father, or the mother barren is.   380
The clouds conceive not rain, or do not pour
In the due birth time, down the balmy shower.
Th' air doth not motherly sit on the earth,
To hatch her seasons, and give all things birth.
Spring-times were common cradles, but are tombs;
And false conceptions fill the general wombs.
Th' air shows such meteors, as none can see,
Not only what they mean, but what they be.
Earth such new worms, as would have troubled much
Th' Egyptian Mages to have made more such.   390
What artist now dares boast that he can bring
Heaven hither, or constellate anything,
So as the influence of those stars may be
Imprisoned in an herb, or charm, or tree,
And do by touch, all which those stars could do?
The art is lost, and correspondence too.
For heaven gives little, and the earth takes less,
And man least knows their trade, and purposes.
If this commerce 'twixt heaven and earth were not
Embarred, and all this traffic quite forgot,   400
She, for whose loss we have lamented thus,
Would work more fully and powerfully on us.
Since herbs, and roots by dying, lose not all,
But they, yea ashes too, are medicinal,
Death could not quench her virtue so, but that
It would be (if not followed) wondered at:
And all the world would be one dying swan,
To sing her funeral praise, and vanish then.
But as some serpents' poison hurteth not,
Except it be from the live serpent shot,   410
So doth her virtue need her here, to fit
That unto us; she working more than it.
But she, in whom, to such maturity
Virtue was grown, past growth, that it must die,
She, from whose influence all impressions came,

But, by receivers' impotencies, lame,
Who, though she could not transubstantiate
All states to gold, yet gilded every state,
So that some princes have some temperance;
Some counsellors some purpose to advance   420
The common profit; and some people have
Some stay, no more than kings should give, to crave;
Some women have some taciturnity;
Some nunneries, some grains of chastity.
She that did thus much, and much more could do,
But that our age was iron, and rusty too,
She, she is dead; she's dead: when thou know'st this,
Thou know'st how dry a cinder this world is.
And learn'st thus much by our anatomy,
That 'tis in vain to dew, or mollify   430
It with thy tears, or sweat, or blood: nothing
Is worth our travail, grief, or perishing,
But those rich joys, which did possess her heart,
Of which she's now partaker, and a part.
But as in cutting up a man that's dead,   *Conclusion*
The body will not last out to have read
On every part, and therefore men direct
Their speech to parts, that are of most effect;
So the world's carcase would not last, if I
Were punctual in this anatomy.   440
Nor smells it well to hearers, if one tell
Them their disease, who fain would think they're well.
Here therefore be the end: and, blessed maid,
Of whom is meant whatever hath been said,
Or shall be spoken well by any tongue,
Whose name refines coarse lines, and makes prose song,
Accept this tribute, and his first year's rent,
Who till his dark short taper's end be spent,
As oft as thy feast see this widowed earth,
Will yearly celebrate thy second birth,   450
That is, thy death. For though the soul of man
Be got when man is made, 'tis born but then
When man doth die. Our body 's as the womb,
And as a midwife death directs it home.
And you her creatures, whom she works upon
And have your last, and best concoction

From her example, and her virtue, if you
In reverence to her, do think it due,
That no one should her praises thus rehearse,
As matter fit for chronicle, not verse,   460
Vouchsafe to call to mind, that God did make
A last, and lasting'st piece, a song. He spake
To Moses, to deliver unto all,
That song: because he knew they would let fall
The Law, the prophets, and the history,
But keep the song still in their memory.
Such an opinion (in due measure) made
Me this great office boldly to invade.
Nor could incomprehensibleness deter
Me, from thus trying to imprison her.   470
Which when I saw that a strict grave could do,
I saw not why verse might not do so too.
Verse hath a middle nature: heaven keeps souls,
The grave keeps bodies, verse the fame enrols.

Of the Progress of the Soul

THE SECOND ANNIVERSARY

Nothing could make me sooner to confess   *The entrance*
That this world had an everlastingness,
Than to consider, that a year is run,
Since both this lower world's, and the sun's sun,
The lustre, and the vigour of this all,
Did set; 'twere blasphemy, to say, did fall.
But as a ship which hath struck sail, doth run,
By force of that force which before, it won,
Or as sometimes in a beheaded man,
Though at those two red seas, which freely ran,   10
One from the trunk, another from the head,
His soul be sailed, to her eternal bed,
His eyes will twinkle, and his tongue will roll,
As though he beckoned, and called back his soul,
He grasps his hands, and he pulls up his feet,
And seems to reach, and to step forth to meet

His soul; when all these motions which we saw,
Are but as ice, which crackles at a thaw:
Or as a lute, which in moist weather, rings
Her knell alone, by cracking of her strings: 20
So struggles this dead world, now she is gone;
For there is motion in corruption.
As some days are, at the Creation named,
Before the sun, the which framed days, was framed,
So after this sun's set, some show appears,
And orderly vicissitude of years.
Yet a new Deluge, and of Lethe flood,
Hath drowned us all, all have forgot all good,
Forgetting her, the main reserve of all,
Yet in this deluge, gross and general,   30
Thou seest me strive for life; my life shall be,
To be hereafter praised, for praising thee,
Immortal Maid, who though thou would'st refuse
The name of mother, be unto my Muse
A father, since her chaste ambition is,
Yearly to bring forth such a child as this.
These hymns may work on future wits, and so
May great grandchildren of thy praises grow.
And so, though not revive, embalm and spice
The world, which else would putrefy with vice.   40
For thus, man may extend thy progeny,
Until man do but vanish, and not die.
These hymns thy issue, may increase so long,
As till God's great *Venite* change the song.
Thirst for that time, O my insatiate soul,
And serve thy thirst, with God's safe-sealing bowl.   *A just*
Be thirsty still, and drink still till thou go;   *disestimation*
'Tis th' only health, to be hydropic so.   *of the*
Forget this rotten world; and unto thee   *world*
Let thine own times as an old story be;   50
Be not concerned: study not why, nor when;
Do not so much, as not believe a man.
For though to err, be worst, to try truths forth,
Is far more business than this world is worth.
The world is but a carcase; thou art fed
By it, but as a worm, that carcase bred;
And why shouldst thou, poor worm, consider more,

When this world will grow better than before,
Than those thy fellow worms do think upon
That carcase's last resurrection.   60
Forget this world, and scarce think of it so,
As of old clothes, cast off a year ago.
To be thus stupid is alacrity;
Men thus lethargic have best memory.
Look upward; that's towards her, whose happy state
We now lament not, but congratulate.
She, to whom all this world was but a stage,
Where all sat hearkening how her youthful age
Should be employed, because in all she did,
Some figure of the Golden Times was hid;   70
Who could not lack, whate'er this world could give,
Because she was the form, that made it live;
Nor could complain, that this world was unfit
To be stayed in, then when she was in it;
She that first tried indifferent desires
By virtue, and virtue by religious fires,
She to whose person Paradise adhered,
As Courts to princes; she whose eyes ensphered
Star-light enough, to' have made the south control,
(Had she been there) the star-full northern pole,   80
She, she is gone; she's gone; when thou know'st this,
What fragmentary rubbish this world is   *Contemplation*
Thou know'st, and that it is not worth a thought;   *of our state in*
He honours it too much that thinks it naught.   *our deathbed*
Think then, my soul, that death is but a groom,
Which brings a taper to the outward room,
Whence thou spiest first a little glimmering light,
And after brings it nearer to thy sight:
For such approaches doth heaven make in death.
Think thyself labouring now with broken breath,   90
And think those broken and soft notes to be
Division, and thy happiest harmony.
Think thee laid on thy death-bed, loose and slack;
And think that but unbinding of a pack,
To take one precious thing, thy soul, from thence.
Think thyself parched with fever's violence,
Anger thine ague more, by calling it
Thy physic; chide the slackness of the fit.

Think that thou hear'st thy knell, and think no more,
But that, as bells called thee to church before,　　　100
So this, to the Triumphant Church, calls thee.
Think Satan's sergeants round about thee be,
And think that but for legacies they thrust;
Give one thy pride, to another give thy lust:
Give them those sins which they gave thee before,
And trust th' immaculate blood to wash thy score.
Think thy friends weeping round, and think that they
Weep but because they go not yet thy way.
Think that they close thine eyes, and think in this,
That they confess much in the world, amiss,　　　110
Who dare not trust a dead man's eye with that,
Which they from God, and angels cover not.
Think that they shroud thee up, and think from thence
They reinvest thee in white innocence.
Think that thy body rots, and (if so low,
Thy soul exalted so, thy thoughts can go),
Think thee a prince, who of themselves create
Worms which insensibly devour their state.
Think that they bury thee, and think that rite
Lays thee to sleep but a Saint Lucy's night.　　　120
Think these things cheerfully: and if thou be
Drowsy or slack, remember then that she,
She whose complexion was so even made,
That which of her ingredients should invade
The other three, no fear, no art could guess:
So far were all removed from more or less.
But as in mithridate, or just perfumes,
Where all good things being met, no one presumes
To govern, or to triumph on the rest,
Only because all were, no part was best.　　　130
And as, though all do know, that quantities
Are made of lines, and lines from points arise,
None can these lines or quantities unjoint,
And say this is a line, or this a point,
So though the elements and humours were
In her, one could not say, this governs there.
Whose even constitution might have won
Any disease to venture on the sun,
Rather than her: and make a spirit fear

That he to disuniting subject were.   140
To whose proportions if we would compare
Cubes, they'are unstable; circles, angular;
She who was such a chain, as Fate employs
To bring mankind all fortunes it enjoys,
So fast, so even wrought, as one would think,
No accident could threaten any link,
She, she embraced a sickness, gave it meat,
The purest blood, and breath, that e'er it eat;
And hath taught us that though a good man hath
Title to heaven, and plead it by his faith,   150
And though he may pretend a conquest, since
Heaven was content to suffer violence,
Yea though he plead a long possession too,
(For they're in heaven on earth, who heaven's works do)
Though he had right, and power, and place before,
Yet death must usher, and unlock the door.
Think further on thy self, my soul, and think   *Incommodities*
How thou at first wast made but in a sink;   *of the soul in*
Think that it argued some infirmity,   *the body*
That those two souls, which then thou found'st in me,   160
Thou fed'st upon, and drew'st into thee, both
My second soul of sense, and first of growth.
Think but how poor thou wast, how obnoxious;
Whom a small lump of flesh could poison thus.
This curded milk, this poor unlittered whelp
My body, could, beyond escape, or help,
Infect thee with original sin, and thou
Couldst neither then refuse, nor leave it now.
Think that no stubborn sullen anchorite,
Which fixed to a pillar, or a grave doth sit   170
Bedded and bathed in all his ordures, dwells
So foully as our souls, in their first-built cells.
Think in how poor a prison thou didst lie
After, enabled but to suck, and cry.
Think, when 'twas grown to most, 'twas a poor inn,
A province packed up in two yards of skin,
And that usurped, or threatened with the rage
Of sicknesses, or their true mother, age.
But think that death hath now enfranchised thee,   *Her liberty*
Thou hast thy expansion now and liberty;   *by death* 180

Think that a rusty piece, discharged, is flown
In pieces, and the bullet is his own,
And freely flies: this to thy soul allow,
Think thy shell broke, think thy soul hatched but now.
And think this slow-paced soul, which late did cleave
To a body, and went but by the body's leave,
Twenty, perchance, or thirty mile a day,
Dispatches in a minute all the way
'Twixt heaven, and earth: she stays not in the air,
To look what meteors there themselves prepare;   190
She carries no desire to know, nor sense,
Whether th' air's middle region be intense,
For th' element of fire, she doth not know,
Whether she passed by such a place or no;
She baits not at the moon, nor cares to try
Whether in that new world, men live, and die.
Venus retards her not, to inquire, how she
Can, (being one star) Hesper, and Vesper be;
He that charmed Argus' eyes, sweet Mercury,
Works not on her, who now is grown all eye;   200
Who, if she meet the body of the sun,
Goes through, not staying till his course be run;
Who finds in Mars his camp, no corps of guard;
Nor is by Jove, nor by his father barred;
But ere she can consider how she went,
At once is at, and through the firmament.
And as these stars were but so many beads
Strung on one string, speed undistinguished leads
Her through those spheres, as through the beads, a string,
Whose quick succession makes it still one thing: 210
As doth the pith, which, lest our bodies slack,
Strings fast the little bones of neck, and back;
So by the soul doth death string heaven and earth,
For when our soul enjoys this her third birth,
(Creation gave her one, a second, grace),
Heaven is as near, and present to her face,
As colours are, and objects, in a room
Where darkness was before, when tapers come.
This must, my soul, thy long-short progress be;
To advance these thoughts, remember then, that she,   220
She, whose fair body no such prison was,

But that a soul might well be pleased to pass
An age in her; she whose rich beauty lent
Mintage to others' beauties, for they went
But for so much, as they were like to her;
She, in whose body (if we dare prefer
This low world, to so high a mark, as she),
The western treasure, eastern spicery,
Europe, and Afric, and the unknown rest
Were easily found, or what in them was best;   230
And when we'have made this large discovery
Of all in her some one part, there will be
Twenty such parts, whose plenty and riches is
Enough to make twenty such worlds as this;
She, whom had they known, who did first betroth
The tutelar angels, and assigned one, both
To nations, cities, and to companies,
To functions, offices, and dignities,
And to each several man, to him, and him,
They would have given her one for every limb;   240
She, of whose soul, if we may say, 'twas gold,
Her body was th' electrum, and did hold
Many degrees of that; we understood
Her by her sight, her pure and eloquent blood
Spoke in her cheeks, and so distinctly wrought,
That one might almost say, her body thought,
She, she, thus richly, and largely housed, is gone:
And chides us slow-paced snails, who crawl upon
Our prison's prison, earth, nor think us well
Longer, than whilst we bear our brittle shell.   250
But 'twere but little to have changed our room,
If, as we were in this our living tomb
Oppressed with ignorance, we still were so.
Poor soul, in this thy flesh what dost thou know?
Thou know'st thyself so little, as thou know'st not,
How thou didst die, nor how thou wast begot.
Thou neither know'st how thou at first cam'st in,
Nor how thou took'st the poison of man's sin.
Nor dost thou (though thou know'st, that thou art so)
By what way thou art made immortal, know.   260
Thou art too narrow, wretch, to comprehend
Even thyself: yea though thou wouldst but bend

Her ignorance
in this life and
knowledge in
the next

To know thy body. Have not all souls thought
For many ages, that our body is wrought
Of air, and fire, and other elements?
And now they think of new ingredients.
And one soul thinks one, and another way
Another thinks, and 'tis an even lay.
Know'st thou but how the stone doth enter in
The bladder's cave, and never break the skin?   270
Know'st thou how blood, which to the heart doth flow,
Doth from one ventricle to th' other go?
And for the putrid stuff, which thou dost spit,
Know'st thou how thy lungs have attracted it?
There are no passages so that there is
(For aught thou know'st) piercing of substances.
And of those many opinions which men raise
Of nails and hairs, dost thou know which to praise?
What hope have we to know ourselves, when we
Know not the least things, which for our use be?   280
We see in authors, too stiff to recant,
A hundred controversies of an ant.
And yet one watches, starves, freezes, and sweats,
To know but catechisms and alphabets
Of unconcerning things, matters of fact;
How others on our stage their parts did act;
What Caesar did, yea, and what Cicero said.
Why grass is green, or why our blood is red,
Are mysteries which none have reached unto.
In this low form, poor soul, what wilt thou do?   290
When wilt thou shake off this pedantery,
Of being taught by sense, and fantasy?
Thou look'st through spectacles; small things seem great
Below; but up unto the watch-tower get,
And see all things despoiled of fallacies:
Thou shalt not peep through lattices of eyes,
Nor hear through labyrinths of ears, nor learn
By circuit, or collections to discern.
In heaven thou straight know'st all, concerning it,
And what concerns it not, shalt straight forget.   300
There thou (but in no other school) mayst be
Perchance, as learned, and as full, as she,
She who all libraries had throughly read

At home, in her own thoughts, and practised
So much good as would make as many more:
She whose example they must all implore,
Who would or do, or think well, and confess
That aye the virtuous actions they express,
Are but a new, and worse edition
Of her some one thought, or one action: 310
She, who in th' art of knowing heaven, was grown
Here upon earth, to such perfection,
That she hath, ever since to heaven she came,
(In a far fairer print), but read the same:
She, she, not satisfied with all this weight,
(For so much knowledge, as would over-freight
Another, did but ballast her) is gone,
As well t' enjoy, as get perfection.
And calls us after her, in that she took,   *Of our*
(Taking herself) our best, and worthiest book.   *company in* 320
Return not, my soul, from this ecstasy,   *this life,*
And meditation of what thou shalt be,   *and in the*
To earthly thoughts, till it to thee appear,   *next*
With whom thy conversation must be there.
With whom wilt thou converse? what station
Canst thou choose out, free from infection,
That will nor give thee theirs, nor drink in thine?
Shalt thou not find a spongy slack divine
Drink and suck in th' instructions of great men,
And for the word of God, vent them again?   330
Are there not some Courts (and then, no things be
So like as Courts) which, in this let us see,
That wits and tongues of libellers are weak,
Because they do more ill, than these can speak?
The poison' is gone through all, poisons affect
Chiefly the chiefest parts, but some effect
In nails, and hairs, yea excrements, will show;
So will the poison of sin, in the most low.
Up, up, my drowsy soul, where thy new ear
Shall in the angels' songs no discord hear;   340
Where thou shalt see the blessed mother-maid
Joy in not being that, which men have said.
Where she is exalted more for being good,
Than for her interest, of motherhood.

Up to those patriarchs, which did longer sit
Expecting Christ, than they'have enjoyed him yet.
Up to those prophets, which now gladly see
Their prophecies grown to be history.
Up to th' apostles, who did bravely run
All the sun's course, with more light than the sun.   350
Up to those martyrs, who did calmly bleed
Oil to th' apostles' lamps, dew to their seed.
Up to those virgins, who thought that almost
They made joint tenants with the Holy Ghost,
If they to any should his temple give.
Up, up, for in that squadron there doth live
She, who hath carried thither, new degrees
(As to their number) to their dignities.
She, who being to herself a State, enjoyed
All royalties which any State employed,   360
For she made wars, and triumphed; reason still
Did not o'erthrow, but rectify her will:
And she made peace, for no peace is like this,
That beauty and chastity together kiss:
She did high justice; for she crucified
Every first motion of rebellious pride:
And she gave pardons, and was liberal,
For, only herself except, she pardoned all:
She coined, in this, that her impressions gave
To all our actions all the worth they have: 370
She gave protections; the thoughts of her breast
Satan's rude officers could ne'er arrest.
As these prerogatives being met in one,
Made her a sovereign State, religion
Made her a Church; and these two made her all.
She who was all this all, and could not fall
To worse, by company, (for she was still
More antidote, than all the world was ill),
She, she doth leave it, and by death, survive
All this, in heaven; whither who doth not strive   380
The more, because she 'is there, he doth not know
That accidental joys in heaven do grow.
But pause, my soul, and study ere thou fall
On accidental joys, th' essential.

*Of essential
joy in this life
and in the next*

Still before accessories do abide
A trial, must the principal be tried.

And what essential joy canst thou expect
Here upon earth? what permanent effect
Of transitory causes? Dost thou love
Beauty? (and beauty worthiest is to move)   390
Poor cozened cozener, that she, and that thou,
Which did begin to love, are neither now.
You are both fluid, changed since yesterday;
Next day repairs, (but ill) last day's decay.
Nor are, (although the river keep the name)
Yesterday's waters, and today's the same.
So flows her face, and thine eyes, neither now
That saint, nor pilgrim, which your loving vow
Concerned, remains; but whilst you think you be
Constant, you'are hourly in inconstancy.   400
Honour may have pretence unto our love,
Because that God did live so long above
Without this honour, and then loved it so,
That he at last made creatures to bestow
Honour on him; not that he needed it,
But that, to his hands, man might grow more fit.
But since all honours from inferiors flow,
(For they do give it; princes do but show
Whom they would have so honoured) and that this
On such opinions, and capacities   410
Is built, as rise, and fall, to more or less,
Alas, 'tis but a casual happiness.
Hath ever any man to' himself assigned
This or that happiness, to arrest his mind,
But that another man, which takes a worse,
Think him a fool for having ta'en that course?
They who did labour Babel's tower to erect,
Might have considered, that for that effect,
All this whole solid earth could not allow
Nor furnish forth materials enow;   420
And that this centre, to raise such a place,
Was far too little, to have been the base;
No more affords this world, foundation
To erect true joy, were all the means in one.
But as the heathen made them several gods,
Of all God's benefits, and all his rods,
(For as the wine, and corn, and onions are

Gods unto them, so agues be, and war)
And as by changing that whole precious gold
To such small copper coins, they lost the old,   430
And lost their only God, who ever must
Be sought alone, and not in such a thrust:
So much mankind true happiness mistakes;
No joy enjoys that man, that many makes.
Then, soul, to thy first pitch work up again;
Know that all lines which circles do contain,
For once that they the centre touch, do touch
Twice the circumference; and be thou such.
Double on heaven, thy thoughts on earth employed;
All will not serve; only who have enjoyed   440
The sight of God, in fulness, can think it;
For it is both the object, and the wit.
This is essential joy, where neither he
Can suffer diminution, nor we;
'Tis such a full, and such a filling good;
Had th' angels once looked on him, they had stood.
To fill the place of one of them, or more,
She whom we celebrate, is gone before.
She, who had here so much essential joy,
As no chance could distract, much less destroy;   450
Who with God's presence was acquainted so,
(Hearing, and speaking to him) as to know
His face, in any natural stone, or tree,
Better than when in images they be:
Who kept, by diligent devotion,
God's image, in such reparation,
Within her heart, that what decay was grown,
Was her first parents' fault, and not her own:
Who being solicited to any act,
Still heard God pleading his safe precontract;   460
Who by a faithful confidence, was here
Betrothed to God, and now is married there,
Whose twilights were more clear, than our midday,
Who dreamed devoutlier, than most use to pray;
Who being here filled with grace, yet strove to be,
Both where more grace, and more capacity
At once is given: she to heaven is gone,
Who made this world in some proportion

A heaven, and here, became unto us all,
Joy (as our joys admit) essential.   470
But could this low world joys essential touch,   *Of accidental*
Heaven's accidental joys would pass them much.   *joys in both*
How poor and lame, must then our casual be!   *places*
If thy prince will his subjects to call thee
My Lord, and this do swell thee, thou art then,
By being a greater, grown to be less man.
When no physician of redress can speak,
A joyful casual violence may break
A dangerous aposteme in thy breast;
And whilst thou joyest in this, the dangerous rest,   480
The bag may rise up, and so strangle thee.
What aye was casual, may ever be.
What should the nature change? Or make the same
Certain, which was but casual, when it came?
All casual joy doth loud and plainly say,
Only by coming, that it can away.
Only in heaven joy's strength is never spent;
And accidental things are permanent.
Joy of a soul's arrival ne'er decays;
For that soul ever joys and ever stays.   490
Joy that their last great consummation
Approaches in the resurrection;
When earthly bodies more celestial
Shall be, than angels were, for they could fall;
This kind of joy doth every day admit
Degrees of growth, but none of losing it.
In this fresh joy, 'tis no small part, that she,
She, in whose goodness, he that names degree,
Doth injure her; ('tis loss to be called best,
There where the stuff is not such as the rest)   500
She, who left such a body, as even she
Only in heaven could learn, how it can be
Made better; for she rather was two souls,
Or like to full, on both sides written rolls,
Where eyes might read upon the outward skin,
As strong records for God, as minds within;
She, who by making full perfection grow,
Pieces a circle, and still keeps it so,
Longed for, and longing for it, to heaven is gone,

Where she receives, and gives addition.   510
Here in a place, where mis-devotion frames   *Conclusion*
A thousand prayers to saints, whose very names
The ancient Church knew not, heaven knows not yet,
And where, what laws of poetry admit,
Laws of religion have at least the same,
Immortal maid, I might invoke thy name.
Could any saint provoke that appetite,
Thou here shouldst make me a French convertite.
But thou wouldst not; nor wouldst thou be content,
To take this, for my second year's true rent,   520
Did this coin bear any other stamp, than his,
That gave thee power to do, me, to say this.
Since his will is, that to posterity,
Thou shouldst for life, and death, a pattern be,
And that the world should notice have of this,
The purpose, and th' authority is his;
Thou art the proclamation; and I am
The trumpet, at whose voice the people came.

The Cross

Since Christ embraced the Cross itself, dare I
His image, th' image of his Cross deny?
Would I have profit by the sacrifice,
And dare the chosen altar to despise?
It bore all other sins, but is it fit
That it should bear the sin of scorning it?
Who from the picture would avert his eye,
How would he fly his pains, who there did die?
From me, no pulpit, nor misgrounded law,
Nor scandal taken, shall this Cross withdraw,   10
It shall not, for it cannot; for, the loss
Of this Cross, were to me another cross;
Better were worse, for, no affliction,
No cross is so extreme, as to have none.
Who can blot out the Cross, which th' instrument
Of God, dewed on me in the Sacrament?
Who can deny me power, and liberty
To stretch mine arms, and mine own cross to be?
Swim, and at every stroke, thou art thy cross,
The mast and yard make one, where seas do toss.   20
Look down, thou spiest out crosses in small things;
Look up, thou seest birds raised on crossed wings;
All the globe's frame, and sphere's, is nothing else
But the meridians crossing parallels.
Material crosses then, good physic be,
And yet spiritual have chief dignity.
These for extracted chemic medicine serve,
And cure much better, and as well preserve;
Then are you your own physic, or need none,
When stilled, or purged by tribulation.   30
For when that Cross ungrudged, unto you sticks,
Then are you to yourself, a crucifix.

As perchance, carvers do not faces make,
But that away, which hid them there, do take:
Let crosses, so, take what hid Christ in thee,
And be his image, or not his, but he.
But, as oft alchemists do coiners prove,
So may a self-despising, get self-love.
And then as worst surfeits, of best meats be,
So is pride, issued from humility,   40
For, 'tis no child, but monster; therefore cross
Your joy in crosses, else, 'tis double loss,
And cross thy senses, else, both they, and thou
Must perish soon, and to destruction bow.
For if the'eye seek good objects, and will take
No cross from bad, we cannot 'scape a snake.
So with harsh, hard, sour, stinking, cross the rest,
Make them indifferent; call nothing best.
But most the eye needs crossing, that can roam,
And move; to th' others th' objects must come home.   50
And cross thy heart: for that in man alone
Points downwards, and hath palpitation.
Cross those dejections, when it downward tends,
And when it to forbidden heights pretends.
And as the brain through bony walls doth vent
By sutures, which a cross's form present,
So when thy brain works, ere thou utter it,
Cross and correct concupiscence of wit.
Be covetous of crosses, let none fall.
Cross no man else, but cross thyself in all.   60
Then doth the Cross of Christ work fruitfully
Within our hearts, when we love harmlessly
That Cross's pictures much, and with more care
That Cross's children, which our crosses are.

Resurrection, imperfect

Sleep sleep old sun, thou canst not have repassed
As yet, the wound thou took'st on Friday last;
Sleep then, and rest; the world may bear thy stay,
A better sun rose before thee today,

Who, not content to enlighten all that dwell
On the earth's face, as thou, enlightened hell,
And made the dark fires languish in that vale,
As, at thy presence here, our fires grow pale.
Whose body having walked on earth, and now
Hasting to heaven, would, that he might allow   10
Himself unto all stations, and fill all,
For these three days become a mineral;
He was all gold when he lay down, but rose
All tincture, and doth not alone dispose
Leaden and iron wills to good, but is
Of power to make even sinful flesh like his.
Had one of those, whose credulous piety
Thought, that a soul one might discern and see
Go from a body, at this sepulchre been,
And, issuing from the sheet, this body seen,   20
He would have justly thought this body a soul,
If not of any man, yet of the whole.
   Desunt caetera.

Upon the Annunciation and Passion falling
upon one day.
1608

Tamely frail body, abstain today; today
My soul eats twice, Christ hither and away.
She sees him man, so like God made in this,
That of them both a circle emblem is,
Whose first and last concur; this doubtful day
Of feast or fast, Christ came, and went away;
She sees him nothing twice at once, who is all;
She sees a cedar plant itself, and fall,
Her maker put to making, and the head
Of life, at once, not yet alive, and dead;   10
She sees at once the virgin mother stay
Reclused at home, public at Golgotha.
Sad and rejoiced she's seen at once, and seen
At almost fifty, and at scarce fifteen.

At once a son is promised her, and gone,
Gabriel gives Christ to her, he her to John;
Not fully a mother, she's in orbity,
At once receiver and the legacy;
All this, and all between, this day hath shown,
Th' abridgement of Christ's story, which makes one   20
(As in plain maps, the furthest west is east)
Of the angel's *Ave*, and *Consummatum est*.
How well the Church, God's court of faculties
Deals, in sometimes, and seldom joining these;
As by the self-fixed pole we never do
Direct our course, but the next star thereto,
Which shows where the 'other is, and which we say
(Because it strays not far) doth never stray;
So God by his Church, nearest to him, we know,
And stand firm, if we by her motion go;   30
His Spirit, as his fiery pillar doth
Lead, and his Church, as cloud; to one end both:
This Church, by letting these days join, hath shown
Death and conception in mankind is one:
Or 'twas in him the same humility,
That he would be a man, and leave to be:
Or as creation he had made, as God,
With the last judgement, but one period,
His imitating spouse would join in one
Manhood's extremes: he shall come, he is gone: 40
Or as though one blood drop, which thence did fall,
Accepted, would have served, he yet shed all;
So though the least of his pains, deeds, or words,
Would busy a life, she all this day affords;
This treasure then, in gross, my soul uplay,
And in my life retail it every day.

A Litany

I

The Father

Father of heaven, and him, by whom
It, and us for it, and all else, for us
   Thou mad'st, and govern'st ever, come
And re-create me, now grown ruinous:
     My heart is by dejection, clay,
     And by self-murder, red.
From this red earth, O Father, purge away
All vicious tinctures, that new fashioned
I may rise up from death, before I am dead.

II

The Son

O Son of God, who seeing two things,   10
Sin, and death crept in, which were never made,
   By bearing one, tried'st with what stings
The other could thine heritage invade;
     O be thou nailed unto my heart,
     And crucified again,
Part not from it, though it from thee would part,
But let it be by applying so thy pain,
Drowned in thy blood, and in thy passion slain.

III

The Holy Ghost

O Holy Ghost, whose temple I
Am, but of mud walls, and condensed dust,   20
   And being sacrilegiously
Half wasted with youth's fires, of pride and lust,
     Must with new storms be weatherbeat;
     Double in my heart thy flame,
Which let devout sad tears intend; and let
(Though this glass lanthorn, flesh, do suffer maim)
Fire, sacrifice, priest, altar be the same.

IV

The Trinity

O Blessed glorious Trinity,
Bones to philosophy, but milk to faith,
   Which, as wise serpents, diversely   30
Most slipperiness, yet most entanglings hath,
      As you distinguished undistinct
      By power, love, knowledge be,
Give me a such self different instinct,
Of these let all me elemented be,
Of power, to love, to know, you unnumbered three.

V

The Virgin Mary

For that fair blessed mother-maid,
Whose flesh redeemed us; that she-cherubin,
   Which unlocked Paradise, and made
One claim for innocence, and disseized sin,   40
      Whose womb was a strange heaven, for there
      God clothed himself, and grew,
Our zealous thanks we pour. As her deeds were
Our helps, so are her prayers; nor can she sue
In vain, who hath such titles unto you.

VI

The Angels

And since this life our nonage is,
And we in wardship to thine angels be,
   Native in heaven's fair palaces
Where we shall be but denizened by thee,
      As th' earth conceiving by the sun,   50
      Yields fair diversity,
Yet never knows which course that light doth run,
So let me study, that mine actions be
Worthy their sight, though blind in how they see.

VII

The Patriarchs

And let thy patriarchs' desire
(Those great grandfathers of thy Church, which saw
    More in the cloud, than we in fire,
Whom Nature cleared more, than us grace and law,
        And now in heaven still pray, that we
            May use our new helps right),   60
Be satisfied, and fructify in me;
Let not my mind be blinder by more light
Nor faith by reason added, lose her sight.

VIII

The Prophets

Thy eagle-sighted prophets too,
Which were thy Church's organs, and did sound
    That harmony, which made of two
One law, and did unite, but not confound;
        Those heavenly poets which did see
            Thy will, and it express
In rhythmic feet, in common pray for me,   70
That I by them excuse not my excess
In seeking secrets, or poeticness.

IX

The Apostles

And thy illustrious zodiac
Of twelve apostles, which engirt this all,
    (From whom whosoever do not take
Their light, to dark deep pits, throw down, and fall,)
        As through their prayers, thou' hast let me know
            That their books are divine;
May they pray still, and be heard, that I go
The old broad way in applying; O decline   80
Me, when my comment would make thy word mine.

X

The Martyrs

And since thou so desirously
Didst long to die, that long before thou couldst,
  And long since thou no more couldst die,
Thou in thy scattered mystic body wouldst
      In Abel die, and ever since
      In thine, let their blood come
To beg for us, a discreet patience
Of death, or of worse life: for oh, to some
Not to be martyrs, is a martyrdom.   90

XI

The Confessors

Therefore with thee triumpheth there
A virgin squadron of white confessors,
  Whose bloods betrothed, not married were;
Tendered, not taken by those ravishers:
      They know, and pray, that we may know,
      In every Christian
Hourly tempestuous persecutions grow,
Temptations martyr us alive; a man
Is to himself a Diocletian.

XII

The Virgins

The cold white snowy nunnery,   100
Which, as thy mother, their high abbess, sent
  Their bodies back again to thee,
As thou hadst lent them, clean and innocent,
      Though they have not obtained of thee,
      That or thy Church, or I,
Should keep, as they, our first integrity;
Divorce thou sin in us, or bid it die,
And call chaste widowhead virginity.

XIII

The Doctors

Thy sacred academe above
Of Doctors, whose pains have unclasped, and taught   110
  Both books of life to us (for love
To know thy Scriptures tells us, we are wrought
     In thy other book) pray for us there
     That what they have misdone
Or mis-said, we to that may not adhere;
Their zeal may be our sin. Lord let us run
Mean ways, and call them stars, but not the sun.

XIV

And whilst this universal choir,
That Church in triumph, this in warfare here,
  Warmed with one all-partaking fire   120
Of love, that none be lost, which cost thee dear,
     Prays ceaselessly, and thou hearken too,
     (Since to be gracious
Our task is treble, to pray, bear, and do)
Hear this prayer Lord, O Lord deliver us
From trusting in those prayers, though poured out thus.

XV

From being anxious, or secure,
Dead clods of sadness, or light squibs of mirth,
  From thinking, that great courts immure
All, or no happiness, or that this earth   130
     Is only for our prison framed,
     Or that thou art covetous
To them whom thou lov'st, or that they are maimed
From reaching this world's sweet, who seek thee thus,
With all their might, Good Lord deliver us.

XVI

From needing danger, to be good,
From owing thee yesterday's tears today,
  From trusting so much to thy blood,
That in that hope, we wound our soul away,

From bribing thee with alms, to excuse   140
　　Some sin more burdenous,
From light affecting, in religion, news,
From thinking us all soul, neglecting thus
Our mutual duties, Lord deliver us.

XVII

From tempting Satan to tempt us,
By our connivance, or slack company,
　　From measuring ill by vicious,
Neglecting to choke sin's spawn, vanity,
　　　　From indiscreet humility,
　　　　Which might be scandalous,   150
And cast reproach on Christianity,
From being spies, or to spies pervious,
From thirst, or scorn of fame, deliver us.

XVIII

Deliver us for thy descent
Into the Virgin, whose womb was a place
　　Of middle kind; and thou being sent
To ungracious us, stayed'st at her full of grace,
　　　　And through thy poor birth, where first thou
　　　　Glorified'st poverty,
And yet soon after riches didst allow,   160
By accepting Kings' gifts in the Epiphany,
Deliver, and make us, to both ways free.

XIX

And through that bitter agony,
Which is still the agony of pious wits,
　　Disputing what distorted thee,
And interrupted evenness, with fits,
　　　　And through thy free confession
　　　　Though thereby they were then
Made blind, so that thou mightst from them have gone,
Good Lord deliver us, and teach us when   170
We may not, and we may blind unjust men.

XX

Through thy submitting all, to blows
Thy face, thy clothes to spoil, thy fame to scorn,
  All ways, which rage, or justice knows,
And by which thou couldst show, that thou wast born,
      And through thy gallant humbleness
        Which thou in death didst show,
Dying before thy soul they could express,
Deliver us from death, by dying so,
To this world, ere this world do bid us go.   180

XXI

When senses, which thy soldiers are,
We arm against thee, and they fight for sin,
  When want, sent but to tame, doth war
And work despair a breach to enter in,
      When plenty, God's image, and seal
        Makes us idolatrous,
And love it, not him, whom it should reveal,
When we are moved to seem religious
Only to vent wit, Lord deliver us.

XXII

In churches, when the infirmity   190
Of him that speaks, diminishes the Word,
  When magistrates do mis-apply
To us, as we judge, lay or ghostly sword,
      When plague, which is thine angel, reigns,
        Or wars, thy champions sway,
When heresy, thy second deluge, gains;
In th' hour of death, th' eve of last judgement day,
Deliver us from the sinister way.

XXIII

Hear us, O hear us Lord; to thee
A sinner is more music, when he prays,   200
  Than spheres, or angels' praises be,
In panegyric alleluias,
      Hear us, for till thou hear us, Lord

We know not what to say.
Thine ear to our sighs, tears, thoughts gives voice and word.
O thou who Satan heard'st in Job's sick day,
Hear thyself now, for thou in us dost pray

XXIV

That we may change to evenness
This intermitting aguish piety,
   That snatching cramps of wickedness   210
And apoplexies of fast sin, may die;
      That music of thy promises,
       Not threats in thunder may
Awaken us to our just offices;
What in thy book, thou dost, or creatures say,
That we may hear, Lord hear us, when we pray.

XXV

That our ears' sickness we may cure,
And rectify those labyrinths aright,
   That we by hearkening, not procure
Our praise, nor others' dispraise so invite,   220
      That we get not a slipperiness,
       And senselessly decline,
From hearing bold wits jest at kings' excess,
To admit the like of majesty divine,
That we may lock our ears, Lord open thine.

XXVI

That living law, the magistrate,
Which to give us, and make us physic, doth
   Our vices often aggravate,
That preachers taxing sin, before her growth,
      That Satan, and envenomed men   230
       Which well, if we starve, dine,
When they do most accuse us, may see then
Us, to amendment, hear them; thee decline;
That we may open our ears, Lord lock thine.

XXVII

That learning, thine ambassador,
From thine allegiance we never tempt,
  That beauty, paradise's flower
For physic made, from poison be exempt,
        That wit, born apt, high good to do,
          By dwelling lazily   240
On Nature's nothing, be not nothing too,
That our affections kill us not, nor die,
Hear us, weak echoes, O thou ear, and cry.

XXVIII

Son of God hear us, and since thou
By taking our blood, owest it us again,
  Gain to thy self, or us allow;
And let not both us and thy self be slain;
        O Lamb of God, which took'st our sin
          Which could not stick to thee,
O let it not return to us again,   250
But patient and physician being free,
As sin is nothing, let it nowhere be.

To Mrs Magdalen Herbert: of St Mary Magdalene

Her of your name, whose fair inheritance
  Bethina was, and jointure Magdalo:
An active faith so highly did advance,
  That she once knew, more than the Church did know,
The Resurrection; so much good there is
  Delivered of her, that some Fathers be
Loth to believe one woman could do this;
  But think these Magdalenes were two or three.
Increase their number, Lady, and their fame:
  To their devotion, add your innocence;   10
Take so much of th' example, as of the name;
  The latter half; and in some recompense
That they did harbour Christ himself, a guest,
  Harbour these hymns, to his dear name addressed. J.D.

La Corona

I

Deign at my hands this crown of prayer and praise,
Weaved in my low devout melancholy,
Thou which of good, hast, yea art treasury,
All changing unchanged Ancient of days,
But do not, with a vile crown of frail bays,
Reward my muse's white sincerity,
But what thy thorny crown gained, that give me,
A crown of glory, which doth flower always;
The ends crown our works, but thou crown'st our ends,
For, at our end begins our endless rest,   10
This first last end, now zealously possessed
With a strong sober thirst, my soul attends.
'Tis time that heart and voice be lifted high,
Salvation to all that will is nigh.

2 *ANNUNCIATION*

Salvation to all that will is nigh,
That all, which always is all everywhere,
Which cannot sin, and yet all sins must bear,
Which cannot die, yet cannot choose but die,
Lo, faithful Virgin, yields himself to lie
In prison, in thy womb; and though he there
Can take no sin, nor thou give, yet he 'will wear
Taken from thence, flesh, which death's force may try.
Ere by the spheres time was created, thou
Wast in his mind, who is thy son, and brother,   10
Whom thou conceiv'st, conceived; yea thou art now
Thy maker's maker, and thy father's mother,
Thou' hast light in dark; and shutt'st in little room,
Immensity cloistered in thy dear womb.

3 *NATIVITY*

Immensity cloistered in thy dear womb,
Now leaves his well-beloved imprisonment,
There he hath made himself to his intent
Weak enough, now into our world to come;

But oh, for thee, for him, hath th' inn no room?
Yet lay him in this stall, and from the orient,
Stars, and wisemen will travel to prevent
Th' effect of Herod's jealous general doom.
See'st thou, my soul, with thy faith's eyes, how he
Which fills all place, yet none holds him, doth lie?   10
Was not his pity towards thee wondrous high,
That would have need to be pitied by thee?
Kiss him, and with him into Egypt go,
With his kind mother, who partakes thy woe.

4 *TEMPLE*

With his kind mother who partakes thy woe,
Joseph turn back; see where your child doth sit,
Blowing, yea blowing out those sparks of wit,
Which himself on those Doctors did bestow;
The Word but lately could not speak, and lo
It suddenly speaks wonders, whence comes it,
That all which was, and all which should be writ,
A shallow seeming child, should deeply know?
His godhead was not soul to his manhood,
Nor had time mellowed him to this ripeness,   10
But as for one which hath a long task, 'tis good,
With the sun to begin his business,
He in his age's morning thus began
By miracles exceeding power of man,

5 *CRUCIFYING*

By miracles exceeding power of man,
He faith in some, envy in some begat,
For, what weak spirits admire, ambitious hate;
In both affections many to him ran,
But oh! the worst are most, they will and can,
Alas, and do, unto the immaculate,
Whose creature Fate is, now prescribe a fate,
Measuring self-life's infinity to a span,
Nay to an inch. Lo, where condemned he
Bears his own cross, with pain, yet by and by   10
When it bears him, he must bear more and die.
Now thou art lifted up, draw me to thee,

And at thy death giving such liberal dole,
Moist, with one drop of thy blood, my dry soul.

6 RESURRECTION

Moist with one drop of thy blood, my dry soul
Shall (though she now be in extreme degree
Too stony hard, and yet too fleshly,) be
Freed by that drop, from being starved, hard, or foul,
And life, by this death abled, shall control
Death, whom thy death slew; nor shall to me
Fear of first or last death, bring misery,
If in thy little book my name thou enrol,
Flesh in that long sleep is not putrefied,
But made that there, of which, and for which 'twas;   10
Nor can by other means be glorified.
May then sin's sleep, and death's soon from me pass,
That waked from both, I again risen may
Salute the last, and everlasting day.

7 ASCENSION

Salute the last and everlasting day,
Joy at the uprising of this sun, and son,
Ye whose just tears, or tribulation
Have purely washed, or burnt your drossy clay;
Behold the Highest, parting hence away,
Lightens the dark clouds, which he treads upon,
Nor doth he by ascending, show alone,
But first he, and he first enters the way.
O strong ram, which hast battered heaven for me,
Mild lamb, which with thy blood, hast marked the path;   10
Bright torch, which shin'st, that I the way may see,
Oh, with thine own blood quench thine own just wrath,
And if thy holy Spirit, my Muse did raise,
Deign at my hands this crown of prayer and praise.

HOLY SONNETS

1

As due by many titles I resign
Myself to thee, O God, first I was made
By thee, and for thee, and when I was decayed
Thy blood bought that, the which before was thine,
I am thy son, made with thyself to shine,
Thy servant, whose pains thou hast still repaid,
Thy sheep, thine image, and, till I betrayed
Myself, a temple of thy Spirit divine;
Why doth the devil then usurp in me?
Why doth he steal, nay ravish that's thy right?   10
Except thou rise and for thine own work fight,
Oh I shall soon despair, when I do see
That thou lov'st mankind well, yet wilt not choose me,
And Satan hates me, yet is loth to lose me.

2

Oh my black soul! now thou art summoned
By sickness, death's herald, and champion;
Thou art like a pilgrim, which abroad hath done
Treason, and durst not turn to whence he is fled,
Or like a thief, which till death's doom be read,
Wisheth himself delivered from prison;
But damned and haled to execution,
Wisheth that still he might be imprisoned;
Yet grace, if thou repent, thou canst not lack;
But who shall give thee that grace to begin?   10
Oh make thyself with holy mourning black,
And red with blushing, as thou art with sin;
Or wash thee in Christ's blood, which hath this might
That being red, it dyes red souls to white.

3

This is my play's last scene, here heavens appoint
My pilgrimage's last mile; and my race
Idly, yet quickly run, hath this last pace,
My span's last inch, my minute's latest point,
And gluttonous death will instantly unjoint
My body, and soul, and I shall sleep a space,
But my'ever-waking part shall see that face,
Whose fear already shakes my every joint:
Then, as my soul, to heaven her first seat, takes flight,
And earth-born body, in the earth shall dwell,   10
So, fall my sins, that all may have their right,
To where they are bred, and would press me, to hell.
Impute me righteous, thus purged of evil,
For thus I leave the world, the flesh, the devil.

4

At the round earth's imagined corners, blow
Your trumpets, angels, and arise, arise
From death, you numberless infinities
Of souls, and to your scattered bodies go,
All whom the flood did, and fire shall o'erthrow,
All whom war, dearth, age, agues, tyrannies,
Despair, law, chance, hath slain, and you whose eyes,
Shall behold God, and never taste death's woe.
But let them sleep, Lord, and me mourn a space,
For, if above all these, my sins abound,   10
'Tis late to ask abundance of thy grace,
When we are there; here on this lowly ground,
Teach me how to repent; for that's as good
As if thou hadst sealed my pardon, with thy blood.

5

If poisonous minerals, and if that tree,
Whose fruit threw death on else immortal us,
If lecherous goats, if serpents envious
Cannot be damned; alas, why should I be?
Why should intent or reason, born in me,
Make sins, else equal, in me more heinous?
And mercy being easy, and glorious

To God, in his stern wrath, why threatens he?
But who am I, that dare dispute with thee
O God? Oh! of thine only worthy blood,   10
And my tears, make a heavenly Lethean flood,
And drown in it my sin's black memory;
That thou remember them, some claim as debt,
I think it mercy, if thou wilt forget.

6

Death be not proud, though some have called thee
Mighty and dreadful, for, thou art not so,
For, those, whom thou think'st, thou dost overthrow,
Die not, poor death, nor yet canst thou kill me;
From rest and sleep, which but thy pictures be,
Much pleasure, then from thee, much more must flow,
And soonest our best men with thee do go,
Rest of their bones, and soul's delivery.
Thou art slave to fate, chance, kings, and desperate men,
And dost with poison, war, and sickness dwell,   10
And poppy, or charms can make us sleep as well,
And better than thy stroke; why swell'st thou then?
One short sleep past, we wake eternally,
And death shall be no more, Death thou shalt die.

To E. of D. with Six Holy Sonnets

See Sir, how as the sun's hot masculine flame
    Begets strange creatures on Nile's dirty slime,
    In me, your fatherly yet lusty rhyme
(For, these songs are their fruits) have wrought the same;
But though the engendering force from whence they came
    Be strong enough, and nature do admit
    Seven to be born at once, I send as yet
But six; they say, the seventh hath still some maim.
    I choose your judgement, which the same degree
    Doth with her sister, your invention, hold,   10
As fire these drossy rhymes to purify,
    Or as elixir, to change them to gold;

You are that alchemist which always had
Wit, whose one spark could make good things of bad.

*   *   *

7

Spit in my face you Jews, and pierce my side,
Buffet, and scoff, scourge, and crucify me,
For I have sinned, and sinned, and only he,
Who could do no iniquity, hath died:
But by my death cannot be satisfied
My sins, which pass the Jews' impiety:
They killed once an inglorious man, but I
Crucify him daily, being now glorified.
Oh let me then, his strange love still admire:
Kings pardon, but he bore our punishment.   10
And Jacob came clothed in vile harsh attire
But to supplant, and with gainful intent:
God clothed himself in vile man's flesh, that so
He might be weak enough to suffer woe.

8

Why are we by all creatures waited on?
Why do the prodigal elements supply
Life and food to me, being more pure than I,
Simple, and further from corruption?
Why brook'st thou, ignorant horse, subjection?
Why dost thou bull, and boar so sillily
Dissemble weakness, and by'one man's stroke die,
Whose whole kind, you might swallow and feed upon?
Weaker I am, woe is me, and worse than you,
You have not sinned, nor need be timorous.   10
But wonder at a greater wonder, for to us
Created nature doth these things subdue,
But their Creator, whom sin, nor nature tied,
For us, his creatures, and his foes, hath died.

9

What if this present were the world's last night?
Mark in my heart, O soul, where thou dost dwell,

The picture of Christ crucified, and tell
Whether that countenance can thee affright,
Tears in his eyes quench the amazing light,
Blood fills his frowns, which from his pierced head fell,
And can that tongue adjudge thee unto hell,
Which prayed forgiveness for his foes' fierce spite?
No, no; but as in my idolatry
I said to all my profane mistresses,   10
Beauty, of pity, foulness only is
A sign of rigour: so I say to thee,
To wicked spirits are horrid shapes assigned,
This beauteous form assures a piteous mind.

10

Batter my heart, three-personed God; for, you
As yet but knock, breathe, shine, and seek to mend;
That I may rise, and stand, o'erthrow me, and bend
Your force, to break, blow, burn, and make me new.
I, like an usurped town, to another due,
Labour to admit you, but oh, to no end,
Reason your viceroy in me, me should defend,
But is captived, and proves weak or untrue,
Yet dearly'I love you, and would be loved fain,
But am betrothed unto your enemy,   10
Divorce me, untie, or break that knot again,
Take me to you, imprison me, for I
Except you enthral me, never shall be free,
Nor ever chaste, except you ravish me.

11

Wilt thou love God, as he thee? then digest,
My soul, this wholesome meditation,
How God the Spirit, by angels waited on
In heaven, doth make his temple in thy breast.
The Father having begot a Son most blessed,
And still begetting, (for he ne'er begun)
Hath deigned to choose thee by adoption,
Coheir to' his glory, 'and Sabbath's endless rest;
And as a robbed man, which by search doth find
His stol'n stuff sold, must lose or buy it again: 10

The Son of glory came down, and was slain,
Us whom he had made, and Satan stol'n, to unbind.
'Twas much, that man was made like God before,
But, that God should be made like man, much more.

12

Father, part of his double interest
Unto thy kingdom, thy Son gives to me,
His jointure in the knotty Trinity
He keeps, and gives me his death's conquest.
This Lamb, whose death with life the world hath blessed,
Was from the world's beginning slain, and he
Hath made two wills, which with the legacy
Of his and thy kingdom, do thy sons invest.
Yet such are thy laws, that men argue yet
Whether a man those statutes can fulfil;   10
None doth, but thy all-healing grace and Spirit
Revive again what law and letter kill.
Thy law's abridgement, and thy last command
Is all but love; oh let that last will stand!

13

Thou hast made me, and shall thy work decay?
Repair me now, for now mine end doth haste,
I run to death, and death meets me as fast.
And all my pleasures are like yesterday,
I dare not move my dim eyes any way,
Despair behind, and death before doth cast
Such terror, and my feebled flesh doth waste
By sin in it, which it towards hell doth weigh;
Only thou art above, and when towards thee
By thy leave I can look, I rise again;   10
But our old subtle foe so tempteth me,
That not one hour I can myself sustain;
Thy grace may wing me to prevent his art,
And thou like adamant draw mine iron heart.

14

O might those sighs and tears return again
Into my breast and eyes, which I have spent,

That I might in this holy discontent
Mourn with some fruit, as I have mourned in vain;
In mine idolatry what showers of rain
Mine eyes did waste! what griefs my heart did rent!
That sufferance was my sin, now I repent;
Because I did suffer I must suffer pain.
Th' hydroptic drunkard, and night-scouting thief,
The itchy lecher, and self tickling proud
Have the remembrance of past joys, for relief
Of coming ills. To poor me is allowed
No ease; for, long, yet vehement grief hath been
The effect and cause, the punishment and sin.

15

I am a little world made cunningly
Of elements, and an angelic sprite,
But black sin hath betrayed to endless night
My world's both parts, and, oh, both parts must die.
You which beyond that heaven which was most high
Have found new spheres, and of new lands can write,
Pour new seas in mine eyes, that so I might
Drown my world with my weeping earnestly,
Or wash it, if it must be drowned no more:
But oh it must be burnt; alas the fire
Of lust and envy have burnt it heretofore,
And made it fouler; let their flames retire,
And burn me O Lord, with a fiery zeal
Of thee and thy house, which doth in eating heal.

16

If faithful souls be alike glorified
As angels, then my father's soul doth see,
And adds this even to full felicity,
That valiantly I hell's wide mouth o'erstride:
But if our minds to these souls be descried
By circumstances, and by signs that be
Apparent in us, not immediately,
How shall my mind's white truth by them be tried?
They see idolatrous lovers weep and mourn,
And vile blasphemous conjurers to call

On Jesus' name, and pharisaical
Dissemblers feign devotion. Then turn
O pensive soul, to God, for he knows best
Thy true grief, for he put it in my breast.

17

Since she whom I loved hath paid her last debt
To nature, and to hers, and my good is dead,
And her soul early into heaven ravished,
Wholly in heavenly things my mind is set.
Here the admiring her my mind did whet
To seek thee God; so streams do show the head,
But though I have found thee, and thou my thirst hast fed,
A holy thirsty dropsy melts me yet.
But why should I beg more love, when as thou
Dost woo my soul, for hers offering all thine: 10
And dost not only fear lest I allow
My love to saints and angels, things divine,
But in thy tender jealousy dost doubt
Lest the world, flesh, yea Devil put thee out.

18

Show me dear Christ, thy spouse, so bright and clear.
What, is it she, which on the other shore
Goes richly painted? or which robbed and tore
Laments and mourns in Germany and here?
Sleeps she a thousand, then peeps up one year?
Is she self truth and errs? now new, now outwore?
Doth she, and did she, and shall she evermore
On one, on seven, or on no hill appear?
Dwells she with us, or like adventuring knights
First travail we to seek and then make love?   10
Betray kind husband thy spouse to our sights,
And let mine amorous soul court thy mild dove,
Who is most true, and pleasing to thee, then
When she' is embraced and open to most men.

19

Oh, to vex me, contraries meet in one:
Inconstancy unnaturally hath begot

A constant habit; that when I would not
I change in vows, and in devotion.
As humorous is my contrition
As my profane love, and as soon forgot:
As riddlingly distempered, cold and hot,
As praying, as mute; as infinite, as none.
I durst not view heaven yesterday; and today
In prayers, and flattering speeches I court God: 10
Tomorrow I quake with true fear of his rod.
So my devout fits come and go away
Like a fantastic ague: save that here
Those are my best days, when I shake with fear.

Good Friday, 1613. Riding Westward

Let man's soul be a sphere, and then, in this,
The intelligence that moves, devotion is,
And as the other spheres, by being grown
Subject to foreign motions, lose their own,
And being by others hurried every day,
Scarce in a year their natural form obey:
Pleasure or business, so, our souls admit
For their first mover, and are whirled by it.
Hence is't, that I am carried towards the west
This day, when my soul's form bends toward the east.   10
There I should see a sun, by rising set,
And by that setting endless day beget;
But that Christ on this Cross, did rise and fall,
Sin had eternally benighted all.
Yet dare I' almost be glad, I do not see
That spectacle of too much weight for me.
Who sees God's face, that is self life, must die;
What a death were it then to see God die?
It made his own lieutenant Nature shrink,
It made his footstool crack, and the sun wink.   20
Could I behold those hands which span the poles,
And tune all spheres at once, pierced with those holes?
Could I behold that endless height which is
Zenith to us, and to'our antipodes,

Humbled below us? or that blood which is
The seat of all our souls, if not of his,
Made dirt of dust, or that flesh which was worn,
By God, for his apparel, ragged, and torn?
If on these things I durst not look, durst I
Upon his miserable mother cast mine eye,   30
Who was God's partner here, and furnished thus
Half of that sacrifice, which ransomed us?
Though these things, as I ride, be from mine eye,
They are present yet unto my memory,
For that looks towards them; and thou look'st towards me,
O Saviour, as thou hang'st upon the tree;
I turn my back to thee, but to receive
Corrections, till thy mercies bid thee leave.
O think me worth thine anger, punish me,
Burn off my rusts, and my deformity,   40
Restore thine image, so much, by thy grace,
That thou mayst know me, and I'll turn my face.

A Hymn to Christ, at the Author's last going into Germany

In what torn ship soever I embark,
That ship shall be my emblem of thy ark;
What sea soever swallow me, that flood
Shall be to me an emblem of thy blood;
Though thou with clouds of anger do disguise
Thy face; yet through that mask I know those eyes,
   Which, though they turn away sometimes,
     They never will despise.

I sacrifice this Island unto thee,
And all whom I loved there, and who loved me;   10
When I have put our seas 'twixt them and me,
Put thou thy sea betwixt my sins and thee.
As the tree's sap doth seek the root below
In winter, in my winter now I go,
   Where none but thee, th' eternal root
     Of true love I may know.

Nor thou nor thy religion dost control,
The amorousness of an harmonious soul,
But thou wouldst have that love thyself: as thou
Art jealous, Lord, so I am jealous now,   20
Thou lov'st not, till from loving more, thou free
My soul; who ever gives, takes liberty:
   O, if thou car'st not whom I love
     Alas, thou lov'st not me.

Seal then this bill of my divorce to all,
On whom those fainter beams of love did fall;
Marry those loves, which in youth scattered be
On fame, wit, hopes (false mistresses) to thee.
Churches are best for prayer, that have least light:
To see God only, I go out of sight: 30
   And to 'scape stormy days, I choose
     An everlasting night.

Hymn to God my God, in my Sickness

Since I am coming to that holy room,
  Where, with thy choir of saints for evermore,
I shall be made thy music; as I come
  I tune the instrument here at the door,
  And what I must do then, think now before.

Whilst my physicians by their love are grown
  Cosmographers, and I their map, who lie
Flat on this bed, that by them may be shown
  That this is my south-west discovery
  Per fretum febris, by these straits to die,

I joy, that in these straits, I see my west;
  For, though their currents yield return to none,
What shall my west hurt me? As west and east
  In all flat maps (and I am one) are one,
  So death doth touch the resurrection.

Is the Pacific Sea my home? Or are
   The eastern riches? Is Jerusalem?
Anyan, and Magellan, and Gibraltar,
   All straits, and none but straits, are ways to them,
   Whether where Japhet dwelt, or Cham, or Shem.   20

We think that Paradise and Calvary,
   Christ's Cross, and Adam's tree, stood in one place;
Look Lord, and find both Adams met in me;
   As the first Adam's sweat surrounds my face,
   May the last Adam's blood my soul embrace.

So, in his purple wrapped receive me Lord,
   By these his thorns give me his other crown;
And as to others' souls I preached thy word,
   Be this my text, my sermon to mine own,
   Therefore that he may raise the Lord throws down.   30

A Hymn to God the Father

I

Wilt thou forgive that sin where I begun,
   Which is my sin, though it were done before?
Wilt thou forgive those sins, through which I run,
   And do them still: though still I do deplore?
     When thou hast done, thou hast not done,
       For, I have more.

II

Wilt thou forgive that sin by which I have won
   Others to sin? and, made my sin their door?
Wilt thou forgive that sin which I did shun
   A year, or two: but wallowed in, a score?   10
     When thou has done, thou hast not done,
       For I have more.

III

I have a sin of fear, that when I have spun
My last thread, I shall perish on the shore;
Swear by thyself, that at my death thy Sun
Shall shine as it shines now, and heretofore;
And, having done that, thou hast done,
I fear no more.

Notes

1 *Satire 1* (*'Away thou fondling motley humourist'*). Date: probably 1593. Partly based on Horace, *Satires*, I. ix.

l. 1. *fondling motley humourist*. Foolish, changeable, whimsical person.

l. 2. *chest*. Donne's study at Lincoln's Inn.

l. 6. *the Philosopher*. Aristotle.

l. 7. *jolly*. Arrogant, overbearing.

l. 18. *parcel gilt*. Partly gilded.   *with forty dead men's pay*. A common swindle was for officers to keep dead men's names on the muster roll and draw their pay.

l. 22. *blue coats*. Servants wearing the blue livery of lower retainers.

l. 27. *monstrous . . . Puritan*. A joke: the 'humourist' is like a Puritan in punctilious conduct, but addicted to ceremony, which Puritans condemned.

l. 30. *broker*. Pawnbroker.

2 l. 36. *Jointures*. Marriage settlements.

l. 46. *beast's skin*. See Gen. 3: 21.

l. 55. *black feathers . . . musk-colour hose*. Apparently fashionable around 1593. 'Musk' was dark brown.

l. 58. *Infanta of London, heir to an India*. The richest heiress in London, whose wealth matches that of the Indies. No particular heiress seems intended. 'Infanta' was properly a Spanish princess.

l. 68. *the wall*. Taking the wall side of the footway, out of range of splashes, implied social superiority.

3 l. 74. *smacks*. i.e. his lips.

ll. 80–1. *horse . . . elephant . . . ape*. Well-known performing animals in Donne's London, trained to bow at Queen Elizabeth's name but not the King of Spain's.

l. 88. *drinking*. The usual word for smoking.

l. 97. *pink, panes*. Decorative eyelets and panels.

4 *Satire 2* (*'Sir; though (I thank God for it)'*). Date: probably 1594. The lawyer-poet Coscus has not been identified. An anonymous sonnet sequence *Zepheria* using legal conceits appeared in 1594.

l. 12. *prompts*. Helps his illiterate neighbour to read the 'neck-verse' and claim benefit of clergy.

4 l. 20. *Pistolets*. A pun: firearms or Spanish coins.

l. 32. *dildoes*. Objects used as substitutes for an erect penis.

l. 37. *canonists*. Canon-lawyers.

5 l. 59. *Sclavonians*. Slavs; speakers of barbarous tongues.

l. 66. *bill*. A pun: halberd (watchman's weapon) or legal document.

l. 68. *suretyship*. Accepting responsibility for another's debt; a blameless reason for imprisonment.

l. 71. *wring*. Force a way through the crowd in court.

l. 78. *Mount*. Mount St Michael, Land's End.

6 l. 86. *pulling prime*. Playing primero, a kind of poker.

l. 96. *power and glory clause*. The doxology ('For thine is the kingdom . . .') was not in the Latin version of the Lord's Prayer Luther would have used as a friar, but he added it in his German translation.

l. 101. *vouched texts*. Biblical passages cited by controversialists to support arguments.

l. 104. *not built, nor burnt*. The woods have not been used for estate purposes but sold to profit the lawyers.

l. 107. *means bless*. Moderation is a blessing.

ll. 111–12. *my words . . . laws*. This satire infringes no law, despite the current spate of legislation.

Satire 3('Kind pity chokes my spleen'). Date: probably 1594 or 1595. Not the poem of a convinced Catholic. Donne's brother Henry, imprisoned for harbouring a priest, died in Newgate in 1593. This may have impelled Donne to reconsider his religious allegiance.

l. 1. *spleen*. Seat of laughter in Elizabethan physiology.

7 l. 7. *blinded*. Without the light of the Gospel; so too 'blind', l. 12.

l. 9. *them*. The virtuous heathen (e.g. Socrates). Whether they would be saved was much debated.

l. 13. *imputed faith*. Credited to them as faith, so earning salvation—an un-Protestant idea, which would have scandalized Luther and Calvin.

l. 17. *mutinous*. The Dutch had been in revolt against their Spanish Catholic overlords since 1568.

l. 24. *Children*. See Dan. 3: 11–30.

l. 25. *limbecks*. Alembics, in which distilled fluid resembles sweat.

l. 35. *to be quit*. As quittance (reward) for your soul.

8 l. 48. *statecloth*. Canopy over the throne. Courtiers made obeisance to it even in the monarch's absence.

l. 50. *Geneva*. Home of Calvinism.

l. 62. *values*. A fine.

l. 77. *protest*. Be a Protestant.

9 l. 92. *vicars*. God's agents.

ll. 96–7. *Philip . . . Gregory . . . Harry . . . Martin*. Philip II of Spain; Pope Gregory XIV; Henry VIII, responsible for the English Reformation; Martin Luther.

Satire 4 ('Well; I may now receive'). Date: probably 1597. Partly based on Horace, *Satires* I. ix.

l. 1. *receive*. i.e. the sacrament.

l. 10. *Statute's curse*. Penalty laid down by anti-Catholic Statute of 1580 for attending Mass.

10 l. 22. *Guiana's rarities*. Said by Raleigh in the description of his 1595 voyage to include cannibals and Amazons.

l. 24. *Danes' Massacre*. Carried out on King Ethelred's orders in 1012.

l. 33. *tufftaffaty*. Tufted taffeta.

l. 34. *rash*. Silk twill.

l. 48. *Jovius . . . Surius*. Catholic historians condemned for innaccuracy by Protestants.

11 l. 54. *Calepine's Dictionary*. An eleven-language dictionary, published in 1590.

l. 55. *Beza*. 1519–1605, Calvinist theologian and translator of the Bible.

l. 59. *Panurge*. Character in Rabelais.

ll. 67–8. *Not alone . . . is*. An allusion to Cato's saying, recorded by Cicero, that he was 'never less alone than when alone'.

l. 68. *Spartans' fashion*. According to Plutarch, the Spartans made slaves drunk so young men would become disgusted with drunkenness.

l. 69. *taste*. Retain its efficacy.

l. 70. *Aretine's pictures*. A reference to notoriously obscene depictions of the sex act by Giulio Romano, illustrating Aretino's sonnets.

l. 84. *he follows me*. The speaker, deliberately misunderstanding the courtier's affected use of 'your' as a kind of indefinite article, points to his French servant.

11 l. 86. *grogaram.* A French silk cloth.

12 l. 97. *Holinsheds . . . Halls . . . Stows.* Raphael Holinshed, Edward Hall, and John Stow all published chronicles of England, containing much imaginary material.

l. 104. *licence.* The granting of monopolies to courtiers for the import, export, or sale of commodities was a contemporary scandal.

l. 106. *span-counter . . . blow-point.* Games rather like marbles, played with counters and the 'points' (tags) that fastened hose to doublet.

l. 112. *Gallo-Belgicus.* An annual register of news, *Mercurius Gallo-Belgicus,* begun 1588.

l. 114. *Spaniards . . . Amiens.* From Armada year, 1588, to Mar. 1597 when the Spaniards took Amiens.

l. 123. *entailed.* Already allocated to future holders.

l. 126. *Dunkirkers.* Pirates from Dunkirk, an infamous haven.

l. 129. *Circe's prisoners.* In Homer, *Odyssey* x.

13 l. 158. *who dreamed he saw hell.* Dante.

l. 169. *waxen garden.* An Italian waxwork garden, exhibited in London.

l. 171. *Presence.* The presence chamber at Court.

14 l. 175. *mews.* Stables.

l. 176. *Balloon.* A kind of volley-ball.

l. 186. *Cheapside books.* Clothiers' ledgers, recording customers' debts.

l. 189. *cochineal.* An expensive cargo prized by privateers preying on the Spanish South American fleet.

l. 197. *Heraclitus.* Called the weeping philosopher.   *Macrine.* No specific courtier seems intended here.

l. 199. *moschite.* Mosque.

l. 204. *Dürer's rules.* Anatomical proportions worked out by Albrecht Dürer and published in 1528.

15 l. 216. *Pursuivant.* Government officer who searched out Catholics.

l. 233. *Ascaparts.* Ascapart was a giant in the romance of Bevis of Hampton.

l. 242. *Maccabees' modesty.* See 2 Macc. 15: 38. The books of Maccabees were not thought 'canonical' (genuinely biblical) by Protestants.

Satire 5 ('Thou shalt not laugh'). Date: probably 1598. Addressed to Donne's employer Sir Thomas Egerton, Lord Keeper, who was investigating the extortions of legal officials ('officers').

l. 2. *he.* Castiglione, author of *The Courtier.*

16 l. 9. *all things be in all*. A Paracelsian doctrine: all matter contains common elements.

l. 39. *gamesters*. Gamblers (i.e. suitors).

l. 42. *Angelica*. In Ariosto's *Orlando Furioso*, Angelica escapes while rival suitors fight for her—like disputed estates vanishing in legal fees.

l. 44. *letter, or fee*. Bribery or corruption.

17 l. 56. *only who have*. See Matt. 25: 29.

l. 57. *Judges are gods*. See Ps. 82: 2, 6.

l. 59. *angels*. A pun: gold coins or the heavenly orders ('Dominations', etc.).

l. 63. *so 'tis*. That's how things are.

l. 66. *pursuivant*. See note to Satire 4, l. 216.

l. 79. *barest thou*. Take off your hat.

l. 82. *these*. Legal officials.

l. 83. *Urim and Thummim*. Hebrew: 'lights and perfections'. See Exod. 28: 30.

18 l. 85. *Great Carrack*. *Madre de Dios*, a Spanish ship with a rich cargo of pepper, was captured in 1592.

l. 86. *leese*. Lose.

l. 87. *Haman*. Not the biblical Haman but an unidentified antiquary ('Hammond' in some MSS) whose collection apparently fetched little.

l. 90. *swimming dog*. In Aesop, the dog opened its mouth to grab the meat carried by its own reflection, so lost the meat.

19 *Elegy 1: The Bracelet*. Date: probably 1593.

l. 9. *angels*. English gold coins.

l. 10. *solder*. Used to patch damaged coins.

l. 23. *rot*. Syphilis.

20 l. 31. *pistolets*. Spanish gold coins.

l. 39. *Visit all countries*. Spain used gold from the Americas for religious warfare and influence-seeking in northern Europe, destabilizing national economies (ll. 40–2).

l. 44–5. *chemics . . . soul*. Alchemists tried to extract the 'soul' of a mineral, to convert it to gold.

l. 59. *conjurer*. An astrologer, whose diagrams would divide the heavens into compartments according to the zodiacal signs and planets, allocating each to certain trades and professions, some disreputable. Astrologers were frequently consulted about lost property.

21 l. 78. *Virtues, Powers, and Principalities.* Angelic ranks above angels and archangels. Donne punningly alludes to gold's control over earthly virtue and authority.

22 *Elegy 2: To his Mistress Going to Bed.* Date: 1593–6.

l. 7. *breastplate.* Jewelled stomacher.

l. 9. *chime.* Of her chiming watch.

l. 11. *busk.* Corset.

l. 12. *stand.* Word-play: (*a*) remain; (*b*) have an erection (see ll. 4 and 24).

l. 21. *Mahomet's paradise.* Contained beautiful nymphs or 'houris'.

23 l. 36. *Atlanta's balls.* Golden apples thrown before Atlanta by Hippomenes to distract her (Ovid, *Metamorphoses* x).

l. 42. *imputed grace.* In Calvinist theology, the grace by which Christ's merits were 'imputed' to the elect.

l. 46. *Here is no penance, much less innocence.* Some MSS and the first printed text (1669) read, more kindly, 'There is no penance due to innocence'.

l. 48. *than a man.* Word-play: (*a*) than a man wears; (*b*) than a man, covering you.

Elegy 3: Jealousy. Date: 1593–6. Takes some ideas from Ovid, *Amores* I. iv. 15–32 and 51–4.

l. 4. *sere-bark.* Dry encrustation.

24 l. 33. *Thames' right side.* Southwark, an unruly district of brothels and playhouses.

Elegy 4: The Anagram. Date: 1593–6. The paradoxical 'praise of ugliness' was a fashion imported from Italy.

25 l. 35. *husbands.* Husbandmen, farmers.

l. 41. *When Belgia's cities, the round countries drown.* When Dutch cities open the dikes and flood the land around for defensive purposes.

l. 50. *tympany.* Wind, causing stomach swelling.

l. 53. *dildoes, bedstaves . . . velvet glass.* Instruments used by women for masturbating.

l. 54. *Joseph.* Repelled Potiphar's wife's approaches in Gen. 39.

Elegy 5: Change. Date: 1593–6.

l. 1. *faith . . . good works.* Key terms in the Protestant–Catholic dispute about salvation, here used jokingly of love.

l. 3. *apostasy.* Word-play: (*a*) lapse from true faith; (*b*) falling backwards, for sex.

26 l. 15. *our clogs, and their own.* Our encumbrances, and answerable only to themselves (with word-play: their own encumbrances, too).

Elegy 6: The Perfume. Date: 1593–6.

l. 2. *escapes.* Secret love affairs.

27 l. 6. *hydroptic.* Bloated; suffering from dropsy.

ll. 7–8. *glazed . . . cockatrice.* Wearing spectacles, as if to guard against the legendary cockatrice or basilisk, which killed by its look.

28 l. 52. *oppressed.* Pressing with large weights on the chest was used to make prisoners talk.

l. 67. *loathsome . . . simply alone.* The ingredients of perfume (e.g. civet from the civet cat's anal glands; musk from the musk deer) are, in themselves, repellent.

l. 69. *soon decay.* Is volatile.

l. 70. *rare.* Word-play: (*a*) tending to rarify; (*b*) precious.

Elegy 7: His Picture. Perhaps written when Donne joined up for the Cadiz expedition, 1596.

l. 4. *we.* Himself, as ghost, and his picture. ('Shadow' could mean 'portrait'.)

29 *Elegy 8: On Sir Thomas Egerton.* Date: September 1599. Egerton, elder son of Donne's employer, was killed in Ireland on 23 Aug. 1599. He had sailed with Donne on Essex's naval expedition to the Azores in 1597. Donne follows Ovid's classical example in including a funeral elegy among his love elegies.

l. 23. *children.* Egerton had three young daughters.

30 *Elegy 9 ('Oh, let me not serve so').* Date: probably 1599–1601.

l. 2. *honours' smokes.* Honorific but unpaid offices.

ll. 8–9. *shall pay|Themselves.* Making love to her will be its own reward, by contrast with the worthless rewards mentioned in ll. 1–3.

l. 9. *dead names.* Empty titles.

l. 10. *in ordinary.* Used in official titles to mean the regular, full-time holder of a post.

31 ll. 45–6. *recusant . . . excommunicate*. Recusants refused to acknow-
ledge the authority of the Church, so would not fear excommunica-
tion.

Elegy 10: Love's War. Date: proably 1599–1601. Partly based on
Ovid, *Amores* I. ix.

l. 1. *war*. Imperative: let other men wage war.

l. 3. *scrupulous*. Involving matters of right and wrong.

l. 5. *Flanders*. The Low Countries, where Spain ('the master') was
warring (perhaps justifiably, Donne implies) against her rebellious
'men' (the Netherlanders).

l. 10. *and our God of late*. The French King, Henry of Navarre,
converted to Catholicism in 1593.

l. 11. *our angels*. English gold, with which Elizabeth had backed
Henry before his conversion.

l. 17. *Spanish journeys*. Privateering voyages against the Spanish
treasure fleets.

32 l. 37. *engines*. Cannon.

Elegy 11: On his Mistress. Date: probably 1599–1601.

l. 14. *page*. The mistress-disguised-as-page motif suggests Donne's
familiarity with drama, especially Shakespeare's comedies.

33 ll. 21–3. *Boreas' . . . Orithea*: In Ovid, Boreas, the north wind, carries
off Orithea to wed. Plato, in the *Phaedrus*, suggests the girl was really
blown over a cliff and killed.

l. 37. *know thee, and know thee*. Pierce your disguise and ravish you.

l. 38. *indifferent*. Bisexual.

l. 41. *Lot's fair guests*. In Gen. 19: 4.

l. 42. *spongy hydroptic*. Referring to Holland's watery, reclaimed
terrain.

l. 46. *King*. Presumably Love. Compare 'The Ecstasy' l. 68.

34 *Elegy 12 : ('Nature's lay idiot')*. Date: probably 1599–1601.

l. 1. *Nature's lay idiot*. By nature, an uninitiated simpleton.

l. 15. *household charms, thy husband's name to teach*. Homely magic,
used by girls to identify their future husbands.

l. 20. *his*. Her husband's.

Elegy 13: Love's Progress. Date: probably 1599–1601.

l. 4. *bear-whelp*. Bears were supposed to lick newborn cubs into shape.

36 ll. 51–2. *Islands Fortunate . . . Canary*. The Fortunate Islands were identified with the Canaries, through which the 'first meridian' of longitude was thought to pass, and which yielded a light wine.

l. 58. *remora*. Legendary sucking fish, which could stop a ship.

l. 61. *Sestos and Abydos*. On opposite shores of the Hellespont, homes of Hero and Leander, the 'two lovers'.

l. 74. *symmetry*. Correspondence; ll. 77–80 spell this out.

37 l. 96. *clyster*. Enema.

Elegy 14: The Comparison. Date: 1601? This poem was probably not in the lost manuscript 'book' of thirteen elegies circulated among Donne's friends, but appears with the elegies in some MSS, and may be of similar date. It follows a sixteenth-century Italian fashion for paradox and anti-woman obscenity.

l. 10. *Sanserra's starved men*. The Protestants besieged in Sancerre in 1573. Their endurance became legendary.

l. 13. *stones in saffroned tin*. Fake gold.

l. 16. *fatal ball which fell on Ide*. The golden apple of discord, on Mount Ida.

l. 23. *chest*. The *pyxis* which in Apuleius's *Golden Ass* Psyche takes down to Hell to fetch the ointment of beauty from Proserpina.

l. 24. *urn*. In Homer, *Iliad*, Jove has two urns, one of good one of evil fortune.

38 l. 31. *quarters*. Of executed criminals.

ll. 35–6. *chemic's . . . limbeck*. The alchemist, with his retort. See 'The Bracelet' ll. 44–6.

l. 49. *turtles*. Turtle doves.

Elegy 15: The Autumnal. Date: perhaps 1600. Written, according to Walton, for and about Magdalen Herbert, the poet George Herbert's mother, who was 32 in 1600.

39 l. 16. *anachorit*. Anchorite. Compare 'The Second Anniversary' ll. 169–72.

l. 25. *underwood*. Brushwood.

l. 29. *Xerxes' strange Lydian love, the platan tree*. Herodotus tells of Xerxes' love for a plane tree. Planes were thought to be sterile (l. 32).

l. 42. *To vex their souls at Resurrection*. Dispersed teeth made resurrection of the body problematic.

39 l. 47. *lation*. Astronomical term for movement.

40 *Sappho to Philaenis*. Date: perhaps 1601. Sappho was a Greek woman poet of Lesbos. This letter to a lesbian lover is modelled on Ovid's *Heroides*.

l. 3. *that draws Nature's works*. Referring to the power of Orpheus's song.

l. 25. *Phao*. Phaon, a male lover of Sappho.

42 *Epithalamion Made at Lincoln's Inn*. Date: probably 1595, after the publication of Spenser's *Epithalamion*. It is not known what, if any, marriage Donne's poem celebrated.

l. 16. *angels*. Gold coins.

l. 29. *fellowships*. The Inns of Court.

43 l. 57. *nill*. Will not.

44 l. 90. *embowel*. Disembowel (for sacrifice).

An Epithalamion, or Marriage Song on the Lady Elizabeth and Count Palatine being Married on St Valentine's Day. Date: February 1613. Elizabeth was daughter of James I. She married Frederick, Elector Platine, amid sumptuous public festivities.

l. 5. *marriest*. Birds were supposed to mate on St Valentine's day.

45 l. 9. *speed*. Succeed in love. Being black (ugly) he might be expected to fail.

47 l. 94. *acquittances*. Acknowledgements of debts paid.

l. 98. *turtles*. Doves.

l. 112. *enlarge*. Prolong.

48 *To Mr T. W. ('Pregnant again')*. Date: late 1592? 'T. W.' was probably Thomas, the younger brother (b. 1576) of Rowland Woodward (see headnote to 'To Mr Rowland Woodward', below).

l. 13. *gluttons*. Who destroy (eat) what they love, as T. W. does Donne.

To Mr S. B. ('O thou which to search out'). Date: 1592? when Samuel Brooke (brother of Christopher: see headnote to 'The Storm', below) probably matriculated at Trinity College, Cambridge. Samuel later took orders and officiated at Donne's marriage.

l. 8. *Heliconian spring*. Source of poetic inspiration.

l. 10. *schismatics with you*. Cambridge was a notorious Puritan centre.

49 *To Mr T. W. ('At once, from hence')*. Date: 1592–3? For 'T. W.' see headnote to 'To Mr T. W.', above.

l. 12. *sacrament*. Pledge of a covenant (usually between God and man).

To Mr E. G. ('Even as lame things'). Date: summer 1593, when London was emptied by the plague. (ll. 7–10). 'E. G.', is the satirist Everard Guilpin, connected with the Guilpins of Suffolk (l. 19), who entered Gray's Inn from Emmanuel College, Cambridge, in 1591.

l. 2. *slimy*. The sun on the slime of the Nile was supposed to breed snakes.

l. 4. *that Parnassus*. Guilpin inherited a house on Highgate Hill.

l. 6. *overseen*. Spied on, presumably by government agents, following the arrest of his brother Henry in May 1593 for harbouring a Catholic priest.

50 l. 17. *Russian merchants*. Muscovy Company merchants built up stock in summer, when northern seas were navigable, and sold in winter, when they froze.

The Storm. Date 1597. Having enlisted as a soldier to fight the Spanish, Donne set sail with Essex's fleet for the Azores on 5 July. The storm he describes struck a few days later and drove the fleet back to Plymouth. Christopher Brooke was a close friend of Donne's who helped at his secret marriage to Ann More (1602), for which both men were briefly imprisoned.

l. 4. *Hilliard*. Nicholas Hilliard, foremost Elizabethan miniature painter.

l. 18. *lie but for fees*. Remain in gaol, having served their sentence, only because they cannot pay the gaoler's fees.

l. 22. *Sara*. See Gen. 18: 12, 21: 6–7.

l. 24. *bring friends one day's way*. Accompany departing guests for their first day's journey: an ancient courtesy.

51 l. 33. *Jonas*. See Jonah 1: 5–6.

52 l. 72. *Fiat. Fiat Lux*. 'Let there be light', Gen. 1: 3.

The Calm. Date: 1597. After setting sail again from Plymouth (see note to 'The Storm', above) Donne was becalmed off Terceira on 9–10 Sept.

l. 3. *fable*. Aesop's fable of the frogs who ask for King Stork instead of dull old King Log ('block'), and are eaten.

l. 12. *becomes one spout*. Streams with molten lead from its roof.

52 l. 16. *frippery.* Old clothes shop.

l. 17. *No use of lanthorns.* Because there was no wind to blow out candles, though unprotected.

l. 23. *calenture.* A madness which seized sailors in the Tropics, causing them to jump into the sea, mistaking it for green fields.

l. 28. *walkers in hot ovens.* See Dan. 3: 11–30.

l. 29. *these.* The 'great fishes' (l. 24): sharks.

l. 30. *brimstone bath.* Sulphur baths, used against venereal disease.

53 l. 33. *Bajazet encaged.* In Marlowe's *Tamburlaine*, the Scythian shepherd Tamburlaine has the Turkish Emperor Bajazeth caged and mocks him.

l. 36. *th' Emperor.* Tiberius. Ants ate his pet snake, Suetonius relates.

l. 37. *galleys.* Boats rowed by chained slaves.

l. 38. *our Venice's.* The group of immobile ships resembles Venetian buildings, with canals between.

l. 53. *Nothing.* Orthodox Christian belief was that God created everything out of nothing.

To Mr Rowland Woodward ('Like one who in her third widowhood'). Date: 1598? Written according to one MS, *Dalla Corte* ('From the Court'), so after Donne had become Egerton's secretary. Woodward, the son of a London vintner (b. 1573), entered Lincoln's Inn in 1591.

54 l. 26. *oil.* Liquid form of metal which alchemists ('physicians') would try to combine with the essence ('soul') of a pure, unmixed substance ('simples') by heat (e.g. by packing them in horse-dung, as Paracelsus advised).

55 *To Sir Henry Wotton ('Here's no more news').* Date: headed in two MSS '20 July 1598. At Court'. Wotton and Donne were undergraduates together at Hart Hall, Oxford, and stayed friends.

l. 2. *Cadiz'or Saint Michael's tale.* Wotton and Donne had been on the Cadiz and Azores (St Michael's Islands) expeditions in 1596–7.

l. 15. *Indian 'gainst Spanish hosts.* The massacres of unarmed South American Indians by colonizing Spaniards had become an international scandal.

l. 23. *egregious gests.* Ostentatious doings.

l. 24. *chests.* Chess, regarded in the sixteenth century as a moral allegory of life.

56 *To Sir Henry Wotton, at his going Ambassador to Venice.* Date: July 1604, when Wotton left England to take up his post.

ll. 21–2. *not to be changed . . . fit.* Donne will not cease to love until Wotton has become so eminent that only honour, not love, is appropriate.

l. 24. *it.* Fortune.

ll. 29–30. *your spirits . . . furnace.* Wotton's abilities are like alchemical essences ('spirits') to be refined by heat (activity).

57 l. 39. *stairs.* See Gen. 28; 12.

58 *Epigrams.* Several of the epigrams relate to the Cadiz expedition of 1596, and none is definitely datable later than 1602 (see notes to individual poems). They appear, grouped together, in the order printed here, in an MS in the hand of Donne's friend Rowland Woodward.

Hero and Leander

l. 2. *one fire.* Mutual love.

Pyramus and Thisbe

ll. 1–2. *by themselves . . . Slain.* They were killed by themselves (suicide) and by each other, because it was for love. For the story, see Shakespeare, *A Midsummer Night's Dream,* v. i.

Niobe

l. 1. *children's birth, and death.* In myth, after the deaths of her twelve children Niobe turned to stone.

A Burnt Ship. Date: June 1596? Probably refers to the destruction of the Spanish galleon *San Felipe* off Cadiz, in which Donne took part.

59 *Fall of a Wall.* Date: 1596? Seemingly refers to the death of an English soldier, Captain Sydenham, at Corunna (1589) which Donne probably heard about from veterans on the Cadiz expedition.

Cales and Guiana. Date: probably August 1597. Addressed to Essex and Raleigh, urging them to follow the 1596 sack of Cadiz ('Cales') with a voyage to Guiana.

Sir John Wingfield. Date: probably June 1596. Wingfield, hero of the capture of Cadiz ('that late island') on 21 June, was killed in the day's fighting and buried in the cathedral.

l. 1. *th' old Pillars.* The mountains guarding the Straits of Gibraltar, known as the Pillars of Hercules, were regarded as the limit of the old world.

A Licentious Person

60 l. 1. *sins and hairs.* See Ps. 40: 12. Syphilis was supposed to cause baldness.

Disinherited

l. 2. *good title.* A good legal claim (because he is now one of the poor).

The Liar

l. 4. *Spanish dieting.* Spaniards were notoriously poor and famished.

Mercurius Gallo-Belgicus. An annual register of (often unreliable) news.

l. 1. *Aesop's fellow-slaves.* They claimed to know everything; Aesop said that left nothing for him to know.

61 l. 5. *Thy credit lost thy credit.* Your credulousness prompted my incredulity.

l. 8. *Greek.* Greeks were proverbially untruthful.

An Obscure Writer

ll. 1–2. *grieved | To be understood.* Because he thinks unintelligibility a sign of depth.

Raderus. Date: 1602?, when Matthew Rader's expurgated edition of Martial appeared.

l. 3. *Katherine.* Unidentified. Presumably a queen who suppressed brothels so the Court would have a monopoly of vice.

Ralphius

l. 2. *keeps his bed.* A pun. The (pawn) broker (*a*) stays sympathetically in bed when his customer is ill; (*b*) retains the bed Ralphius has pawned.

62 *The Progress of the Soul.* Date: 1601. Donne's prefatory Epistle is dated 16 August. Accordingly to Ben Jonson, Donne's satirical epic (of which this unfinished first canto is apparently all he wrote) was going to trace the soul of the apple plucked by Eve through the bodies of heretics from Cain to Calvin. But Donne implies that the soul, after witnessing 'every great change' in the course of history (l. 69), and inhabiting the bodies of Mahomet and Luther (ll. 66–7), will end up in England (ll. 57–60), and in a man ('he', Epistle l. 38). One MS reads 'she' for 'he' here, and if this were correct, taken together with ll. 61–5 of the poem, it would clearly suggest Queen Elizabeth as the soul's last home. It has also been suggested that 'he' might be

Robert Cecil and that, as a follower of Essex, Donne might be attacking the powerful Cecil faction at court.

Title. Infinitati Sacrum. Sacred to Infinity. Presumably a joke about the poem's unfinished state. *Metempsychosis.* The doctrine that souls could transmigrate between creatures (plants, animals, humans), usually traced to Pythagoras (Epistle ll. 24–5). *Poêma Satyricon.* A satirical poem. Donne uses Latinized forms of Greek words, as a mock-learned flourish.

Epistle

l. 2. *picture.* Perhaps the description of himself which follows, or an actual portrait which he intended to accompany the poem.

l. 8. *sine talione.* Without retaliation.

l. 10. *Trent Council.* The Council of Trent (1542) introduced an 'Index' of books (but not, as Donne suggests, authors) forbidden to Catholic readers.

The Progress of the Soul

63 l. 3. *the law.* The Mosaic Law.

ll. 7–8. *gold Chaldee . . . Roman iron.* Donne combines the Four Monarchies (Babylon, Persia, Greece, Rome) with the four 'ages' of the earth, from Golden to Iron.

l. 9. *Seth's pillars.* The Jewish historian Josephus said that Seth, son of Adam, and his children, inscribed their scientific discoveries on pillars of stone and brick.

l. 16. *Danow.* Danube.

l. 17. *western land of mine.* America and the West Indies, source of gold.

l. 19. *before thee, one day.* Plants (and so vegetable souls) were created on the third day; the sun, on the fourth (Gen. 1: 14–19).

l. 21. *Janus.* Noah.

l. 24. *vivary.* Menagerie (i.e. the Ark).

64 l. 41. *lustres.* Periods of five years. Donne was almost 30.

l. 52. *this sea.* His projected epic.

l. 55. *light, and light.* Neither 'dark' nor 'heavy'.

l. 60. *Tigris, and Euphrates.* Mesopotamia; the traditional site of Eden.

65 l. 61. *the great soul.* See headnote, above.

l. 68. *th' Empire, and late Rome.* Rome in Imperial and later eras.

l. 70. *fatal.* Because the Tree of Knowledge brought death.

l. 77. *Stood in the self same room.* A Judaeo-Christian tradition sited

Eden and Golgotha in the same place. (This would not tally, though, with l. 60.)

66 l. 98. *Were prisoners judges.* If fallen man ('prisoner' of sin) were judge, God's treatment of Adam, and fallen man, would seem harsh.

l. 108. *then.* In Gen. 2 the fruit is forbidden before Eve's creation.

67 l. 150. *His apples . . . kill.* Mandrakes were used as aphrodisiacs and to procure abortions.

68 l. 165. *moist red eyes.* The name of Cain, Eve's son, was translated 'constant weeping'.

l. 169. *Unvirtuous.* Without medicinal powers ('virtues').

69 l. 195. *last.* The reading of one MS. Others, and the first edition of Donne's *Poems* (1633) read 'taste'.

70 l. 217. *Asked . . . leave.* Potatoes, mandrakes, and the flesh and eggs of sparrows (proverbially lecherous) were used as aphrodisiacs.

71 l. 264. *whether she . . . breathe.* How fish breathed was still disputed in Donne's day.

ll. 267–8. *faith | Cares not.* Science is reason's province, not faith's.

l. 270. *makes a board.* Goes to and fro.

72 l. 274. *sea pie.* Oyster-catcher.

l. 290. *Fasts, and Lents.* To help the fishing industry, the Elizabethan government made Wednesdays and Saturdays fish-days, when eating meat was punishable by law. The Church forbade meat in Lent.

l. 294. *gluttony's best orator.* Ease (leisure) incites to greed.

l. 300. *the other.* The bird's soul enters a venal State official.

73 l. 304. *Morea.* The Peloponnese.

l. 307. *hopeful promontory.* Cape of Good Hope.

l. 320. *seas above the firmament.* See Gen. 1: 7.

74 l. 336. *crab and goat.* Tropics of Cancer and Capricorn.

l. 351. *thresher.* The fox-shark, which lashes its enemy with its tail.

75 l. 385. *no knees.* A popular belief, repeatedly denied by elephant-experts from Aristotle on.

76 l. 406. *the first type.* Abel, the first shepherd, is prototype of pastors and rulers.

77 l. 436. *Son to himself, and father too.* Because the wolf's soul enters its cub.

l. 439. *Moaba.* The names of Adam's children here and in ll. 457, 487, and 509 are not biblical but based on rabbinical tradition.

78 l. 480. *hath no gaol.* Does not imprison desire.

79 l. 494. *equal fires.* Constant temperatures, such as alchemy required.

l. 503. *sinewy strings.* Nerves and sinews.

80 l. 516. *Cain's race.* See Gen. 4: 17-22.

l. 517. *Seth . . . astronomy.* According to Josephus (see l. 9, note).

81 *SONGS AND SONNETS.* Date: none of these poems can be dated precisely, and there is no evidence for dating any of them before 1602 (see note to *A Valediction: of the Book*). References to the king's hunting in *The Sun Rising*, to his favourites in *The Anniversary*, to his face on coins in *The Canonization*, and to effigies of him in *Farewell to Love*, must, if they allude to James I, date these poems after his accession in 1603. *Twickenham Garden* must be dated after 1607, when Lady Bedford went to live at Twickenham.

The Flea. Flea-poems were common in sixteenth-century Europe.

The Good Morrow

82 l. 3. *country.* An indecent pun. See *Hamlet*, III. ii. 123.

l. 4. *seven sleepers.* Legendary Christian youths walled up alive in the persecution of Decius (AD 249) who slept for 187 years.

l. 19. *Whatever dies, was not mixed equally.* Galenic medicine attributed disease to disproportion of humours in the body.

Song ('Go, and catch a falling star')

l. 2. *mandrake.* See *The Progress of the Soul*, ll. 130-60.

The Undertaking

84 l. 2. *Worthies.* Nine famous warriors, celebrated in pageants.

l. 6. *specular stone.* Transparent building stone, mentioned by Pliny, and regarded as a lost secret of the ancients.

85 *The Sun Rising.* The reference to James I's passion for hunting dates this poem after 1603.

l. 17. *th'Indias of spice and mine.* The East and West Indies.

l. 24. *alchemy.* Sham gold.

86 *The Indifferent.* Based on Ovid, *Amores* II. iv.

Love's Usury

87 l. 9. *think any rival's letter mine.* Waylay, open, and read others' mail.

87 ll. 10–11. *at next nine . . . promise*. Be shamefully late for assignations.

l. 11. *mistake*. Take for, and take (make love to) instead of.

l. 15. *quelque-choses*. Fancy foreign dishes; here, dressed-up city madams.

The Canonization

l. 7. *stamped*. On coins.

88 l. 15. *plaguy bill*. Weekly lists of deaths were printed in London during plague outbreaks.

l. 20. *fly*. Butterfly or moth, often shown in emblems fluttering round a candle ('taper').

l. 23. *hath more wit*. Makes more sense. The lovers illustrate how a single creature, the mythical phoenix, could contain both sexes.

l. 26. *die*. Refers, as often, to orgasm. The lovers' 'mysterious' resurrection may blasphemously allude to Christ's.

l. 41. *glasses*. Alchemical vessels, into which the 'soul' (quintessence) is driven.

The Triple Fool

89 l. 6. *lanes*. Rivers, thought by some classical writers to filter the salt from seawater.

The Legacy

92 l. 6. *something*. i.e. his heart (see l. 12); his heart is also the 'me' of l. 7.

l. 9. *Tell her*. The early editions do not use inverted commas, so it is impossible to decide where the speech starting 'Tell her' ends. It might end at 'kill me' (l. 11) or at 'gone' (l. 12) or at 'lie' (l. 14), or even at the end of the poem; and 'that is you, not I' (l. 10) might be part of the speech or an explanatory interjection. This uncertainty compounds the poem's dazzling complication.

l. 18. *colours . . . corners*. Specious appearances and secret places.

A Fever

93 l. 13. *schools*. Academic theologians. The 'fire' is foretold in 2 Pet. 3: 7.

l. 21. *meteors*. Thought of as impure and so transient, burning themselves out, unlike the permanent stars in the 'firmament'.

Air and Angels

94 l. 17. *would sink admiration*. Her beauty would overwhelm mere admiration, as opposed to love.

l. 19. *Every thy hair.* Even one of your hairs (the 'scattering bright' extremities of ll. 21–2).

ll. 23–4. *Then as . . . wear.* Angels were supposed to make themselves visible by taking bodies of condensed air, purest of the elements (though less pure than angels, since they were spirits).

l. 25. *sphere.* Embodiment.

Break of Day. Date: before 1612, when it was printed with music in William Corkine's *Second Book of Airs*.

l. 12. *him.* Indicating the poem is spoken by a woman.

95 *The Anniversary.* Date: probably after 1603, since James I's weakness for 'favourites' seems to be alluded to (l. 1).

l. 18. *inmates.* Lodgers.

96 *A Valediction: of my Name in the Window*

l. 6. *either rock.* Diamonds were classified in Donne's day into those originating in new or old rock.

l. 8. *through-shine.* Transparent.

l. 12. *I am you.* Because her reflected face has his name on it.

l. 25. *all my souls.* Refers to the Aristotelian doctrine that man has three souls: a soul of growth, which plants also have; a sensitive soul, common to men and animals; and a rational, immortal soul which is man's distinctive possession.

l. 30. *will come again.* As the scattered body will be recompacted and rejoin the soul in heaven at the Resurrection, so, if she has his soul, his body will come back to her.

97 l. 48. *Genius.* Guardian angel.

l. 57. *superscribing.* Addressing the letter; writing to his rival she will mistakenly put Donne's name on it.

l. 65. *Impute this idle talk, to that I go.* Attribute my foolishness (the poem) to the fact that I am near death, and so distracted.

98 *Twickenham Garden.* Date: after 1607 when Donne's patronness, Lucy Countess of Bedford, went to live at Twickenham Park.

l. 9. *serpent.* Perhaps a phallic double meaning.

l. 27. *truth.* i.e. to her husband.

A Valediction: of the Book. Date: probably after 1602; see note to l. 9.

l. 3. *esloign.* Remove.

99 l. 6. *Sibyl's glory*. The Sibyls in classical times were inspired prophetesses.

l. 7. *Her who from Pindar could allure*. The historian Aelian says Pindar was defeated in a poetic contest by Corinna, a woman poet of Thebes.

l. 8. *her, through whose help Lucan is not lame*. His wife; according to legend she helped him write the *Pharsalia*.

l. 9. *her, whose book (they say) Homer did find*. The legend that a woman called Phantasia wrote Homer's epics was first given common currency by Lipsius in a book published in 1602.

l. 15. *the faith of any ground*. The trustworthiness of any doctrine.

l. 22. *for Love's clergy only*. Only for initiates (who will understand the 'cypher'), not for common people.

l. 32. *amuse*. Puzzle.

l. 39. *how prerogative these states devours*. How special privileges, such as are granted to monarchs (or women), encroach on men's rights.

100 ll. 48–9. *Love and . . . proceed*. The nature of statecraft, as of love, will not stand scrutiny.

l. 53. *will their nothing see*. Will see a reflection of their own craft, which is negligible compared to love.

ll. 61–3. *to conclude . . . eclipses be*. Noting the time at which an eclipse occurred at different spots on the earth's surface gave a method of calculating their relative longitude. Donne puns on 'longitude' (*a*) geographical position; (*b*) duration.

Love's Growth

101 l. 18. *Stars by the sun are not enlarged, but shown*. There was an old belief that stars derived their light from the sun. (Compare Dryden, *Religio Laici* l. 1, 'Dim as the borrowed beams of moon and stars').

Love's Exchange

102 l. 5. *who were their own before*. Who were already damned (being Love's fellow-devils).

l. 11. *A* non obstante *on nature's law*. A licence exempting him from natural, unfalsified expressions of feeling.

l. 25. *condition*. Make conditions of surrender.

103 l. 42. *anatomies*. Bodies for dissection.

Confined Love

l. 12. *jointures*. Money or property allocated to the wife in a marriage settlement.

l. 14. *we.* Suggests a woman speaker.

The Dream ('Dear love, for nothing less than thee')

104 l. 20. *Profane.* Since she knows men's thoughts she must be not an angel but God, and it would be profanity to doubt it.

A Valediction: of Weeping

105 l. 8. *that thou.* That reflection of you.

l. 9. *on a divers shore.* The tear that has fallen between the lovers is an emblem of the sea that will divide them.

Love's Alchemy

106 l. 7. *no chemic yet the elixir got.* No alchemist has discovered the Philosophers' Stone.

l. 12. *winter-seeming summer's night.* Short as a summer night, cold as winter.

l. 15. *man.* Servant.

l. 22. *that day's.* The wedding day, with its vulgar festivity.

l. 24. *mummy, possessed.* Dead flesh, once you have had them; or, possibly, dead flesh possessed by a demon. 'Mummy', flesh preserved in bitumen, was imported from Egypt and used in medicine.

The Curse

ll. 11–12. *no touch|Of conscience, but of fame.* Not saving contrition, but just concern about the scandal of loving so despised a woman.

l. 14. *scarceness.* Poverty.

l. 16. *incestuously an heir begot.* Committed adultery with a near kinswoman, begetting an heir to an estate that would otherwise have passed to him.

107 l. 24. *be circumcised for bread.* Become a Jew to attract Jewish charity.

108 *A Nocturnal upon St Lucy's Day, being the shortest day.* 13 Dec., St Lucy's Day, when the sun entered the sign of the Goat (l. 39), was popularly thought the shortest. Conjectured associations of the poem with the Countess of Bedford seem unlikely. She did not die until 1627. Donne's wife died in 1617, and may be the subject. Or the dead woman may be imaginary.

l. 3. *flasks.* Powder-flasks, i.e. the stars (see 'Love's Growth', l. 18, and note).

l. 6. *The general balm th' hydroptic earth hath drunk.* The earth, raging with thirst as if dropsical, has soaked up the balm of 'balsamum' regarded in Paracelsian medicine as the vital life-preserving essence.

108 l. 7. *The bed's-feet.* This phrase meant simply 'the foot of the bed' in seventeenth-century English. Traditionally life ebbed from the feet up (see Shakespeare, *Henry V*, II. iii. 20–5). Donne imagines the process unnaturally reversed.

l. 13. *new alchemy.* The usual alchemical aim was to extract from bodies their 'quintessence' (l. 15) or 'elixir' (l. 29), which was thought of as a celestial substance latent in all things. Love's alchemy is 'new', because he extracts a quintessence from nothing, reducing Donne, in his 'limebeck' or chemical retort (l. 21), to the quintessential nothing—more essentially nothing even than the nothingness out of which God created the world (l. 29).

109 ll. 33–4. *yea plants, yea stones detest, | And love.* A belief deriving from Pliny, still widespread in the seventeenth century, and thought to be corroborated by, for example, the lodestone.

110 *The Bait.* A parody of Marlowe's *The Passionate Shepherd to his Love*, first published 1599. An anonymous reply to Marlowe, which possibly also influenced Donne, appeared in *England's Helicon* (1600).

l. 17. *angling reeds.* Fishing rods.

l. 23. *sleavesilk.* Silk that could be 'sleaved' (unravelled).

The Broken Heart

112 l. 14. *chaws.* Chews.

l. 15. *chain-shot.* Cannon balls chained together.

l. 16. *fry.* Young fish.

A Valediction: forbidding Mourning. Walton, Donne's friend and first biographer, says he wrote this poem on leaving his wife to travel abroad in 1611. Modern commentators doubt Walton's reliability.

113 l. 9. *Moving of th' earth.* Earthquakes, taken as portents.

l. 11. *trepidation.* Astronomer's term for oscillation of the ninth (crystalline) 'sphere', imperceptible on earth ('innocent'), but supposedly affecting the other concentric 'spheres' composing the Ptolemaic universe.

l. 13. *sublunary.* Beneath the moon's sphere, in the part of the cosmos subject, unlike the upper heavens, to change and decay.

The Ecstasy

114 l. 6. *balm.* See 'A Nocturnal Upon St Lucy's Day' l. 6, note.

l. 11. *pictures*. Reflections.

l. 16. *her*. This word shows the poem is addressed to a third party, not the woman who shared the ecstasy.

l. 27. *concoction*. Refinement (of metals or minerals by heat).

l. 36. *both one, each this and that*. The two souls joined are one soul, but each united soul also contains two souls (his and hers).

115 l. 52. *intelligences . . . sphere*. The spheres of the cosmos were supposed to be directed by spirits or 'intelligences'.

l. 55. *sense*. Sense perception and sensuousness.

l. 57. *influence*. In Paracelsus' doctrine this denoted the force of the stars, which reached man by mixing with the air.

l. 62. *Spirits*. Subtle vapours which were believed to arise from the blood and join soul to body.

116 l. 76. *Small change*. The hypothetical pure lover (ll. 21–8) will see little difference between the dialogue of souls and the love-making of bodies.

Love's Deity

l. 5. *produced a destiny*. Imposed a fate (i.e. to love unrequited).

l. 6. *vice-nature, custom*. 'Custom is second nature' was a saying.

l. 18. *purlieu*. Domain, which now extends over activities (l. 17) that do not properly belong to love.

117 l. 26. *loves*. i.e. someone else.

Love's Diet

l. 24. *entail*. The list of heirs to an estate.

118 l. 25. *buzzard*. An inferior hawk.

l. 29. *spring*. Hawking term for making a bird break cover.

The Will

l. 3. *Argus*. Mythical hundred-eyed giant.

l. 12. *ingenuity*. Ingenuousness.

l. 14. *any, who abroad hath been*. Travellers were notorious bores.

l. 15. *Capuchin*. Friar vowed to poverty.

ll. 19–20. *faith . . . good works*. Puritans (schismatics) believed in salvation through faith alone, and rejected the Catholic doctrine of salvation through works.

119 l. 40. *brazen medals*. Ancient bronze coins, collected as curiosities and useless as currency.

The Funeral

120 l. 9. *sinewy thread*. The nerves.

l. 19. *idolatry*. The worship of objects.

l. 23. *bravery*. Defiance.

The Blossom

l. 12. *forbidden*. This suggests that the lady is married, so divinely proscribed like the tree in Eden.

l. 15. *that sun*. The lady.

121 l. 31. *some other part*. The phallus.

The Primrose. Date: possibly 1613. In the second edition of Donne's *Poems* (1635) the poem is subtitled 'being at Montgomery Castle, upon the hill, on which it is situate'. Donne visited the castle, home of the Herbert family, in spring 1613.

l. 8. *true love*. Primroses with four or six petals, instead of the common five, were called 'true loves' and thought lucky for lovers.

122 l. 24. *mysterious*. Five, the number of the pentangle, was thought magical, since it contained the first odd and the first even numbers.

l. 27. *take*. Consort sexually with.

The Relic

123 l. 17. *Mary Magdalen*. The saint was always depicted with long golden hair.

l. 18. *A something else*. Probably 'A Jesus Christ'. There was a blasphemous tradition linking him and Mary Magdalen as lovers. The age of 'mis-devotion' would forget Christ's body had not remained in any grave.

l. 30. *nature, injured by late law, sets free*. Love, naturally free, is restricted by laws (of marriage).

The Damp

l. 5. *damp*. Poisonous mist.

124 l. 21. *die*. Have an orgasm: a common double meaning.

l. 24. *have odds enough*. Have the advantage of. That women had superior stamina in love-making was a common belief.

The Dissolution

l. 5. *involve*. Include. At her death her elements—earth (despair), air (sighs), fire (passion), and water (tears)—enter his body and over-burden it.

l. 12. *security*. Carelessness. He thoughtlessly squandered his sighs, passion, etc., in the pursuit of love.

l. 18. *break*. Go bankrupt.

125 *A Jet Ring Sent*. Jet was used for cheap rings.

l. 8. *fling*. To 'jet' meant to throw.

Negative Love

l. 5. *sense*. Sensuality.

ll. 11–12. *can by no way be expressed|But negatives*. St Thomas Aquinas wrote that it was impossible to say what God was, only what He was not.

l. 18. *speed*. Succeed in getting what he wants.

126 *The Prohibition*. In one MS the third stanza is headed 'T. R.', suggesting it may be by Donne's friend Sir Thomas Roe.

l. 11. *officer*. Executioner.

l. 18. *neither's office do*. Cancel each other out.

l. 19. *die*. See 'The Damp' l. 21 and note.

l. 22. *stage*. A living exhibition of her power. The captives at a Roman triumph were afterwards slaughtered.

The Expiration. Date: before 1609 when it was printed, with music, in Ferrabosco's *Airs*.

The Computation

127 l. 1. *since yesterday*. The poem's years add up to 2,400: 100 for each hour since he saw her.

The Paradox

l. 3. *He thinks that else none can*. The lover thinks no one but a perfect lover can say 'I love', and that no one is really in love but him. The paradox is he cannot himself say 'I love', because, according to the poem's logic, love kills instantly.

l. 14. *the light's life*. The sun.

Farewell to Love

128 l. 1. *Whilst yet to prove*. While I was still inexperienced.

l. 10. *As they wax lesser, fall, as they size, grow*. Things desired, but not known, grow or diminish as our desire for them does.

l. 12. *His highness sitting in a golden chair.* A toy or gingerbread king, bought at a fair.

l. 22. *cocks and lions.* Exempt, according to Galen, from post-coital depression.

ll. 28–30. *Because that other . . . posterity.* Nature may have made men feel sad after sex to put them off. Because the brevity of the enjoyment, and of sexual arousal, would incline them, otherwise, to repeat the act often ('posterity' meaning successive acts of love, as well as children).

129 l. 31. *Since so.* Since this is so.

l. 40. *worm-seed.* A plant used as an anaphrodisiac.   *tail.* Penis.

130 *The Dream* ('*Image of her*'). Printed as a love elegy in 1633 and 1635, but as one of the *Songs and Sonnets* in MSS.

l. 8. *the more, the less we see.* The brighter the object the less distinctly we see it, because dazzled.

l. 11. *meaner.* More moderate.

l. 24. *snuff.* Burnt-out piece of wick.

131 *To Sir Henry Goodyer* ('*Who makes the past*'). Date: 1608? Donne lived at Mitcham (l. 48) from 1605 to 1610. Goodyer apparently went abroad in 1609, perhaps following Donne's advice in this letter.

l. 4. *pair of beads.* Rosary.

l. 16. *women's milk, and pap.* See Heb. 5: 12–14.

132 l. 34. *make your hawk's praise yours.* The hawk lessens as it soars; Goodyer's spendthrift ways lessen him.

l. 44. *fruit-trenchers.* Wooden fruit plates, adorned with moral maxims.

To the Countess of Bedford ('*Reason is our soul's left hand*'). Date: probably 1608. The Countess was a favourite lady-in-waiting of Queen Anne and a leading figure in the Jacobean court. A cultured and influential woman, she befriended Donne and helped him financially.

l. 6. *want.* Do without.

133 l. 16. *catholic.* General, universal; not a reference to Roman Catholicism.

l. 22. *balsamum.* See 'A Nocturnal upon St Lucy's Day' l. 6, and note.

l. 27. *mithridate.* Antidote against poisons.

l. 35. *home.* Heaven (her proper residence as an 'angel').

134 *To the Countess of Bedford* ('*You have refined me*'). Date: 1608? In

MSS this poem follows 'Reason is our soul's left hand', suggesting closeness of date.

l. 13. *this place.* Twickenham Park, bought by the Countess in 1607.

l. 20. *both computations.* The two ways of computing the day were 'artificial day' (sunrise to sunset) and 'natural day' (24 hours). The Countess, as sun, makes a new world where it is light all the time, so the 'artificial day' idea becomes redundant (l. 24).

135　l. 41. *schools.* Theological controversialists.

l. 48. *Escurial.* The massive place cum monastery built by Philip II near Madrid in 1584, which makes other churches seem mere 'chapels'.

ll. 61-2. *nice thin . . . repress.* Wiredrawn theology may advantage the heresy it attacks.

136　*To Mrs M. H.* ('Mad paper stay'). Date: probably late 1608. For Magdalen Herbert ('M. H.'), see headnote to *Elegy 15*, above. In February 1609, at the age of 40, she married her second husband, Sir John Danvers (see Donne's coy references to a man friend, ll. 37–52) who was 20.

l. 8. *thou shouldst be wicked too.* Donne sarcastically puts wickedness as well as unworthiness among qualities requisite for worldly success.

137　l. 43. *protest.* Demand (a legal sense).

l. 46. *oaths.* Not to remarry.

l. 47. *Reserved.* Qualified, guarded.

To the Countess of Bedford at New Year's Tide ('This twilight of two years'). Date: c.25 Mar. (New Year's Day in the seventeenth-century calendar) 1610(?). For the Countess see headnote to 'To the Countess of Bedford' ('Reason is our soul's left hand'), above.

138　l. 20. *strong extracts.* Concentrates. Alchemical processes needed gentle heat, not powerful agents (like the Countess's name).

l. 25. *too much grace might disgrace.* Her grace, truly described, would raise incredulity, so bring her and the poem into discredit.

l. 38. *security.* Freedom from care.

139　l. 43. *Indifferent . . . got.* Most court activities are morally neutral.

l. 50. *using.* As an occasion for virtue.

l. 63. *dis-enrol.* From the Book of Life, listing the redeemed.

l. 65. *private gospel.* Assurance of individual salvation.

139 *To the Countess of Bedford* (*'Honour is so sublime perfection'*). Date: unknown. Perhaps 1610.

    l. 4. *these*. Earth and water.

    l. 6. *those*. Fire and air.

140   l. 8. *whom they . . . show*. Kings show whom they would have us honour.

    l. 12. *dung*. See 'To Mr Rowland Woodward', l. 26, note.

    l. 18. *Sicil Isle*. Sicily, site of Etna.

    l. 21. *But one*. Except for God.

    l. 29. *specular stone*. See 'The Undertaking', l. 6, note.

    l. 35. *Have birthright*. According to Aristotle, a vegetative and sensible soul existed in each individual before the rational soul.

141   l. 42. *her yea, is not her no*. Discretion and religion do not disagree.

    l. 44. *break them*. By preferring discretion to religion or vice versa. *wit*. Intelligence.

    ll. 47–8. *The pieceless centres . . . the lines*. The indivisible point at the centre of a circle (symbol of perfection) is the source of every radius.

To the Countess of Huntingdon (*'Man to God's image'*). Date: probably 1610. Elizabeth Stanley (b. 1587) was stepdaughter to Donne's employer, Egerton, and married Henry Hastings, later Earl of Huntingdon, in 1601. Donne had probably not seen her since his expulsion from York House. His friend Goodyer encouraged him to address a verse-letter to her, in hope of patronage, and he reluctantly complied.

    l. 3. *Canons . . . invade*. Canon law will not let women into the ministry.

    l. 6. *new star*. Novae had been sighted in 1572, 1600, and 1604, causing surprise, because the firmament was presumed changeless (l. 8).

142   l. 18. *towards earth doth bend*. It was believed the sun was nearer the earth than in the past, and that this presaged the world's end.

    l. 36. *low names*. The names of woman, wife, and mother, which make the Countess visible to the world; otherwise, as pure virtue, she would be invisible.

143   l. 41. *one*. Her husband.

144 *To Sir Edward Herbert, at Juliers*. Date: 1610. Edward Herbert (who became Lord Herbert of Cherbury, 1629) was brother of George Herbert and eldest son of Donne's friend Magdalen Herbert. He

was poet, philosopher, diplomat, and traveller, and also, as his *Autobiography* shows, ludicrously vain. The siege of Juliers (Jülich, West Germany) was part of a local dispute between Protestant and Catholic princes. The Protestants (including Herbert) took the town in August 1610. Donne's poem is in part a reply to Herbert's satire 'The State Progress of Ill', and picks up from it the idea of the ark and of man taming the beasts within himself.

l. 1. *beasts*. The allegory of the beasts (animal passions) in man is from Plato's *Republic*.

l. 10. *disafforested*. Converted from forest to arable land.

l. 11. *Empaled*. Fenced.

l. 16. *devils*. See Matt. 8: 30–4; Mark 5: 2–14; Luke 8: 27–33.

l. 19. *our first touch*. As soon as they enter our bodies.

l. 24. *Hemlock*. Food for birds, but kills men.

l. 27. *specific poison*. Van Forrest, the Dutch authority on poisons, whom Donne read, says some kill by heat, cold, or corrosion (l. 26), some by their 'specific form' or mysterious antipathy (l. 29) to man.

l. 31. *his*. His own.

l. 34. *what she was*. Before the Fall.

145 l. 43. *calentures*. See 'The Calm' l. 23, note.

l. 44. *icy*. Benumbing. Herbals listed poppies as cold, dry plants.

To the Countess of Bedford ('Though I be dead'). Date: spring 1612. In France with Sir Robert Drury from November 1611 to April 1612, Donne had heard that the Countess and other great ladies were offended by his lavish praise of Elizabeth Drury in 'The First Anniversary' (1611).

l. 19. *half rights seem too much*. To give only half her due of praise would sound excessive.

146 l. 26. Desunt caetera. The rest is missing.

Epitaph on Himself. Date: unknown, but perhaps spring 1612 (see previous poem). It may be the Countess's displeasure that has 'killed' Donne.

OMNIBUS. To everyone.

l. 14. *glass*. Brittle (because alive), and vessels of the soul.

147 *Elegy on the Lady Markham* ('Man is the world'). Date: May 1609. Bridget, Lady Markham, cousin and close friend of Lady Bedford, died aged 30 on 4 May.

147 l. 8. *above our firmament.* See Gen. 1: 7, 9. These are spiritual, as opposed to worldly, tears.

l. 11. *are sin.* Immoderate grief shows failure to accept God's will.

l. 12. *God's 'No'.* Gen. 9: 11, 15.

l. 22. *take up porcelain.* That porcelain was made by burying clay was a popular error.

148 l. 36. *to death.* Mortally.

l. 38. *this, and that virginity.* Neither reluctance to die, nor willingness to sin, blemished her purity.

l. 44. *all, sinners be.* Rom. 3: 23.

l. 49. *cherubins.* See Exod. 25: 18–20. Why angels should need wings was much debated. Aquinas said they could move anywhere instantaneously.

To the Lady Bedford ('*You that are she and you*'). Date: probably May 1609. The evidence of the MSS suggests this was a covering letter for the elegy on Lady Markham (above)—the 'she' of this poem.

l. 6. *were to be so, when they were not yet.* Was destined before they were born.

149 l. 7. *Cusco, and Musco.* Cuzco (Peru) and Moscow represent opposite ends of the earth.

l. 23. *this all.* The world, which will have its dead bodies re-compacted at the general resurrection.

l. 34. *both rich Indies.* See 'The Sun Rising' l. 17 and note.

l. 41. *doubt.* Suspect.

l. 44. *Judith.* The apocryphal Book of Judith tells of a beautiful heroine who was also, like Lady Markham, a widow.

150 *Elegy on Mistress Bulstrode* ('*Death I recant*'). Date: August 1609. Cecilia Bulstrode (b. 1584, d. 4 Aug. 1609), close friend and kinswoman of Lady Bedford, was a court lady of dubious reputation. A reply to this elegy survives by Lady Bedford.

l. 10. *well preserved.* By their goodness, acting as preservative.

l. 17. *rounds.* Encompasses.

l. 22. *without creation.* See Wisd. 1: 12: 'God made not death'.

l. 24. *four monarchies.* Babylon, Persia, Greece, Rome.   *antichrist.* Orthodox Christianity, drawing on biblical prophecies, taught that after Christ's thousand-year reign on earth (the Fifth Monarchy), Antichrist would be destroyed. For Death's death see 1 Cor. 15: 26.

l. 34. *Reserve but few.* See Matt. 20: 16: 'few are chosen'.

152 *An Elegy upon the Death of Mistress Bulstrode ('Language thou art too narrow').* Date: August 1609 (see previous poem).

l. 9. *owe all that we be.* See Gen. 3: 16: 'in sorrow thou shalt bring forth children'.

l. 10. *fifth and greatest monarchy.* See 'Elegy on Mistress Bulstrode' l. 24, note. For sorrows attendant on the Second Coming see Matt. 24: 6–31.

l. 24. *crystal ordinance.* Apparently, artillary made of glass, which would unite military strength with purity (translucence), but would also, inevitably, shatter.

l. 27. *rebel.* Against sorrow, because they rejoice she is in heaven ('better').

l. 34. *The ethics.* Moral treatises.   *virtues cardinal.* Prudence, justice, temperance, fortitude.

l. 37. *no more than let in death.* She kept out sin, but let in death, which we all derive from Adam's Fall.

153 l. 44. *a holiday.* A saint's day to celebrate.

l. 45. *bush.* See Exod. 3: 2.

l. 52. *that order.* Seraphim, nearest to God. The tradition that the fallen angels came from the highest orders derived from Ezek. 28: 12–19.

l. 58. *lemnia.* A red clay, mentioned by Pliny as antidote to poisons; in alchemy, an ingredient of the Philosophers' Stone.

l. 60. *spruce.* In Donne's day, an exotic wood from Prussia (Spruce-Land), used for coffers and chests.

l. 62. *waste a stoic's heart.* Even a Stoic, proof against passion on principle, could not bear all the grief alone.

To the Countess of Bedford ('To have written then'). Date: soon after 4 Aug. 1609 (see l. 68, note).

l. 2. *simony.* Buying something sacred (repaying her letter by replying).

ll. 5–6. *this . . . that.* Writing . . . not writing.

154 l. 14. *Here Peter . . . fane.* St Peter's, Rome, was supposed to occupy the site of a Temple of Jupiter; St Paul's, London, of a Temple of Diana.

l. 37. *new philosophy.* Copernican astronomy.

l. 47. *he.* Christ; see Luke 9: 62.

154   l. 50. *cockle*. A weed.

155   l. 55. *dignities*. Titles (of the body as casket, temple, and palace of the soul).

ll. 57–8. *For, bodies . . . naturally free*. Bodies are not essentially inferior to souls. Bodies will be made immortal, at the resurrection, and souls, too, have to be preserved from death by God, not being immortal by nature.

l. 67. *Virginia*. Re-colonized in 1607 and 1609.

l. 68. *Two new stars*. Lady Markham (d. 4 May 1609) and Cecilia Bulstrode (d. 4 Aug. 1609); see pp. 147 and 150, 242.

ll. 69–70. *Why grudge we . . . company?* Why do we not send our souls to join theirs, which would dignify us, not heaven?

l. 72. *two truths*. Others' vice and her virtue. She believes in neither.

l. 77. *one*. Humility.

l. 78. *suspicion*. Of her own virtue.

l. 81. *aspersion*. Admixture.

l. 83. *purge vice with vice*. Use evil (cruelty, etc.) to root out evil.

156   *A Funeral Elegy*. Date: probably December 1610. This poem and the *Anniversaries* were written to commemorate Elizabeth Drury, the only surviving daughter of Sir Robert Drury of Hawstead, Suffolk, who died in December 1610, aged 14. Donne had never met her, but his sister Anne had known the Drurys from 1598 on, and probably encouraged Donne to commemorate Elizabeth so as to attract Sir Robert's patronage. The attempt was successful: Donne accompanied the Drurys on their European travels from November 1611 to September 1612, and on their return Sir Robert provided the Donnes with a rent-free house in Drury Lane.

l. 8. *Escurials*. See 'To the Countess of Bedford' l. 48, note (p. 239).

l. 18. *house*. Her body, 'tabernacle' (l. 16) of the Holy Ghost.

157   l. 41. *Afric Niger*. Associated in Donne's day (following Pliny) with the upper Nile, which flows partly underground.

l. 68. *new stars*. See 'To the Countess of Huntingdon' l. 6, note.   *artist*. Astronomer.

l. 73. *balsamum*. Precious aromatic resin.

158   *An Anatomy of the World. The First Anniversary*. Date: probably July–October 1611. Elizabeth Drury has been dead 'some months' (l. 39). The poem was published in or before November. For the occasion, see headnote to 'A Funeral Elegy', above.

159 l. 8. *standing house.* Palace, permanent residence.

160 l. 57. *balm.* See 'A Nocturnal upon St Lucy's Day' l. 6, note.

161 l. 110. *kill ourselves.* The idea that sex shortens life came from Aristotle.

l. 112. *There is not now that mankind.* The belief that men were shorter, weaker, lived less long, etc., than in the past was commonplace, and drew on the writings of Church Fathers, especially St Cyprian.

l. 115. *stag, and raven.* Longer-lived than man, according to Pliny.
     long-lived tree. Oak.

l. 122. *confessed, and recompensed the meat.* Food, it was believed, had been anciently more nourishing. The curse on the land (Gen. 3: 17–18), and the effect of the Flood on the soil, had marred it.

l. 128. *Methusalem.* Lived 969 years (Gen. 5: 27).

162 l. 134. *three lives.* Leases for 'three lives' lasted till the death of the last survivor of three named leasees.

l. 145. *adds to'our length.* It was believed that imperfections of physique and stature would be made good in resurrected bodies.

l. 159. *new diseases.* Syphilis; also influenza, of which the first epidemic struck England in 1612.

163 l. 172. *Help . . . allow.* Granted man's other faults are remediable, or take effect gradually.

l. 173–4. *depart | With.* Part with.

l. 180. *poisonous tincture.* Original sin. The alchemical 'tincture' was a pure essence.

l. 187. *banquet.* Nibble at (seventeenth-century 'banquet' meant dessert course).

l. 206. *element of fire.* The idea that a sphere of fire surrounded the Earth was disproved by Kepler.

l. 207. *sun is lost, and th' earth.* Copernicus's theory that the Earth circled the sun was corroborated by early seventeenth-century astronomy, but much disputed.

164 l. 234. *single money.* Small change.

165 l. 252. *round proportion.* As against Plato's notion that heavenly bodies moved in perfect circles, Ptolemy constructed a complex, though still geocentric, model (ll. 253–7) that was compatible with observed readings.

l. 258. *eight and forty.* Ptolemy's universe had 48 constellations.

l. 260. *New stars.* See 'To the Countess of Huntingdon' l. 6, note.

165 l. 274. *fall'n nearer us.* It was widely believed that the sun was getting nearer, partly because Ptolemy's readings put it further off than later estimates.

l. 285. *round proportion.* Renaissance cosmographers taught that the Earth was a perfect sphere: mountains and ocean depths being negligible irregularities (l. 300). Others believed the Earth's original roundness had been destroyed by the Flood.

l. 286. *Tenerife.* The Pico de Teide on Tenerife (12,172 ft.) was a standard example of huge height. Estimates ranged from 7 to 70 miles.

166 l. 295. *vault infernal.* Authorities on Hell sited it inside the Earth, and keenly disputed its diameter.

l. 311. *that ancient.* Perhaps Pythagoras, but the idea was common-place.

l. 316. *the forms from objects flow.* The usual Renaissance theory of vision, derived from Aristotle, was that objects emitted rays to the eye.

l. 317. *those great Doctors.* Augustine and Ambrose both likened the Ark's proportions to the human body's.

167 l. 335. *Since most men . . . they be.* Reputation is generally an accurate guide to character; hence the need for 'discretion' in behaviour.

l. 343. *turquoise.* Believed to reflect its wearer's health.

l. 345. *gold falls sick.* Gold amalgam, combining gold and mercury, is paler than gold.

l. 366. *diaphanous.* Like the white light of eternity. Her 'miracle' was being both coloured and transparent.

168 l. 380. *father . . . mother.* Sky and earth.

l. 387. *meteors.* Included, in Donne's day, everything in the sphere of the air (rain, lightning, etc.).

l. 389. *new worms.* Species of snakes from Africa and America.

l. 390. *Egyptian Mages.* Adept at snake magic; see Exod. 7: 10-12.

l. 392. *constellate.* Use the power of the constellations in cures or charms.

169 l. 426. *iron.* Accounts of the world's decay gave the 'ages' as Gold, Silver, Brass, and Iron.

l. 440. *punctual.* Proceeding point by point.

170 l. 462. *a song.* See Deut. 31: 19, 31-43.

Of the Progress of the Soul. The Second Anniversary. Date: probably

December 1611–January 1612. Written in Amiens (where Donne was with Sir Robert Drury), sent to England, and published in or before May 1612. For the occasion see 'A Funeral Elegy', headnote.

171 l. 23. *some days.* See Gen. 1: 5, 8, 13, 16–19.

l. 42. *vanish, and not die.* See 1 Cor. 15: 51–2.

l. 44. *God's great* Venite. The Day of Judgement; for *Venite* ('Come') see Matt. 25: 34.

l. 46. *safe-sealing bowl.* The communion chalice.

l. 48. *hydropic.* Thirsty, like a sufferer from dropsy.

172 l. 75. *tried.* Tested against the standard of.

ll. 79–80. *made the south . . . pole.* Made the southern hemisphere starrier than the northern (which, in Donne's day, was thought the starrier).

l. 92. *Division.* A run of short notes in music.

173 l. 120. *Saint Lucy's night.* 12–13 Dec., considered the longest of the year (but still, Donne means, just a few hours).

l. 124. *ingredients.* The four elements.

l. 127. *mithridate.* An antidote against poison, containing many ingredients (Pliny mentions 54).

l. 131. *quantities.* Geometrical figures.

l. 134. *say this is a line, or this a point.* Points have position but no magnitude; lines, length but no breadth.

174 l. 140. *disuniting.* Division. Spirits were by definition indivisible.

l. 143. *chain.* The golden chain in Homer, *Iliad*, viii. 19, was allegorized in the Renaissance as Fate's chain of cause and effect.

l. 152. *content to suffer violence.* See Matt. 11: 12.

l. 158. *sink.* Sewer.

l. 162. *second soul of sense, and first of growth.* See 'A Valediction: of my Name in the Window' l. 25 and note.

l. 165. *curded milk.* See Job 10: 10.

175 l. 181. *piece.* Gun.

l. 193. *element of fire.* See 'The First Anniversary' l. 206, note.

l. 195. *baits.* Stops for refreshment.

l. 198. *Hesper, and Vesper.* Both names for Venus as evening star.

l. 199. *Argus.* Hundred-eyed giant, charmed to sleep and killed by Mercury in Ovid, *Metamorphoses*, i. 622–721.

l. 204. *his father.* Saturn.

175 l. 219. *long-short.* Long in distance, but quickly covered.

176 ll. 235–6. *betroth | The tutelar angels.* Embrace a belief in guardian angels.

l. 242. *electrum.* An alloy, four parts gold to one of silver.

l. 260. *By what way . . . immortal.* It was disputed whether the soul was immortal by nature, or by God's sustaining power.

177 l. 266. *new ingredients.* Salt, sulphur, and mercury, according to the new medicine of Paracelsus.

ll. 271–2. *how blood . . . other go.* A much-disputed question, prior to Harvey's discovery of the circulation of the blood.

l. 277. *those many opinions.* Medical authorities variously classed nails and hair as skin, bones, organs, or excrements (waste products).

l. 284. *catechisms and alphabets.* Rudiments.

l. 292. *sense, and fantasy.* The current theory of perception, derived from Aristotle, was that sense perception carried an impression to a part of the mind called fantasy, which made an image (phantasm) of the object.

l. 299. *it.* Heaven.

178 l. 332. *like.* Similar to one another.

l. 342. *that, which men have said.* Some theologians claimed Mary was free of original sin. Donne disagrees: she rejoices to be redeemed by her son.

179 l. 382. *accidental joys in heaven do grow.* Whereas heaven's essential joy (the sight of God) is immutable, subsidiary joys (e.g. the conversation of the saints) can increase.

180 l. 406. *that . . . more fit.* Man might become more worthy of his Creator.

l. 418. *for that effect.* To reach heaven (Gen. 11: 4).

181 l. 432. *thrust.* Crowd.

l. 440. *All will not serve.* You will not be able to imagine the sight of God, even if you think twice as much about heaven as about earth.

182 l. 470. *as our joys admit.* In so far as earthly joy allows.

l. 473. *casual.* (*a*) In a philosophical sense, related to attributes ('accidents'), not essences; (*b*) subject to chance.

l. 479. *aposteme.* Abscess.

l. 500. *the stuff is not such as the rest.* The material (of her creation) is superior in kind, not degree.

l. 508. *Pieces.* Adds to.

183 l. 511. *place.* Amiens (see headnote).

l. 514. *what laws of poetry admit.* Invocation to pagan deities, muses, etc., allowed by poetic licence.

l. 528. *The trumpet.* Calling the Israelites to meet, Num. 10: 2–3.

184 *The Cross.* Date: unknown; perhaps 1607, or earlier. In 1604 James rejected Puritan demands for the abolition of the sign of the cross in baptism. Donne's poem contributes to the controversy on the royal side.

l. 12. *cross.* Affliction. Donne plays on this sense throughout.

l. 15. *instrument.* Agent (i.e. priest).

l. 16. *Sacrament.* Baptism.

l. 27. *extracted chemic medicine.* An 'essence' as used in Paracelsian medicine.

185 l. 46. *snake.* The snake hidden under flowers was a common emblem (see 'The Comparison' l. 46).

ll. 51–2. *in man alone . . . hath palpitation.* An Aristotelian doctrine.

Resurrection, imperfect. Date: unknown; perhaps 1608. 'Imperfect' means unfinished.

l. 1. *repassed.* Recovered from (Donne's coinage). For the 'wound' see Matt. 28: 45.

186 l. 12. *mineral.* Stones and metals were believed to 'ripen' in the earth: Christ, in the grave, ripened into a redeemer.

l. 14. *tincture.* Essence of gold—the 'Philosophers' Stone'.

l. 23. Desunt caetera. 'The rest is lacking'.

Upon the Annunciation and Passion falling upon one day. 1608. Date: 25 Mar. 1608 was both Good Friday and the Feast of the Annunciation.

l. 4. *a circle.* Symbol of perfection. Christ's beginning and end as man, coming together, suggest circularity.

l. 8. *cedar.* Symbol of Christ; see Ezek. 18: 22.

187 l. 16. *he her to John.* See John 19: 26.

l. 17. *orbity.* Bereavement.

l. 22. Ave *and* Consummatum est. Gabriel's greeting (*Ave Maria*) and Christ's dying words ('It is finished').

l. 26. *next.* Nearest; the Pole Star.

l. 38. *one period.* The same point in time (since God is eternal His acts are simultaneous).

188 *A Litany.* Date: probably winter 1608/9, when Donne was confined to bed with a severe attack of neuritis.

   l. 7. *red earth.* 'Adam' was thought to mean 'red earth' in Hebrew.

   l. 25. *intend.* Intensify.

189 l. 29. *Bones . . . faith.* The mystery of the Trinity is hard for reason to digest but easy for faith.

   l. 32. *distinguished undistinct.* At once separate and inseparable.

   l. 33. *power, love, knowledge.* Attributes of the Trinity's three persons.

   l. 34. *such self different.* Similarly, separate/inseparable.

   l. 40. *disseized.* Dispossessed.

   l. 46. *nonage.* Minority.

   l. 49. *denizened.* Naturalized.

190 l. 57. *cloud . . . fire.* See Exod. 13: 21.

   l. 58. *Nature . . . grace and law.* They saw more by the light of nature than we do with the Old and New Testaments.

   ll. 66-7. *made of two | One law.* Foretold in the Old Testament the events of the New.

   l. 80. *The old broad way in applying.* The traditional, straightforward method of scriptural interpretation.

   l. 81. *my comment . . . mine.* My commentary would substitute my own meaning for the Bible's.

191 l. 85. *thy scattered mystic body.* The Church, of which Abel and his sheep were a symbol.

   l. 92. *confessors.* Those who remain true to their faith under persecution, but are not martyred.

   l. 99. *Diocletian.* Roman emperor AD 284-305, who persecuted Christians.

192 l. 110. *Doctors.* Theologians.

   l. 111. *Both books.* The Bible, and God's register of the saved.

   l. 117. *Mean ways.* Middle courses.

193 l. 142. *light affecting, in religion, news.* Frivolously espousing new religious beliefs.

   l. 147. *measuring ill by vicious.* Excusing sin by comparing it with vice rather than with virtue.

   l. 149. *indiscreet humility.* Over-humble attitudes which make people despise Christians.

l. 164. *still the agony of pious wits.* Scholars agonize over the disputed reasons for Christ's 'agony' (Matt. 26: 37–8).

l. 167. *thy free confession.* See John 18: 5–8. Those who 'fell to the ground' were, some commentators thought, blinded.

l. 171. *blind unjust men.* Deliberately deceive persecutors (a reference to the Catholic defence of 'equivocation').

194 l. 175. *born.* Human, not supernaturally exempt from pain.

l. 178. *Dying . . . express.* Christ 'gave up the ghost' voluntarily (Mark 15: 37).

l. 193. *lay or ghostly sword.* Punishment for secular or spiritual offence.

l. 198. *sinister.* Leading to hell.

195 l. 206. *Job's sick day.* See Job 2: 4–7.

l. 215. *book . . . creatures.* The Bible and the Book of Nature.

ll. 219–20. *by hearkening . . . invite.* Encourage flatterers and scandal-mongers, by lending a ready ear.

l. 227. *make us physic.* Make us an example.

ll. 232–3. *may see then . . . decline.* May see us hear them, for our good, but You refuse to hear them.

196 l. 243. *thou ear, and cry.* God is source of prayer, as well as hearer.

l. 245. *By taking . . . again.* By taking on human nature, have also taken on the obligation to save us.

l. 252. *nothing.* That sin had no essence, but was merely privation of good, was a common theological view.

To Mrs Magdalen Herbert: of St Mary Magdalene. Date: probably 1609. For Mrs Herbert see headnote to *Elegy 15*, above.

ll. 1–2. *Her of your name . . . Bethina . . . Magdalo.* John 11 identifies the 'sinner' who anointed Christ's feet (Luke 7) as Mary, sister of Martha and Lazarus, of Bethany ('Bethina'). According to Church tradition, Mary Magdalene who stood by the cross (Luke 8) was the same woman, and her family had estates at Magdala.

l. 5. *The Resurrection.* First witnessed by Mary (John 20).

l. 8. *think these Magdalenes were two or three.* Some commentators argued that the actions ascribed to Mary Magdalene were those of several women.

l. 12. *The latter half.* The later, devout Mary, not the 'sinner'.

l. 13. *did harbour Christ himself, a guest.* In John 12: 1–8.

196 l. 14. *hymns*. The poems Donne sent were probably, but not certainly, the *La Corona* sequence.

197 *La Corona*. The 'Crown' of linked sonnets was an Italian form. There was also a way of saying the Rosary called 'The Corona of Our Lady', dividing the beads into seven sections. Date: probably 1609 (see previous note).

198 4 *Temple*. See Luke 2: 42–9.

l. 9. *His godhead was not soul to his manhood*. Christian doctrine stipulates that Christ became a man, with a human soul.

6 *Resurrection*

199 l. 7. *last death*. Hell (see Rev. 2: 11).

l. 10. *of which, and for which*. Flesh returns to dust, its origin, and is made ready for resurrection and heaven, its goal.

7 *Ascension*

l. 7. *show alone*. Display only himself (see Col. 2: 15).

l. 9. *ram*. Punning on (*a*) battering ram; (*b*) the ram in the thicket (Gen. 22: 13), seen by biblical interpreters as a symbol of the Saviour.

200 *Holy Sonnet* 1 (*'As due by many titles'*). Date: this and the five Holy Sonnets that follow were probably written in 1609.

l. 5. *I am thy son, made with thyself to shine*. See Matt. 13: 43.

Holy Sonnet 3 (*'This is my play's last scene'*)

201 l. 7. Several MSS have another version of this line ('Or presently, I know not, see that face'), which suggests Donne, like other 'advanced' thinkers, suspected the soul might not go to heaven (or hell) at death, but sleep in the grave till the Last Judgement.

l. 13. *Impute*. According to Protestant doctrine, no soul can be saved through its own righteousness, only through Christ's 'imputed' to it.

Holy Sonnet 4 (*'At the round earth's imagined corners'*)

l. 1. *corners*. See Rev. 7: 1.

l. 4. *souls*. The belief (seemingly Donne's here) that the soul dies, and later rises from the grave, was a version of the heresy known as Mortalism. (see *Holy Sonnet* 3 l. 7, above).

l. 7. *you*. Those alive on the Last Day (see 1 Cor. 15: 51–2).

Holy Sonnet 6 (*'Death be not proud'*)

202 l. 14. *And death . . . shalt die.* See 1 Cor. 15: 26, 54. Donne's line may echo Shakespeare, Sonnet 146 (published 1609): 'And death once dead, there's no more dying then'.

To E. of D. with Six Holy Sonnets. Date: probably 1609, when Richard Sackville, who was to be a lifelong friend and patron of Donne, became Earl of Dorset, aged 19. The Holy Sonnets sent may have been 1–6 above.

ll. 6–7. *nature do admit . . . at once.* Pliny's *Natural History* reported septuplets in Egypt.

203 *Holy Sonnet* 7 (*'Spit in my face you Jews'*). Date: unknown. This and the following nine Holy Sonnets may have been written soon after the first six (see above), but there is no evidence.

l. 8. *Crucify him daily.* See Heb. 6: 6.

l. 11. *Jacob came.* See Gen. 28: 1–36.

Holy Sonnet 11 (*'Wilt thou love God . . .'*)

204 l. 4. *his temple.* See 1 Cor. 6: 19.

l. 6. *still begetting.* God's acts are eternal, without beginning or end.

Holy Sonnet 12 (*'Father, part of his double interest'*)

205 l. 6. *from the world's beginning.* See Rev. 13: 8.

l. 7. *two wills.* The Old and New Testaments.

l. 12. *law and letter.* See 2 Cor. 3: 6 and John 1: 17.

l. 13. *abridgement.* See Mark 12: 29–31.   *last command.* See John 13: 34.

Holy Sonnet 13 (*'Thou hast made me'*)

l. 14. *adamant.* A magnet.

Holy Sonnet 14 (*'O might those sighs and tears'*)

206 l. 5. *idolatry.* Worship of women.

l. 9. *hydroptic.* Thirsty, as if through dropsy.

Holy Sonnet 15 (*'I am a little world'*)

l. 6. *new spheres.* Ptolemy had added a ninth sphere, the Primum Mobile, beyond the fixed stars; later astronomers posited tenth and eleventh spheres.   *new lands.* If this refers to Galileo seeing 'new lands' in the moon through his telescope, the poem must be dated after the publication of his *Sidereus Nuncius* (1610). But the reference may be to voyages of discovery.

206   l. 9. *drowned no more.* See Gen. 9: 11.

l. 10. *burnt.* See 2 Pet. 3: 7, 12.

l. 13. *zeal.* See Ps. 69: 9.

Holy Sonnet 16 ('*If faithful souls . . .*')

l. 2. *As angels.* Angelic knowledge was supposed to be intuitive not inferential.   *father's.* Donne's father had died in 1576, when Donne was barely 4. He was almost certainly, like Donne's mother, a Roman Catholic.

l. 10. *conjurers.* Magicians.

207   *Holy Sonnet* 17 ('*Since she whom I loved*'). Date: probably 1617. Donne's wife died on 15 Aug., aged 33.

l. 2. *to hers, and my good.* Her death is for her good, since she is in heaven, and for Donne's since it fixes his mind on 'heavenly things'.

Holy Sonnet 18 ('*Show me dear Christ*'). Date: probably 1620, following the defeat (29 Oct.) of the Protestants (under James I's son-in-law the Elector Palatine) by the Catholics at the Battle of the White Mountain (outside Prague). This disaster prompts Donne to ask God to reveal the True Church—the bride ('spouse') of the Lamb, described in Rev. 19.

l. 2. *she.* The Roman Church.

l. 5. *Sleeps she a thousand.* Was the True Church in abeyance for centuries prior to the Protestant Reformation?

l. 6. *self truth.* Infallible, as the Roman Church claims to be.

l. 8. *one . . . seven . . . no hill.* Mount Moriah, where Soloman built the Temple; or the seven hills of Rome; or Geneva, by its lake.

l. 12. *dove.* See S. of S. 5: 2; the Song was interpreted as expressing Christ's love for his Church.

Holy Sonnet 19 ('*Oh, to vex me . . .*'). Date: unknown; perhaps 1620 or later. In the Westmoreland MS (written by Donne's friend Rowland Woodward) this comes last of the *Holy Sonnets*, after 'Show me dear Christ', which may imply late date.

208   *Good Friday, 1613. Riding Westward.* Date: Good Friday fell on 2 April 1613. Donne was riding to visit Sir Edward Herbert (see

headnote to 'To Sir Edward Herbert, at Juliers', above) at Montgomery Castle.

ll. 1–2. *sphere . . . intelligence.* Referring to the Platonic idea that the celestial spheres were driven by spirits or 'intelligences'.

l. 4. *foreign motions.* The outer spheres of the Ptolemaic universe were supposed to influence the motions of the inner.

l. 17. *must die.* See Exod. 33: 20.

l. 20. *footstool crack, and the sun wink.* See Matt. 27: 45 and 51, and Isa. 66: 1.

209 l. 26. *The seat . . . of his.* Blood was thought by some the residence of the soul. Whether or not this was so with Christ (says Donne) all our souls depend on his redeeming blood.

A Hymn to Christ, at the Author's last going into Germany. Date: 1619. Donne went as chaplain with the Earl of Doncaster's diplomatic mission (May 1619–January 1620). Other evidence shows he was depressed at this time and feared he would not return.

210 l. 17. *control.* Forbid.

Hymn to God my God, in my Sickness. Date: November or early December 1623. An epidemic of relapsing fever swept London in 1623. Victims died in two or three days. Donne fell ill late in November, but was out of danger by 6 Dec. His first biographer, Walton, dates this poem 23 Mar. 1631, during his last illness, but is probably wrong.

l. 9. *south-west.* South (heat) and west (sunset), signifying death by fever.

l. 10. Per fretum febris. 'Through the strait' (or 'the raging heat', Lat. *fretum* can mean either) 'of fever'.

211 l. 18. *Anyan, and Magellan, and Gibraltar.* The Anian Strait was between America and Eastern Asia, so could provide a North-West passage to the Pacific and the East Indies as the Straits of Magellan provided a South-West passage.

l. 20. *where Japhet dwelt, or Cham, or Shem.* Of Noah's sons, Japhet inherited Europe, Ham Africa, Shem Asia.

l. 22. *stood in one place.* See *The Progress of the Soul* l. 77, and note.

l. 30. *Therefore . . . throws down.* Donne's 'text' is not biblical, but see Job 22: 29.

A Hymn to God the Father. Date: November–December 1623, during Donne's illness.

211 l. 1. *that sin where I begun.* Original sin.

　　l. 5. *done.* Punning on 'Donne'.

212 l. 15. *Sun.* Punning on Son; the sun symbolized God's mercy.

Further Reading

BIOGRAPHY

R. C. Bald, *John Donne: A Life* (Oxford, 1970).

BIBLIOGRAPHY AND REFERENCE

G. L. Keynes, *A Bibliography of John Donne*, 4th edition (Oxford, 1973).
J. R. Roberts, *John Donne: An Annotated Bibliography of Modern Criticism, 1912–1967* (University of Missouri Press, 1973).
—— *John Donne: An Annotated Bibliography of Modern Criticism, 1968–1978* (Columbia, Mo., 1982).
H. C. Combs and Z. R. Sullens, *A Concordance to the English Poems of John Donne* (Chicago, 1940).

CRITICISM

Useful selections of the earlier criticism are:
J. R. Roberts (ed.), *Essential Articles for the Study of John Donne's Poetry* (Hassocks, Sussex, 1975).
A. J. Smith (ed.), *John Donne: The Critical Heritage* (London, 1975).

J. R. Roberts's bibliographies (above) list criticism up to 1978. Books relating wholly or partly to Donne since that date include:
D. Aers, B. Hodge, and G. Kress, *Literature, Language and Society in England, 1580–1680* (Dublin, 1981).
C. Belsey, *Desire: Love Stories in Western Culture* (Oxford, 1994).
J. Carey, *John Donne: Life, Mind and Art* (London, 1981).
S. Davies, *John Donne* (Plymouth, 1994).
T. Docherty, *John Donne, Undone* (London, 1986).
B. K. Lewalski, *Protestant Poetics and the Seventeenth-Century Religious Lyric* (Princeton, 1979).
A. F. Marotti, *John Donne, Coterie Poet* (Madison, Wis., 1986).
D. Novarr, *The Disinterred Muse: Donne's Texts and Contexts* (Ithaca, NY, 1980).
A. C. Partridge, *John Donne, Language and Style* (London, 1978).
A. Sinfield, *Literature in Protestant England, 1560–1660.* (Princeton, 1983).
W. Zander, *The Poetry of John Donne: Literature and Culture in the Elizabethan and Jacobean Period* (Brighton, 1982).

John Donne Journal: Studies in the Age of Donne (1982–) is published twice a year by the English Department of North Carolina State University, Raleigh, ed. M. T. Hester and R. V. Young.

Index of Poem Titles and
First Lines

OXFORD

MORE OXFORD PAPERBACKS

This book is just one of nearly 1000 Oxford Paperbacks currently in print. If you would like details of other Oxford Paperbacks, including titles in the World's Classics, Oxford Reference, Oxford Books, OPUS, Past Masters, Oxford Authors, and Oxford Shakespeare series, please write to:

UK and Europe: Oxford Paperbacks Publicity Manager, Arts and Reference Publicity Department, Oxford University Press, Walton Street, Oxford OX2 6DP.

Customers in UK and Europe will find Oxford Paperbacks available in all good bookshops. But in case of difficulty please send orders to the Cash-with-Order Department, Oxford University Press Distribution Services, Saxon Way West, Corby, Northants NN18 9ES. Tel: 01536 741519; Fax: 01536 746337. Please send a cheque for the total cost of the books, plus £1.75 postage and packing for orders under £20; £2.75 for orders over £20. Customers outside the UK should add 10% of the cost of the books for postage and packing.

USA: Oxford Paperbacks Marketing Manager, Oxford University Press, Inc., 200 Madison Avenue, New York, N.Y. 10016.

Canada: Trade Department, Oxford University Press, 70 Wynford Drive, Don Mills, Ontario M3C 1J9.

Australia: Trade Marketing Manager, Oxford University Press, G.P.O. Box 2784Y, Melbourne 3001, Victoria.

South Africa: Oxford University Press, P.O. Box

WORLD'S ⚙ CLASSICS

WILLIAM WORDSWORTH

Selected Poetry

Edited by Stephen Gill and Duncan Wu

Wordsworth was one of the most illustrious of the Romantic poets. In this selection generous extracts are given from his important work *The Prelude*, together with many of his shorter poems. The reader will find classics such as *Tintern Abbey*, *Westminster Bridge* and 'I wandered lonely as a cloud' well represented. Notes and introduction are provided by Wordsworth's biographer, Stephen Gill, and Duncan Wu.

WORLD'S ✿ CLASSICS
OXFORD

ALEXANDER POPE

Selected Poetry

Edited by Pat Rogers

Pope has been acknowledged as the most important poet of the first half of the eighteenth century. This selection includes his brilliant poems *An Essay on Criticism*, *Windsor Forest*, and his masterpiece of social satire, *The Rape of the Lock*. Together with a representative sample of Pope's other verse, Pat Rogers gives an eloquent defence of Pope's poetic practice.

WORLD'S ⚙ CLASSICS

OXFORD

SAMUEL TAYLOR COLERIDGE

Selected Poetry

Edited by Heather Jackson

Coleridge was one of the most significant figures in the development of Romantic poetry. This new selection represents the full range of his poetic gifts, from his early polemic poetry such as the *Sonnets on Eminent Characters*, to the maturity of the blank verse poems, *Fears in Solitude* and *Frost at Midnight*. Also included are the wonderful works, *Kubla Khan* and *The Rime of the Ancient Mariner*.

WORLD'S ⚙ CLASSICS

LORD BYRON

Selected Poetry

Edited by Jerome J. McGann

Byron was one of the most acclaimed writers of his time, and he continues to be a highly popular Romantic poet with readers today. His mastery of a sweeping range of topics and forms is clearly reflected in this selection, which includes extracts from all his major poems such as *Childe Harold*, *Beppo*, and *Don Juan*, together with many shorter lyrics.

WORLD'S ✦ CLASSICS
OXFORD

JOHN DRYDEN

Selected Poetry

Edited by Keith Walker

Dryden was the leading poet of his day, and dominated the literary scene with satires such as *MacFlecknoe* and *Absalom and Achitophel*. This selection represents the full range of his talent and pays particular attention to his classical translations, which gave new life to English verse. These include extracts from Horace, Lucretius, Ovid, and Virgil's *Aeneid*, as well as his own fables and reworkings of some of Chaucer's tales.

WORLD'S ⚙ CLASSICS
OXFORD

SIR PHILIP SIDNEY
Selected Poetry
Edited by Katherine Duncan-Jones

Sidney, a contemporary of Shakespeare, is now considered to be one of the most important poets of the Elizabethan era. In addition to a number of shorter lyrics, this selection by a leading Sidney scholar includes poems from *The Old Arcadia*, together with his most substantial works *Astrophil and Stella*, the first sonnet sequence ever written in English, and *The Defence of Poesy*.

WORLD'S ❁ CLASSICS

OXFORD

ANDREW MARVELL

Selected Poetry

Edited by Keith Walker and Frank Kermode

Marvell is regarded as one of the finest Metaphysical poets. His brilliant use of conceits and luxuriant imagery is ever-present in this selection which includes much of his lyrical poetry together with some of his more political works. Such famous poems as *To his Coy Mistress*, the Mower poems, and *On a Drop of Dew* can all be found, with informative notes and introduction by Frank Kermode and Keith Walker.

THE OXFORD AUTHORS

General Editor: Frank Kermode

THE OXFORD AUTHORS is a series of authoritative editions of major English writers. Aimed at both students and general readers, each volume contains a generous selection of the best writings—poetry, prose, and letters—to give the essence of a writer's work and thinking. All the texts are complemented by essential notes, an introduction, chronology, and suggestions for further reading.

Matthew Arnold
William Blake
Lord Byron
John Clare
Samuel Taylor Coleridge
John Donne
John Dryden
Ralph Waldo Emerson
Thomas Hardy
George Herbert and Henry Vaughan
Gerard Manley Hopkins
Samuel Johnson
Ben Jonson
John Keats
Andrew Marvell
John Milton
Alexander Pope
Sir Philip Sidney
Oscar Wilde
William Wordsworth

Oxford
Paperback
Reference

THE CONCISE OXFORD COMPANION
TO ENGLISH LITERATURE

*Edited by Margaret Drabble and
Jenny Stringer*

Derived from the acclaimed *Oxford Companion to English Literature*, the concise maintains the wide coverage of its parent volume. It is an indispensable, compact guide to all aspects of English literature. For this revised edition, existing entries have been fully updated and revised with 60 new entries added on contemporary writers.

* **Over 5,000 entries on the lives and works of authors, poets and playwrights**

* **The most comprehensive and authoritative paperback guide to English literature**

* **New entries include Peter Ackroyd, Martin Amis, Toni Morrison, and Jeanette Winterson**

* **New appendices list major literary prize-winners**

From the reviews of its parent volume:

'It earns its place at the head of the best sellers: every home should have one'
Sunday Times